Federal Contracting Answer Book

Second Edition

Federal Contracting Answer Book

Second Edition

Terrence M. O'Connor
Mary Ann P. Wangemann

ſſſ
MANAGEMENTCONCEPTS
Vienna, Virginia

ʃʃʃ
MANAGEMENTCONCEPTS
8230 Leesburg Pike, Suite 800
Vienna, Virginia 22182
(703) 790-9595
Fax: (703) 790-1371
www.managementconcepts.com

Printed in the United States of America

Library of Congress Cataloging-in-Publication Data

O'Connor, Terrence M.
  Federal contracting answer book/Terrence M. O'Connor, Mary Ann P. Wangemann. — 2nd ed.
    p. cm.
  ISBN 978-1-56726-245-2
    1. Public contracts—United States.   2. Government purchasing—United States.   I. Wangemann, Mary Ann P.   II. Title.

  HD3861.U6 O267 2009
  658.7'23—dc21

                                                        2009020008

10   9   8   7   6   5   4   3   2

About the Authors

Terrence M. O'Connor, LL.M., is Special Counsel (Government Contracts) with the law firm of Albo & Oblon, L.L.P. in Arlington, Virginia.

He has practiced government contract law for almost 40 years. After graduating from Notre Dame Law School, he began practicing law at the National Capital Planning Commission in Washington, D.C., and later moved to the Appalachian Regional Commission.

After 15 years as a federal government attorney, Mr. O'Connor went into private practice as a government contract litigation attorney. He has tried government contract cases before the U.S. Court of Federal Claims, U.S. Court of Appeals for the Federal Circuit, and various boards of contract appeals (BCAs), including the ASBCA and the CBCA as well as some of its predecessors: the GSBCA, DOTBCA, AGBCA, IBCA, and VABCA. Mr. O'Connor has also litigated government contract protests before the Government Accountability Office (GAO). He received his Master of Laws (Government Procurement) degree from The George Washington University Law Center.

His publications include *Understanding Government Contract Law* and *Federal Procurement Ethics: The Complete Legal Guide*. He also writes a monthly column on recent court, GAO, and BCA decisions for the *Federal Acquisition Report*. Since 1985, he has been an instructor for Management Concepts, teaching classes including Advanced Federal Contract Law, Construction Contracting, and Federal Real Property

Lease Law. He also conducts training sessions for the National Contract Management Association (NCMA).

Mary Ann P. Wangemann, CPCM, PMP, has worked in the government marketplace for the last 25 years. She is currently responsible for the Management Concepts Federal Acquisition Certification–Project/Program Management product line. Previously, she started up mySBX to help connect small businesses together to work on federal business opportunities. For the previous 20 years she was with EDS, managing programs and working in every aspect of federal procurement and contract performance: strategic planning, marketing, sales support, proposal development, business management, contracts administration, technical and management solution development and delivery, and contract startup and shutdown. As an EDS Fellow, she evaluated technology and business trends, set strategic direction, evaluated intellectual property, and provided thought leadership at EDS.

Dr. Wangemann holds a doctoral degree in Human Resource Management from The George Washington University. Her dissertation, *Executive Decision Making in an Organizational Learning Context*, has been published nationally and internationally. She also holds a master's degree in information systems and business administration from the Johns Hopkins University, a bachelor's degree from the University of Maryland at Baltimore County, and a contract management certificate from the University of Virginia.

She received the National Contract Management Association's National Education Award in 1996 and the Blanche Witte Award for Excellence in the field of contract management in 2000. She was named Outstanding Woman of Loudoun County in 2000 and an NCMA Fellow and Center for Excellence in Government Principal.

To Carol, the love of my life

To Kathleen, Maura, and Tate, the loves of my life

and with thanks to Cathy Kreyche and Myra Strauss, who make writing a joy

and extra thanks to Lena Johnson for the help with this second edition.

Finally, I'd like to thank Barbara Beach for getting me into the writing arena in the first place.

Terry O'Connor

*   *   *

To my parents, Robert and Lorraine Pater, for teaching me how to go after my dream

To my daughter, Lorraine Ann Wangemann, whom I encourage to dream

Mary Ann Wangemann

Table of Contents

Preface

As a new administration begins, we are entering a new era of government contracting and a new way of getting things done at the federal level. As contracting professionals, we are called upon to understand these complexities and to help inform our colleagues both in industry and in the government how to navigate these new waters.

We spend our days tracking the changes, the new ways of doing things, and the nuances of the regulations. We have written this book to help you take advantage of what we have learned. We use the question and answer format because we think it can best give you fast, accurate, and straightforward answers to your most pressing questions about procurement.

We have updated this book to take into account the new streamlined ways of doing things. We've added topics such as cost and price analysis so we can share the government's view with you about what it looks for in proposals. We cover the changes in the ethics regulations so that you can do it all according to the letter of the law. As anyone in the field knows, we are dealing with a topic area that changes routinely to accommodate national priorities. Therefore, we anticipate that our readers will use this book as a foundation to gain a broad understanding of the changes in our marketplace and then rely on the latest regulations and contract terms and conditions to govern their business decisions. We hope you enjoy this book and that it helps you understand the big picture as well as the details of federal contracting.

Terrence M. O'Connor
Mary Ann P. Wangemann

CHAPTER 1
Introduction to the Federal Marketplace

The U.S. federal government spends billions of dollars annually to meet its agencies' missions; it offers opportunities for any business sector and provides a stable business base for companies interested in working with the federal government. But, what exactly is the federal government marketplace? How does it differ from the commercial marketplace? What makes it so appealing to pursue? A company interested in doing business with the federal government needs to understand the components of the government marketplace and the legislation that defines the various elements of that market. The techniques for entering the government marketplace are important for both large and small businesses.

1. What is the federal government market?

The *federal government market* consists of the sellers—contractors—who provide products and services to buyers—people working in the federal government. The sellers in this marketplace include individual entrepreneurs, small businesses, and large businesses. The buyers work for civilian agencies, such as the departments of Education, Energy, and Transportation, as well as Department of Defense (DoD) service branches such as the Navy, Army, and Air Force. The goods and services that are exchanged in this marketplace include:

- Normal consumer goods such as socks, pastries, computers, and cleaning supplies

- Services such as information technology, biometric scanning, consulting, or teaching

- Government-unique items such as F-22s, missile guidance systems, and M1 tanks.

2. How is conducting business with the federal government different from conducting business with commercial companies?

In addition to the sheer size difference between the federal government and a commercial company, there are several distinctions between conducting business with a federal agency versus a commercial company.

Use of Federal Acquisition Regulation—Most federal agencies (other than the Central Intelligence Agency and the United States Postal Service, for example) use the Federal Acquisition Regulation (FAR) to provide direction and govern their federal procurements. The FAR is managed by the FAR Council as part of the Office of Federal Procurement Policy. The FAR provides direction on items such as the underlying principles of federal procurement; appropriate behavior for government and contractor personnel; applicable contract clauses based on contract type; dispute procedures; and recommendations for how government personnel should evaluate contractor proposals. The government regularly reviews the regulations and relies on industry to help define and update outdated regulations to keep them in line with best business practices. The FAR is developed with contractor input, but it is finalized, interpreted, and designed to protect the government's interests. The Federal Acquisition Streamlining Act (FASA), enacted in 1994, lessened the regulations and paperwork required to conduct business with the government.

In contrast, a commercial company may select its business partners in any manner it chooses. Contracts between two commercial entities use the Uniform Commercial Code (UCC). The UCC is designed to protect the buyer and seller equally.

Types of Purchases—One similarity, of course, is that, like commercial companies, the government buys commercially available items or products and services that are available for sale on the open marketplace. In fact, the Federal Acquisition Reform Act (FARA), also known as the Clinger-Cohen Act, further mandated the government's use of commercial items to meet contractual requirements. FARA exempted commercial off-the-shelf (COTS) items from certain FAR requirements and simplified the procedure for acquiring them. Although the government procures a great deal of COTS items, there is still a tremendous market for research and development, defense, and civilian products and services that commercial companies do not need.

Socioeconomic Objectives—The government focuses on two perspectives as it awards contracts. The first is that it wants to protect the taxpayers' money, so it works hard at securing the best possible value contract. To accomplish this, it enforces strict guidelines to keep competition open. Specifically, through the Procurement Integrity Act, the government punishes companies suspected of trying to get an "inside track" on a procurement. Second, the government tries to meet socioeconomic objectives through its procurement actions. To accomplish this, it establishes set-aside programs designed to give small businesses the opportunity to compete for federal business. These set-asides target, for example, small disadvantaged businesses, labor surplus area businesses, and veteran-owned businesses. Through programs like these, the government encourages and helps small businesses obtain federal business even though procuring goods or services from these smaller companies may be more expensive for the government.

A commercial company can award contracts in any manner it chooses and may choose not to run a competition at all. Further, a company pays attention to the socioeconomic objectives only through its own beneficence, not because it was mandated by Congress or an executive agency.

Government Authority—Another important difference in contracting with the federal government versus a commercial company is that the government has the right to know all. The federal government differs from a commercial company in that the government can audit all contractor pricing, costing, and invoicing documents for noncommercial items. When bidding on a government contract, a contractor must detail the costs for direct, overhead, general and administrative (G&A) expenses, and profit amounts on the proposal cover sheet. The government reserves the right to audit any documentation to determine whether the price is fair and reasonable. This is not the norm in the commercial marketplace. The government has relaxed these requirements significantly in the FARA for commercial items. In a commercial contract between two companies, typically only the line item and total price are given.

Close Monitoring—Finally, government contracts require close monitoring. Skillful contract management is required for success and profit in the regulated government environment. A contractor's management team must constantly monitor the project to ensure strict adherence to the stringent government requirements. For example, if a company performs work in a manner different from the proposal, it must obtain contracting officer (CO) approval. (The CO is the only person who can bind the government in a contract action.) If a company changes the dials on the widget it is making for the government, the CO must approve that change. Commercial contracts often maintain the same level of monitoring and thus can cause significant problems downstream between the two organizations. Further, any government funding expenditure is subject to scrutiny.

Something as innocuous as paying for lunch at a contractor and government function falls within the realm of procurement law. For these reasons, a contractor management team must understand the government regulations and contractual obligations, and clearly communicate these requirements to the people working for the government.

3. Why do business with the federal government?

Doing business with the federal government pays off for many reasons:

1. *Government contracts can be profitable*—Profit margins on federal contracts are low compared with the profit margins that can be realized in the private sector. Profit is handled differently depending on the contractual relationship between the contractor and the government. Some contracts do not allow the contractor to receive any more than a 10 percent profit. In firm fixed price contracts, the contractor determines up front how much the entire contract will cost. Once the amount is agreed upon with the government, the contractor will receive that much money. A contractor could make more than 10 percent profit in a firm fixed price contract if it manages the contract well. Cost plus award fee contracts allow the government to assess a contractor's performance throughout the life of the contract and to make decisions periodically on the amount of fee or profit the contractor receives.

   Although profit may not seem like a motivator to get into the government marketplace, it is considered a positive reason to pursue government business because of the size of government contracts. Ten percent of ten million dollars is *a lot* of money. Once a company becomes proficient at bidding and running a government contract, the profit associated with government business can become the financial foundation for a company.

2. *Government contracts allow a company's skill base to broaden*—Many skills are required on government contracts. The technology required on government programs can allow companies and their employees to broaden their skills. Often, skills that are required on government deals can be transferred to the company's commercial side. The airline industry, for example, has used many of the parts developed for DoD aircraft on its commercial planes.

3. *Government contracts build a solid financial base*—Government contracts may last up to 10 years or longer if permitted by the FAR. The longevity of contracts builds a solid financial base of backlog business for the company.

4. *Government contracts provide employment opportunities*—In today's scaled-down workforce, new government contracts represent jobs for employees. Federal government contracts are relatively secure. Regulations are in place requiring government personnel to have funds appropriated and obligated before they give a contractor a contract or delivery order. This guarantees a contractor payment for acceptable goods or services and provides a steady revenue stream.

5. *Government contracts help small businesses*—Employing small businesses (SBs), small, disadvantaged businesses (SDBs), and women-owned businesses helps all parties concerned. The federal government meets its socioeconomic objective to decrease unemployment rates by helping small businesses succeed and grow. Small companies get the expertise of a new marketplace and the opportunity to grow their businesses through gov-

ernment contracting. Finally, when small companies team with large companies, the large companies have the opportunity to meet the requirements placed on them by the federal government to subcontract federal work to SBs and SDBs.

4. What are the roles of each branch of the government in federal procurement?

Each branch of the federal government—executive, legislative, and judicial—plays a unique role in the procurement of goods and services.

The *executive branch* consists of agencies (e.g., National Aeronautics and Space Administration, DoD, Department of Health and Human Services) that develop requirements for what they plan to procure, conduct the source selection process (the way in which the agency will select a procurement winner), and use the goods and services procured.

The *legislative branch* consists of Congress and the Government Accountability Office (GAO), which maintain the funding authority. The legislative branch ensures that government money is spent appropriately through its oversight function. Executive agency representatives present their annual procurement plans at congressional hearings. The agency budgets are either approved and become part of the authorization bill, or disapproved and not funded. A bill is introduced into the House and Senate appropriations committees for a final review. These committees appropriate funds for any authorized project provided that the requested amount either matches or is less than the approved amount. After passing in the House and Senate, the appropriations bill is sent to the President, who has the authority to accept or reject it.

Congress also enacted the FAR in accordance with the requirements of the Office of Federal Procurement Policy Act of 1974 and the Armed Services Procurement Act of 1931. The FAR is prescribed jointly by the secretary of defense, the administrator of general services, and the administrator of NASA. It provides the body of regulation that governs all federal procurements. The latest version of the FAR can be obtained at: http://www.arnet.gov/FAR/. In addition, this site describes how contractors can provide input to FAR updates.

The *judicial branch* consists of the courts that handle disputes arising out of federal government contracts. The U.S. Court of Federal Claims may act as a trial court to determine whether a CO's decision in a contract award or action was correct.

5. What methods can be used to secure a government contract?

Several methods can be used to secure a government contract: work independently, work as a subcontractor, or subcontract work to other companies. Further, a company can either develop or become part of another company's General Services Administration (GSA) schedule contracts.

Work Independently

A company can decide to pursue a particular contract alone without the help of any prime contractor or subcontractors. The do-it-alone approach is useful if the company has all the resources available internally to respond to and meet the government's requirements, including employees with the appropriate skills, raw materials, production capabilities, and appropriate products. To determine whether a company has the necessary resources, it must consider the following aspects:

- Employees with the appropriate skills are required both on a proposal effort and to manage the contract after award. Such employees must be available at the time stipulated by the customer, and those time frames may shift if the customer has a schedule change.

- The company must assess product availability in terms of the amount of time it will take to produce a product from scratch, or the time it will take to make an existing product conform to the customer's specifications.

- Once the company determines that it can develop the product within the designated time frame, it must assess whether it can produce and deliver the product quantities the customer requires in the short time frame typically allowed on a contract.

- The company must consider the availability of all the resources necessary to fulfill the contract requirements in relation to the company's other business objectives. The company may have employees with the appropriate skill sets and adequate production capabilities; however, if the same resources are required in other areas of the business and cannot be spared because the other business areas could suffer irreparably, then the company cannot work on the contract alone. On the other hand, smaller contracts may make it financially feasible for the company to work alone.

If the company decides to pursue a customer contract on its own, the company must accomplish all the marketing activities, proposal development, and contract performance. The benefit to this approach is that the company has complete control and decision-making power over all aspects of the procurement. The company can determine how many resources to apply to the effort, how much risk it is willing to take in pricing the contract, and how it will ultimately satisfy the customer's requirements without consulting other partners. Although this approach allows maximum control, it also places all contract risk on the company. All pre-contract costs must be borne by the company. If the company does not meet the contract's requirements, the company is liable for all contractual remedies. The good news is that working alone allows the company to reap all the financial and reputation benefits associated with successful contract performance.

Work As a Subcontractor

Working as a subcontractor for another company, particularly a large company, offers an excellent opportunity for the subcontractor to meet its own objective of getting into new business without many of the risks associated with doing it alone. Large contractors typically have a lot of experience in each aspect of the procurement cycle and can be an invaluable resource to a company trying to break into new customers or market areas. Often, the subcontracting company benefits from the significant resources available within the larger company. For example, a large company primarily handles many of the costs associated with marketing, proposal development, and solution demonstrations. The subcontractor's responsibility may be limited to writing a few proposal sections or helping with marketing initiatives. The bottom line is that with minimal up-front investment, a company subcontracting to another company can win government business.

The disadvantage of working as a subcontractor for another company is that the prime contractor basically makes all decisions. The subcontracting company can negotiate with the other company to determine a mutually agreeable level of risk, but if the subcontractor does not want to comply with the prime contractor's decisions, the prime contractor may find another subcontractor to do the work. In addition, because the work is not done by just one company, the revenues from the contract do not belong solely to one company. The prime contractor and subcontractor must agree to a revenue-sharing approach. Finally, the prime contractor ultimately controls the program. Therefore, the subcontractor may need to change the way it offers its products or services based on the prime contractor's decision, or risk losing its place on the contract team.

It is important for a subcontractor to understand which other subcontractors are working for the prime contractor. If multiple subcontractors can provide the same product or service, how will the prime contractor divide the work among them? The prime contractor may delineate up front what specific products or services will come from each subcontractor, thereby minimizing any confusion from the beginning. Or it may determine its supplier based on past performance, price, ability to get the job done in the required timeframe, or other criteria. Regardless, a subcontracting company needs to know up front how work will be assigned to it throughout the course of the contract so that it can staff and plan accordingly.

Subcontract Work to Other Companies

Another way to pursue business is to be the prime contractor and subcontract work to other companies. If a company has established credibility, is a recognized industry expert, or brings a unique value-added contribution to a particular deal, it may be possible for the company to prime the deal. In this situation, other companies would subcontract to the company in pursuit of a piece of the business. Although the company would assume much of the risk as the prime contractor, some of that risk would be shared with the subcontractors.

For this approach to work, the prime contractor will need to find subcontractors that are willing to be on the team. The degree to which the prime contractor's team is perceived as a viable contract contender dictates how quickly other companies are willing to join the team. As prime contractor, the company makes most of the decisions and relies on the strengths of other companies to complement its own strengths.

While an automatic assumption might be that the prime contractor is usually a big company and the subcontractors are typically smaller, this is not always the case. For example, for a small business set-aside contract, a small business may prime the deal and work with a large company as a subcontractor. This approach provides the small business the experience of acting in a prime contractor role and meets the government's requirements for at least 51 percent of the work to be done by a small business. The small business benefits from the strength of a large business standing behind it with the personnel, processes, and resources to make the program run successfully.

Develop GSA Schedule Contracts

A less risky approach than running an entire program on its own is for a company to secure a GSA schedule, through which the company can sell its products and services to anyone within the government. GSA schedules are increasing in popularity because once they are established, they are easy to use and are a cost-effective alternative to agency-specific procurements. If the company is interested in competing on a GSA multiple award schedule contract, GSA's website (http://www.gsa.gov) will provide more information.

GSA is the primary supply source for many of the government's commercial item acquisitions. Any government agency can buy off the GSA schedule, thereby saving the expense of putting out a brand new acquisition. Further, GSA works with participating companies to secure most valued customer pricing, or the prices that are available in the commercial marketplace to those customers who buy large quantities of the company's products or services. By securing most valued customer pricing and giving all agencies access to those prices, GSA provides a cost effective alternative to an agency going out and buying products and services on its own.

FARA has raised the threshold for small acquisitions to $5 million for commercial items and has included a commercial services definition. These two changes and the recent changes in the GSA program make it possible for small companies to put their commercial products and services on a GSA schedule contract. GSA schedule contracts allow all government agencies the opportunity to buy a small company's products and services, and GSA provides advertising for small businesses on its web page. The advertising is paid for by the 1 percent industrial funding fee that GSA collects on every delivery order issued under the schedule. An agency wishing to procure goods and services using the GSA schedule contracts can conduct a quick comparison among three or more companies that are on the schedule and award the contract. To stay competitive, a company can always reduce its GSA price if it really wants to acquire certain business. Note: See below how GSA assists small businesses in acquiring a GSA schedule.

6. What assistance does the government provide small businesses seeking to pursue government business?

The government spends approximately $105 billion annually on contracting opportunities, but a small company that does not understand the government process may have difficulty obtaining these contract dollars. The government, unlike commercial entities, must have its acquisition programs meet goals that go beyond mere purchasing. For example, the government has socioeconomic goals to ensure that the U.S. economy prospers and grows. The Small Business Administration (SBA) was designed to help small companies thrive and prosper in the United States. To that end, the SBA uses many initiatives to help small businesses and small, disadvantaged businesses obtain government contracts. For example, the SBA works with many government agencies to develop offices specifically focused on doing business with small companies (as described below in the GSA example).

Small Business Administration

The government established the SBA to help small companies obtain, maintain, and retain government business. The SBA offers seminars, literature, websites, local offices, skilled expertise, one-on-one business advice, and an automated phone system to help small business owners start a business and move into the government marketplace. In addition to the headquarters office in Washington, D.C., and regional offices located throughout the United States, the SBA has personnel who work to identify programs as small business set-asides and who work to enact legislation that helps small businesses obtain and keep federal business. They also help match complementary companies to encourage them to work together on programs that would offer mutual gain.

Industry Classification

The government helps SBs by defining Standard Industrial Classification (SIC) codes that stipulate the qualifications of an SB so it can receive benefits. These industry classification codes are used throughout the entire government to define programmatic requirements, but they are of particular interest to SBs because they delineate the parameters by which a company may define itself as small or small and disadvantaged. The government defines small businesses according to a business' industry, revenue, and number of employees. Each industry has a different threshold for what constitutes a small business. For example, the revenue criterion is a lot higher for construction contracts than for consulting contracts because the government assumes that construction contracts cost more to operate and, therefore, it pays more for them. A $10 million construction contract may represent one program, whereas $10 million in consulting contracts may represent 50 or more separate programs.

8(a) Program

Another initiative that the SBA has is the small and disadvantaged business program. The program is commonly called the *8(a) program* because that is the citation of the part of law that enacted the program. For a company to qualify under the 8(a) program, the company must meet the thresholds for revenue and number of employees for its industry. In addition, at least 51 percent of the business must be owned and operated by a person from a minority ethnicity within the United States. Finally, the company has to enroll and be accepted as part of the 8(a) program.

Set-Aside Programs

It is important for a company to determine if it is an SB or if it qualifies as an SDB because the company can then compete on programs reserved for SBs and SDBs. Such programs are called *small business set-asides*. There are also SDB set-asides and only SDBs can compete on them. By limiting the competition and excluding large companies, the government hopes to encourage small businesses to pursue business opportunities within the federal marketplace.

New Business Relationships

Another benefit of set-aside programs is that they help small companies establish new business relationships with other SBs, SDBs, and large companies. An SB or an SDB can work with a large company on a set-aside program because the only requirement for the program is that the SB or SDB perform at least 51 percent of the work to be performed on the contract. So an SDB can be the prime contractor on a program and subcontract 49 percent or less of the work to an SB or large company to help meet program requirements. Through this working relationship, the small business may be able to secure future business opportunities with the large company.

SB and SDB Agency Goals

The SBA helps small companies by setting goals for government agencies on how much business they must give to SBs. An agency then sets goals for each prime contractor on how much of the agency's contract must be completed by a subcontractor that is an SB. As more and more SBs are established, the SBA increases its goals for agencies. This initiative helps SBs and SDBs because the government must continually seek smaller companies to meet the SBA's requirements.

In addition, agencies establish certain dollar thresholds under which *all* requirements must be set aside for a small business. So if the government identifies a certain requirement and it is under the dollar threshold established, it must go to a small business. The caveat to this requirement is that if a government agency does not believe there are two or more responsible small businesses that can do the work and participate in a competitive procurement, the agency can get approval to open the procurement up for full competition, allowing any size company to participate.

Prime Contractor Requirement

Large prime contractors need SBs and SDBs to meet the program requirements of certain contracts. As the economy moves toward entrepreneurs and start-up companies, the SBA is requiring that a greater percentage of business be given to SBs and SDBs through prime contracts. When a large company works with a small company, the small company helps the large company meet its government-imposed socioeconomic goals. This partnership, in turn, allows the government to meet its socioeconomic objective of keeping people employed through small companies. Most governmental contracts require prime contractors to state how close they can come to meeting an agency's SB/SDB goal. The prime contractors must certify that they will subcontract a certain percentage of the work available on the contract to SB/SDB companies.

Small and Disadvantaged Business Officers

The SBA has small-business liaisons called *small and disadvantaged business officers* who work within agencies and continually try to find new program requirements that could be completed by SBs and SDBs. In addition, the liaisons question government procurement officials about why each piece of business is not an SB or SDB set-aside. The officials must also justify why a small company could not perform the program requirements.

Program Requirements

Once the government decides that a particular program requirement can be performed by an SB or SDB, that requirement remains a set-aside, even if a new contract for the same work must be obtained. For example, a government needs agency data communication lines installed and the SBA determines that there are SBs or SDBs that could do this work. The program requirement would be released in a request for proposals (RFP) that allows only SBs or SDBs to compete for the program. If, after the contract work is over, the agency decides it needs more data communication lines installed, its RFP would have to be released as an SB or SDB set-aside program because it was once classified as such.

Mentor-Protégé Program

Several agencies have developed mentor-protégé programs. These programs team a large government contractor with an SB trying to become a federal contractor. The large company works with the small company on programs, and the large company teaches the small company the federal procurement process. The small company gains expertise and assistance in getting started; the large company gains credit toward its subcontracting plan for its participation in the program.

Probably the most widely known and used mentor-protégé program is one offered by DoD to help small companies gain the skills required to manage federal contracts. To qualify as a mentor under the program, a company must:

- Currently be eligible to receive government contracts

- Have been awarded at least $100 million in DoD contracts in the last fiscal year

- Possess a demonstrated ability to assist protégé development

- Have secretary of defense approval

- Be performing under an active subcontracting plan.

The protégé must meet the following requirements:

- Be an SDB as defined by the SBA

- Be eligible for government contracts.

If a company is interested in participating in the DoD mentor-protégé program, it should review the *Policy and Procedures for the DoD Pilot Mentor-Protégé Program* (DAC 91-10) issued as part of the Department of Defense FAR Supplement dated February 1996.

Easy-to-Use Small Purchase Ordering Procedures

Small purchase ordering procedures allow contractors to compete for work using the Internet. Small purchase ordering procedures allow the government to pay for products or services by using credit cards thereby simplifying the whole financial transaction. The simplified acquisition procedures may be used for all acquisitions under the small-acquisition threshold, which is currently set at $100,000. The only exception is orders placed under an established contract for products and services obtained from a required-sources supply. If the product or service is required for support of humanitarian or peace-keeping missions, the threshold is raised to $200,000.

FAR Part 13 explains methods available to COs for small purchases. As the government raises its threshold on small purchases, it will become significantly easier for a company to work on a contract alone. With these electronic systems, full-scale proposals, which can be costly for small companies, will not be required.

GSA Office of Small Business Utilization

GSA has an Office of Small Business Utilization (OSBU) that advocates for small, minority, veteran, HUBZone, and women business owners. Its mission is to promote increased access to GSA's nationwide procurement opportunities. It monitors and implements small business polices and nurtures entrepreneurial opportunities. OSBU offers programs such as the Veterans Technology Services (VETS), which is a set-aside government-wide acquisition contract (GWAC) exclusively for small technology firms owned by service-disabled veterans. Further, OSBU offers activities such as procurement networking sessions; marketing strategies and techniques workshops; electronic commerce/electronic data interchange training sessions; interagency networking break-fasts; trade missions; roundtables; and procurement conferences. More information is available at www.gsa.gov/sbu.

GSA Advantage

The GSA Advantage system can be thought of as the government-wide electronic mall containing all the products and services that the government routinely buys. Anyone can gain access to the site at https://www.gsaadvantage. gov. A company can use this site to determine the specific products and services purchased by the government and the selling prices being offered by its competitors.

7. What information can a company get from the government? What information from a company can be protected?

A company has two issues involving information the government has. First, how can the company get the information it wants? Second, how can the company protect from disclosure information on itself that is in the hands of the government? A number of laws and regulations are important.

The Freedom of Information Act (FOIA) applies to all government documents, not just procurement documents. The procurement integrity laws tell agencies what documents in the procurement process may be distributed to the general public. These also provide protection for information submitted to the government during the procurement process. And finally, the FAR provides guidance on the kind of information that can be distributed during the sealed bid process and the negotiated procurement process.

The Freedom of Information Act

FOIA is often referred to as a "disclosure statute." It encourages an agency to release information *unless* the document is exempt from disclosure under one of the exemptions in FOIA. For documents involved in the procurement process, the most common problem is identifying what information submitted by the company seeking a government contract may be released to the general public or to a competing company. These cases are referred to as "reverse FOIA" cases because the agency wants to distribute the information of the submitting company but the company wants to prevent its distribution.

Courts have set some clear guidelines.

Whether information submitted to the government is protected as that company's confidential or financial information depends on two factors. "Voluntarily submitted" information is protected only if the information is the kind of information that would customarily not be released to the public by the person from whom it was obtained. On the other hand, information submitted to the government "under compulsion" can be withheld only if the company that submitted the document can show that its disclosure would either "impair the government's ability to obtain necessary information in the future" or "would cause substantial harm to the competitive position of the person from whom the information was obtained." Incidentally, if voluntary or under compulsion information comes within this test, its release is prevented by the Trade Secrets Act. The Trade Secrets Act is a criminal law that makes it a misdemeanor to release information that is protected from disclosure.

For example, a defense contractor who won a contract showing line item costs to the government of certain products fought the release of its line item prices, overhead, profit, and other cost information, arguing that this information was confidential or financial information protected from release under FOIA. The government refused to release overhead and profit figures but was prepared to release the line item prices. An appeals court assumed that the information was provided "under compulsion" and concluded that the contractor's competitors would benefit from release of the information. Disclosing the line item prices would help the company's commercial customers negotiate or "ratchet down" the contractor's prices. In addition, disclosure of its unit prices would help its competitors calculate its actual costs "with a high degree of precision" and thereby help its competitors underbid the company. So that information could not be released. The court did, however, say that the total price of the contract could be released.

To find out more about the Freedom of Information Act and the appropriate forms to use with each agency, go to https://www.USA.gov and search on FOIA.

Federal Acquisition Regulation

The FAR provides guidance on the kind of information that should be released during the negotiated process and during the sealed bid process.

The Negotiated Process
During the negotiated procurement process, no one can get from the government "an offeror's technical solution, including unique technology, innovative and unique uses of commercial items, or any information that would compro-

mise an offeror's intellectual property to another offeror." FAR 15.306(e)(1), (2), and (3). Since the company's intellectual property is a valuable commodity that the government collects during the procurement process, it could be used to get a cheaper price from a competitor. In addition, the FAR states that the government must protect its sources. The government cannot reveal "the names of individuals providing reference information about an offeror's past performance." FAR 15.306(e)(4).

Further, the government can't reveal "an offeror's price without that offeror's permission." The government can, however, tell one or all companies that its price is too high or too low and give them the government estimate for the purchase. FAR 15.306(e)(3). This government release provides the private market an opportunity to test the validity of the government estimates.

The Sealed Bid Process

The FAR guidance for sealed bidding is more general and therefore less helpful to a CO struggling with what can or cannot be released. The FAR states that after a solicitation has been issued, "Discussions regarding a solicitation shall be conducted and technical or other information shall be transmitted only by the contracting officer or superiors having contractual authority or by others specifically authorized. Such personnel shall not furnish any information to a prospective bidder that alone or together with other information may afford an advantage over others. However, general information that would not be prejudicial to other prospective bidders may be furnished upon request; e.g., explanation of a particular contract clause or a particular condition of the schedule in the invitation for bids, and more specific information or clarifications may be furnished by amending the solicitation." FAR 14.409.1.

Keep in mind that by its very nature, a sealed bid process is used only when the government does not anticipate any reason to engage in any individual discussions with the potential bidders. If the government needs additional information, the FAR allows amendments to the solicitation document that are then distributed to all potential bidders.

The Procurement Integrity Act

Companies cannot get two categories of information that are protected by the Procurement Integrity Act: contractor bid or proposal information and source selection material. Therefore, some information a company submits to the government cannot be disclosed even though the government has the data in its possession.

Contractor proposal or bid information includes cost or pricing data; indirect costs and direct labor rates; and proprietary information about manufacturing processes, operations, or techniques. Also protected is "information marked in accordance with 52.215-1(e)." This FAR clause is the instructions for offerors provision. It tells companies to mark the cover page with a certain legend and then to mark each protected page. For the cover page, companies are to "Mark the title page with the following legend: This proposal includes data that shall not be disclosed outside the Government and shall not be duplicated, used, or disclosed—in whole or in part—for any purpose other than to evaluate this proposal. If, however, a contract is awarded to this offeror as a result of—or in connection with—the submission of this data, the Government shall have the right to duplicate, use, or disclose the data to the extent provided in the resulting contract. . . . The data subject to this restriction are contained in sheets [insert numbers or other identification of sheets]." In addition to this cover legend, companies are to also "Mark each sheet of data it wishes to restrict with the following legend: 'Use or disclosure of data contained on this sheet is subject to the restriction on the title page of this proposal.'"

That does not end the matter. What typically happens is overkill. Companies routinely mark every possible page with this legend, protecting information such as the table of contents and pages with one word on them. To limit this, the FAR gives the CO the opportunity to limit which information is protected.

In addition to contractor material, government material is also protected. The FAR defines source selection information to include "bid prices before bid opening, proposed costs *anytime*, source selection plans, technical evaluation plans and evaluations, cost or price evaluations of proposals, competitive range determinations, rankings of bids, proposals, or competitors, reports and evaluations of source selection panels," and a catch-all: "other information marked as 'SOURCE SELECTION INFORMATION—SEE FAR 3.104' based on a case-by-case determination by the head of the agency or designee, or the contracting officer, that its disclosure would jeopardize the integrity or successful completion of the Federal agency procurement to which the information relates."

8. What steps does an agency take in a negotiated procurement to purchase goods and services?

An agency takes a series of steps in purchasing goods and services through a negotiated procurement:

Determine the resources required to meet the operational strategy—The Constitution and subsequent government actions mandate each agency's purpose and mission. The agency develops its operational strategy for accomplishing that mission. In doing so, the agency considers available facilities, personnel, budgets, and other resources. Future budget requirements are driven by resources needed for the operational strategy that are above and beyond the resources currently available.

Assign a program manager and contracting officer—A program manager (PM) and a CO are assigned to work together throughout the life of the procurement cycle. The PM understands the users' requirements and what goods and services are needed to meet them. The CO understands how to obtain the necessary products or services from the contracting community using the federal procurement regulations.

Develop an acquisition strategy—Once the program budget is approved, the PM and CO must decide whether the agency should wait until government resources are available to meet the requirement or procure goods and services from the contractor community. A "make or buy" decision is made for each individual program or project. This decision process is part of the acquisition strategy and includes the contracting process, components of the solicitation, demonstration test and evaluation criteria, bidders' list, methods for obtaining competitors, guidelines for proposal evaluation, cost goals, lifecycle cost projections, data rights, warranties, contractor incentives, contract type, and contract administration details.

Develop an acquisition plan—The next step in the process is to develop the acquisition plan, which includes a plan of action and milestones, statement of need, applicable conditions, cost parameters, standards of performance, delivery requirements, tradeoffs or alternate methods for completing the work, and government program risks associated with contractor performance.

Obtain approval and funding—The PM and CO are required to justify the program need and its approach throughout the procurement cycle. Each agency has its own unique approval cycle, and the size of the procurement dictates review requirements. These reviews ensure that taxpayers' dollars are spent prudently, government assets are used effectively, and the resulting contract meets the agency's objectives.

Establish the source selection authority—The source selection authority (SSA) determines the winning contractor. The SSA and the source selection evaluation board (SSEB) develop and approve a source selection plan. Components of this plan will appear in the RFP. After proposal submission, the SSEB evaluates contractor proposals against the evaluation criteria and makes its recommendation for award to the SSA. The SSA may accept or reject the SSEB's recommendation.

Develop the final RFP—The RFP's statement of work (SOW) describes the work the contractor must perform. Coupled with the SOW, the government includes the other sections of the RFP: cover letter, schedule, packaging, acceptance, delivery, performance, contract administration, FAR clauses, special contract clauses, attachments, proposal instructions, representations, certifications, and evaluation criteria. The RFP is written by the CO and PM with help from the contracting officer's technical representative (COTR), who understands the technical implications of a program and can assist the CO, a government committee, or a government contractor.

Conduct market research—The government is now required under FARA to conduct market research to determine whether products and services required are available commercially. This requirement demonstrates the government's preference to use COTS items where appropriate.

Send out draft or final documents—The government may choose to solicit industry input to determine if the technology requested is feasible, or whether alternate approaches should be considered. The government may choose to send the entire draft RFP or selected sections out for industry comment. This draft document review gives contractors a chance to shape the procurement. Should the government decide to do this, it may then review and incorporate industry comments as deemed appropriate. Otherwise, the government may just decide to issue the RFP in its final format.

Conduct a bidders conference—The government conducts a bidders conference to determine the level of competition and to understand any contractor concerns. In this meeting, the government reviews the agency's mission, program purpose, and milestones, and answers any contractor questions.

Answer industry questions—Throughout the procurement process, the government receives questions from companies. The RFP states a date by which all questions should be submitted to the government. If a company has a question after that date, it should be directed to the CO, who will ensure that the appropriate government personnel provide the answer. Companies submit questions in writing, and the government then provides answers to all the bidding contractors.

Finalize the source selection approach—The government prepares for receipt of company proposals by coordinating the following:

- *Logistics*—Places identified to evaluate and store the proposals

- *Evaluators*—People selected to evaluate contractors' proposals

- *Schedule*—Milestones established for the evaluation process.

Receive company proposals and begin evaluation—Each evaluator is assigned a section or sections of the companies' proposals to review. Depending on the government's RFP, the proposals may be submitted in writing, orally, or both. One evaluator evaluates the same section of each company's proposal so that the evaluations are consistent. Each evaluator reviews the companies' proposals against the evaluation criteria and assigns a score. If the evaluator needs additional information from the company about its solution, the evaluator will issue a clarification report (CR) or a deficiency report (DR), depending on the severity of the issue.

Receive company responses to clarifications and deficiencies—The evaluator receives the company responses to clarifications and deficiencies and determines if the responses are adequate to resolve the issue. The evaluator then assigns a score to the section. If the evaluator still has questions, follow-up clarifications and deficiencies may be issued to the contractor.

Evaluate companies' price proposals—The evaluation price team begins its evaluation of the companies' price proposals to determine if the prices are reasonable. The government can make an award at this point in the process if it chooses.

Initiate audits—The CO may decide to initiate pre-award surveys or other audits of companies if he or she feels it is appropriate. An independent agency usually conducts these audits, and the audit results are presented to the SSA.

Make competitive range determination—During the procurement process, the government may make a competitive range determination. This determination used to be based on the government's belief that, given the current state of the company's proposal, a company could not become eligible for award within the procurement timeframe. Now, with the government moving toward the goal of efficient competition, it may make a competitive range determination by selecting the three or four top proposals and excluding the rest from the competition. Because of this, companies must put forth their best proposal at initial submission. If they don't, they may be excluded from serious consideration. Companies no longer within the competitive range are dropped from the procurement.

Conduct live test demonstrations (LTDs)—If the RFP requires a demonstration, the government conducts LTDs with each company. Before the demonstration, the government must determine how to evaluate the companies' solutions. The results of the LTDs are included in the SSA evaluation. So, for example, if the government determines the response rate in an information technology procurement, it then uses that rate to evaluate one contractor's performance against another's in an evaluation.

Prepare for discussions with companies—The government identifies any outstanding issues in each company's proposal. Each company is then assigned a time to meet with the government to review the issues. Any issue the company has at this time is also discussed.

Call for final proposal revisions—The government then issues a call for final proposal revisions to all companies still within the competitive range. Keep in mind that the government may make awards based on initial offers and a final proposal revision may never be requested.

Negotiate final contract—The government negotiates the final contract with the apparent winner before or after the award is announced.

Award contract—The government then awards the contract to the winning company.

Contract start-up—The government provides guidance to the contractor during contract start-up.

Contract performance—The government monitors, directs, and assesses contractor performance during the contract period.

Contract shutdown—The government works with the contractor to close out the contract. This closeout may be due to termination for default of the contractor, termination for the convenience of the government, or contract completion.

9. What steps must a company take to sell goods and services?

A company must also take a series of steps to sell goods and services to the federal marketplace:

Determine method to sell to the government—At some point, a company decides to pursue federal business or to increase its presence within the federal marketplace. There are many approaches to penetrating the federal marketplace. A company may go after a contract alone, work through the SBA, subcontract to a large company, or prime the contract and subcontract work to other companies. Other alternatives that are available to all size contractors can also be easily used by small businesses. For example, a company may choose to sell its products and services under a GSA schedule. Additionally, a company may choose to market to government agencies and prime contractors to gain access on an existing contract vehicle. It may also choose to pursue micro or small purchases to minimize the required amounts of paperwork necessary to sell to the government. The following steps will vary depending upon which approach is selected.

Assess the corporate organization required for government business—Besides all the normal functions required to pursue business, such as engineering, manufacturing, research and development, marketing, and finance, government contracts may require additional corporate functions. Audit, inspection, acceptance, quality assurance, and contract modifications are all functions that most government contracts require. In addition, the government may require the contractor to adhere to and track capability maturity models, contract data requirements lists, and other government initiatives. Some of these initiatives are minimized when the government buys a commercial product or service because in those procurements the government tries to use many of the same terms and conditions that are used in the commercial marketplace.

Develop a strategic plan to determine how to enter the federal market—The planning process can help a company analyze external and internal conditions, constraints, opportunities, organization, and policies so it can develop assumptions, objectives, programs, projects, schedules, and financials for entering the government marketplace. To develop a plan the company should gather initial data, develop and document the plan, communicate the plan to the people responsible for implementing it, establish a review mechanism to evaluate the plan's success, and develop and use feedback mechanisms to update the plan.

Develop a marketing plan for each program the company decides to pursue—The company can use the same planning methodology to develop a strategy for winning a program. For the marketing plan, the company needs to identify specific projects that will help demonstrate its interest in a particular program. Projects may include advertising, strategic partnerships, or competition analysis.

Assign a program manager and salesperson to pursue the program—Early in the process, few people are involved in the program. Typically, a company will assign a program manager to begin solution development and a salesperson to gather customer and competition information.

Begin marketing a specific program—The marketing plan is implemented for a specific program. Executive government visits are made to the contractor facility, contractors visit the government sites, solution development begins, and so on.

Gather marketing information—The company gathers marketing information throughout the procurement process.

Information on the customer, the competitors, new technology, and industry trends are all part of the procurement strategy. As this information changes, the company may make slight alterations to the procurement strategy.

Analyze the draft RFP—If there is a draft RFP process, it gives industry an understanding of what is being procured and allows the government to solicit industry feedback. The government evaluators assigned to the procurement review these draft documents and incorporate changes as deemed appropriate. The draft RFP can normally be found on the agency's website or on the electronic posting system. When analyzing the RFP, the contractor should determine how much electronic commerce will take place and ensure that it is capable of the electronic interfaces necessary to work with the government.

Shape the procurement—It is in both the government's and the contractor's best interest for the contractor to try to shape the procurement. *Shaping* means that the contractor analyzes the government's draft documents or solicitation requirements and works to get the RFP language more conducive to the company making a positive bid decision. Shaping is favorable to the government because it can help the evaluators determine if they will receive at least three proposals in response to the RFP. Contractors can also use position papers, marketing meetings, and bidders conferences to shape the procurement.

Begin solution development—The draft documents also give the contractor the opportunity to begin developing the solution it intends to bid on the program. Refining the solution occurs throughout the procurement cycle. At this point, the high-level solution components are identified.

Determine acquisition strategy—Once the company identifies high-level components, it can decide whether it should make or buy the components. Due to the government's emphasis on commercial items, contractors should use commercial products wherever applicable.

Establish the external team—The company's decision to make or buy leads to establishing a list of products and services that must be procured from outside sources. The company then contacts the companies providing the needed goods and services for potential teaming partner or subcontractor relationships.

Develop a bid and proposal (B&P) budget—The core team then establishes its best estimate of how much it will cost the company to pursue this piece of business. The team assesses the B&P budget as part of the bid decision criteria.

Understand the competition—The core team analyzes the competition and assesses how its team fares. This analysis also becomes a component of the bid decision criteria.

Determine eligible past performance citations—Due to the government's increased emphasis on past performance, the contractor should determine early on if it has contracts that demonstrate its capabilities in areas similar to those required by the new contract, and if those contracts can be referenced. This determination should be made as soon as possible because if the contractor is performing poorly on existing contracts, it stands little chance of winning future business until the performance problems are resolved.

If a company has no past experience with government contracting, that fact is not considered either a positive or a negative factor in the source selection. It is considered a neutral consideration.

Make an initial bid decision—Based on all information obtained to date, the company decides whether to bid the program.

Receive the RFP and make a final bid decision—Once the final RFP is received and reviewed, the company reassesses its bid decision.

Establish a core team—If the company decides to make a bid, the program manager and the salesperson typically add members to the core team of the program effort.

Develop a proposal plan—The core team develops a proposal plan to help manage the proposal effort.

Develop a proposal management approach—As part of the planning process, the core team establishes the approach to proposal management. Some companies use a standard approach; others develop a new approach for each program they pursue.

Select a proposal team—The remaining members of the proposal team are selected by the salesperson and the program manager. To contain bid and proposal costs, members stay on a proposal effort only as long as they actively contribute to the proposal.

Conduct solicitations—The company issues solicitations for products and services that will be procured from outside sources that do not meet the single or sole source criteria. This is a critical component because the company will later be audited through a Contractor Purchasing System Review (CPSR) to determine if it procured products and services in a competitive manner. Passing the CPSR is required for the contractor to make purchases *on any government contract.*

Develop the technical volume—The technical team finalizes the technical solution and documents it in the technical volume or section of the proposal.

Develop the management volume—The management team finalizes the program management solution and documents it in the management volume.

Develop the price volume—The business team finalizes the business solution and responds to the price requirements of the RFP in the price volume.

Develop the contracts volume—The contract team responds to the contractual requirements of the RFP in the contracts volume.

Develop any other required sections of the proposal—The government may require the company to complete other steps for the contractor proposal. The government reviews the program requirements and the information provided to make a sound judgment of the contractor's abilities. This information may include software development capabilities, live test demonstration (LTD) description, past performance, risk mitigation, or an executive summary. In addition, the government may require a copy of the slides that will be used at the oral presentation of the proposal to the government.

Resolve outstanding issues—The government requests that companies ask all questions during the question phase of the procurement cycle. However, the company should not hesitate to ask questions after that point; it is in both the government's and the company's best interest that the company continue to ask questions. The company must pose all questions in writing to the CO.

Determine the review team approach and members—Each company handles proposal reviews differently. The company should determine the approach and members up front to ensure a successful review.

Finalize the solution—At some point, the company will have to finalize its solution so that the production process may begin. After this point, changes should be kept to an absolute minimum, with the ramifications of the changes carefully considered.

Manage change—Government amendments, program delays, or product inability to meet requirements are all valid reasons for changing the solution after it is considered final. The important thing for the company to do is to manage the changes and the ripple effects caused by the changes throughout the proposal.

Develop the proposal—The proposal development process goes on throughout the procurement process. At this point in the cycle, the company outlines and writes proposal sections, designs graphics, and carefully weaves winning themes throughout the proposal.

Conduct the proposal review process—Most companies conduct a review of the technical, business, and management solutions. At the end of the proposal process, the company reviews each requirement and its associated response to ensure that all requirements have been addressed.

Produce and deliver the proposal—After the review teams' comments are incorporated into the proposal, the team produces the final version of the proposal. The company submits the completed proposal and required number of copies to the government at the authorized location by the designated time.

Respond to CRs/DRs—The contractor must respond to the government's CRs and DRs. The contractor does this by answering the question posed and by updating its proposal to reflect any new information.

Develop an LTD plan—The LTD, if required by the RFP, is typically evaluated. Contractors want to plan carefully to ensure that the LTD is successful.

Conduct an LTD—At the government-designated site, date, and time, the contractor conducts its LTD.

Conduct government site visits—The government may visit the contractor site before award for several reasons, including pre-award survey, audit, or Software Engineering Institute evaluation (for software development contracts only).

Conduct orals—The government may require the contractor to come to the government site and present all or some of its proposed solution orally.

Prepare for discussions—The government may enter into discussions with all contractors still within the competitive range, or it may wait until an apparent winner is selected and conduct discussions with only that contractor. The contractor prepares for discussions by developing a list of items for discussion and possible resolution of the issues.

Develop a final proposal revision strategy plan—Since the turnaround time is so short on a final proposal revision (FPR), formerly known as the best and final offer, the contractor usually prepares an FPR strategy plan. The plan should delineate how the contractor intends to work with its subcontractors to lower the prices on the program.

Conduct negotiations with subcontractors—To drive the overall contract price down, prime contractors conduct negotiations with subcontractors in an attempt to reduce the subcontractors' prices.

Prepare and submit final proposal revisions—The contractor develops strategies to reduce the contract price and updates final prices to reflect the latest negotiations with the vendors. The company then turns in the FPR to the government. However, in an effort to streamline procurement, the government is trying to award more contracts on the initial offer or first and final offer.

Develop a contract start-up plan—Once the contract is awarded, the government expects the contractor to begin work immediately. Therefore, the contractor develops a plan for how the contract will operate before being informed of an award. The contractor must establish processes and prepare deliverables to accommodate all the initial contract requirements.

Receive notice of contract award—At last the contractor is awarded the contract. Provided no protests are lodged, contract work begins immediately.

Negotiate the prime contract—The government may choose to finalize the prime contract before or after the award is announced.

Finalize subcontracts—The prime contractor and subcontractors may choose to finalize the subcontracts before or after the award is announced.

Conduct contract start-up—The prime contractor then implements the contract start-up processes identified in the contract start-up plan, including locating and training personnel, locating and remodeling office space, implementing operating procedures with subcontractors and internal support organizations, working with the government to determine day-to-day operations, and purchasing materials required for contract work.

Perform contract work—Work is performed throughout the life of the contract. This work includes the following tasks, if they are required by the contract: producing contract deliverables, understanding contractual implications of any decision made, filling delivery orders, managing task orders, managing change to the prime contract, managing change to the subcontracts, managing contract risks, and preparing for audits (such as audits of time cards, rates, or purchasing system).

Develop a contract closeout plan—Eventually, the contract will end because of completion, termination, or the government's decision not to renew contract options. The contractor must develop a plan to close out the contract to ensure that government and corporate assets are protected and to ensure that requirements are met through the last day of the contract period.

Conduct contract closeout—As the contract nears completion, the contractor must conduct the following steps: reassign personnel, dispose of contract resources, return government-furnished property, close out subcontracts, close out prime contracts, and prepare for final audit and payment.

CHAPTER 2
Introduction to Federal Contracting

A prospective contractor needs to understand the numerous terms that are commonly used in the federal government marketplace. Starting off with the document that governs all federal contracts, we discuss the types of regulations that impact federal business. Next we discuss procurement methods and competition types. A discussion of contract vehicles follows, and the chapter wraps up with some of the unique contract set-asides available for contractors.

10. What regulations govern federal acquisition?

A number of regulations have important implications for federal acquisition.

Federal Acquisition Regulation (FAR)

Standard policies and procedures for federal government acquisitions are outlined in the FAR. The FAR is available in bookstores (although no longer available in print from the Government Printing Office, it is still available through commercial companies such as Management Concepts) and online, and should be reviewed to help a company understand the rules of federal procurement. Because the regulations are continually evolving, a contractor should refer to a current edition of the FAR to determine the exact wording of the clauses of interest. The current edition of the FAR can be obtained at the website www.gpo.gov. In addition, www.farsite.hill.af.mil/search.htm allows you to do key word searches on the FAR. The website www.dfsc.dla.mil lists which agencies have been granted FAR exceptions.

Agency-Specific Regulations

Several agencies have developed their own sets of regulations to supplement the FAR; these are designed to work in conjunction with the FAR to accommodate the requirements of a particular agency. For example, the Department of Justice has the Justice Acquisition Regulations, and the Department of Defense has the Defense Federal Acquisition Regulation. Because of these unique requirements, a contractor must always ensure that it has the most current copy of the regulations being used by a particular agency for a procurement.

Procurement Acts and Executive Orders

Never before in the history of procurement have so many new regulations been developed that impact federal acquisition. Former Vice President Al Gore's National Performance Review, which was later changed to the National Partnership for Reinventing Government, has significantly reduced the time, effort, and resources expended on federal procurement. For example, the Federal Acquisition Streamlining Act has significantly altered the complexion of the FAR by simplifying the procurement process and making the regulations shorter and more user-friendly. The Federal Acquisition Reform Act, passed in 1997, significantly affected FAR Parts 5, 13, 14, 15, 19, 23, and 25.

11. What are the standard procurement methods used in federal acquisition?

The government may choose either sealed bid or competitive procurement as the procurement method. The government selects the method based on procurement conditions.

Sealed Bid

The government conducts sealed bid procurements when the procuring agency has determined that the award will be made on the basis of price and that discussions will not be held with the bidders. In this procurement method:

1. The government issues an invitation for bid (IFB) outlining the goods and services to be purchased and the terms and conditions by which those items must be offered.

2. Contractors review the IFB and determine if they can be cost-competitive. If the answer is yes, contractors respond with their price for the work solicited.

3. At a designated time, all bids are opened in a public forum.

4. The low-cost contractor wins the bid provided it is deemed a responsible contractor. (FAR 6.4.)

Competitive Proposals

The government conducts a competitive negotiation if it determines that factors in addition to price must be considered as part of the evaluation process and that discussions with companies may be required. In this procurement method:

1. The government issues an RFP.

2. Each contractor reviews the RFP to decide whether to bid on the program. If the answer is yes, the contractor responds with a proposal.

3. If required, each contractor participates in post-submission activities, such as a live test demonstration, an audit, discussions, and a final proposal revision submission.

4. The government makes an award decision based on factors described in RFP Section M, Evaluation Criteria. (FAR 6.5.)

E-Buy

A third type of procurement method is quickly making its way to the forefront in today's age of high technology. When fully implemented, the General Services Administration (GSA) will require its schedule holder contractors to put their products, services, and prices on the GSA Advantage! system. This system paves the way for the e-Buy program, which allows government procurement officials to solicit price quotes instantaneously from competing product and service providers. In today's procurement environment, the government buyer may solicit quotes from three to four providers that it has some familiarity with. In the e-Buy arena, companies will be categorized according to Dun and Bradstreet's Universal Standard Products and Services Classification (UNSPSC) categories. When a buyer needs something, the buyer will select the appropriate UNSPSC category and all companies within that category will be sent notification about the request for quote (RFQ). Once the RFQ time is closed, the buyer may select the company that represents the best overall value to the government and issue an order to that contractor. This ensures that all companies holding schedules and listed in the GSA Advantage! system will be able to bid on an RFQ.

12. What are competition requirements?

Three main types of competition are used in federal contracting: full and open competition, sole source acquisition, and set-asides.

Full and open competition means that any source (individual or company) may compete. Typically, full competition requires the government to evaluate at least two offers submitted by two different companies before making the award decision.

Sole source acquisition means that the agency contracts with a source after soliciting and negotiating with only one source.

The government is not using sole source acquisitions as much since the Competition in Contracting Act was passed in 1984 (P.L. 98-369) because it can receive better pricing and terms through the competitive process. The government may use sole source acquisitions, however, in extreme situations, such as:

1. Only one source can satisfy the requirements

2. Unusual and compelling urgency

3. National defense

4. Other special circumstances (FAR 6.302).

Set-asides allow the government to use the procurement process to meet socioeconomic objectives by limiting the types of companies allowed to bid on an otherwise competitive bid. The government may require that the team be composed of the following types of companies:

- *Small businesses*—Companies that meet the government's requirements for revenue and size within a particular industry. The government has established Standard Industrial Classification (SIC) codes that categorize the type(s) of work a company performs. If a company applies to the SBA and meets the qualifications, it can be classified as a small business for that particular SIC code and be allowed to compete for small business set-asides within that industry classification. Due to the North American Free Trade Agreements Act and the need for common industry definitions for Canada, Mexico, and the United States, the U.S. Census Bureau is issuing the *North American Industry Classification System Manual.* Once this classification system is implemented, it will replace the standard industrial code system. Additional information can be found at www.census.gov/epcd/www/naics.

- *Small and disadvantaged businesses*—Companies operated and at least 51 percent owned by a person recognized as having minority status. Small and disadvantaged businesses do not have to be part of the SBA's 8(a) program. Companies must be prequalified by the SBA for 8(a) participation, and then they are eligible for contract awards that are 8(a) program set-asides.

- *HubZones*—Businesses located in areas that have been defined by the government as economically depressed due to high unemployment rates.

13. What types of contracts exist in the government marketplace?

The government can use any of the many types of contracts. The contract type selection depends on:

- Whether the items being procured are commercial and available off-the-shelf or require development

- The degree of risk associated with contract performance

- The degree of certainty the government has regarding the quantity and timing of contract purchases.

Contract Types

All contract types are described in the FAR, but the main contract types and characteristics are:

- *Fixed price contracts*—In a fixed price contract, the contractor is held to the dollar amount the company proposed for the goods and services required in the RFP. The contractor is paid this amount regardless of actual costs incurred. In this type of contract, overruns are paid by the company, which benefits from underruns (provided it did not intentionally overbid the contract). Characteristics of a fixed price contract include:

    —Assigns maximum risk and full responsibility for costs and resulting profit or loss to the contractor

    —Provides maximum incentive for the contractor to control costs

—Imposes a minimum administrative burden on both contracting parties.

There are several different types of fixed price contracts: incentive contracts, indefinite delivery/indefinite quantity (ID/IQ) contracts, cost reimbursement contracts, and time and materials contracts.

- *Incentive contracts*—These tie the profit or fee payable under the contract to the contractor's performance, so if a contractor does well it is awarded money in excess of its contract costs. Characteristics of an incentive contract are as follows:

  —Establishes reasonable and attainable targets that are clearly communicated to the contractor

  —Applies incentive increases or decreases to performance targets rather than minimum performance requirements.

- *ID/IQ contracts*—These are used when the exact times and/or quantities of future deliveries are not known at the time of contract award. Characteristics of an ID/IQ contract are as follows:

  —Permits the government to stock at minimum levels

  —Permits flexibility in quantities and delivery scheduling

  —Limits the government's obligation to a minimum quantity specified in the contract

  —Can be fixed price, cost plus, or time and materials.

- *Cost reimbursement (cost plus) contracts*—These allow the contractor to bill the customer for the actual costs incurred, plus a negotiated fee. The fee is an award based on a predetermined fixed amount, an evaluated amount, or incentives. Characteristics are as follows:

—Used for contracts requiring research or development, or when the government does not know the magnitude of the work being contracted

—Risk is shared between the contractor and the government; all of the contractor's expenses are recoverable, but the fee portion can be at risk for poor performance.

• *Time and materials contracts*—These are used for acquiring services on the basis of direct labor hours at a specified fixed hourly rate and materials at cost (including a materials handling fee). Characteristics include the following:

—Minimal risk for the company because all costs are covered and the contract only requires the company's best efforts. However, although all costs are covered, there is some risk for the company because it is locked into the rate proposed. For example, if a contractor bids a $75/hour rate and because of increased salary requirements it would like to charge $85/hour to cover its expenses and protect its profit margin, the government still holds the contractor to providing the service for the agreed upon $75/hour rate.

—Negotiated fixed fee is available to the company, provided that it can operate at the price proposed. If the costs are exceeded, the fee could shrink to zero.

Multiple Award Schedules

There are an increasing number of multiple award schedules (MASs) available for contractors to bid on. MASs are contract vehicles that are awarded to more than one contractor. The MAS gives the government the option of running competitions among the companies selected for award. When a company wins a multiple award schedule, it just wins the right to sell products and services at the prices established by its schedule. The GSA schedules are the most common and popular multiple award schedules. Companies work to get their products and services on the GSA schedule, and anyone from any agency within the government can buy off the schedule. In addition, the government can request that the company provide a discount from the schedule-established prices.

Blanket Purchase Agreements

The establishment of blanket purchase agreements (BPAs) is another popular trend in government contracting. BPAs are typically tied to a GSA schedule but are established between an agency and a company and list specific products and services that the company can sell to that agency. Like MASs, BPAs help to simplify the acquisition process because the terms and conditions are negotiated up front, and any orders placed against the MAS or BPA must comply with them.

14. Are there any types of small procurements that can be accomplished without all the paperwork associated with a full and open competition?

The government realizes that it is a waste of contractors' time and taxpayers' dollars to procure every product or service using the detailed processes described in this book. To help reduce government administrative overhead burden, the government, in FAR Part 13, identifies two types of small procurements that have simplified procedures for purchasing the necessary goods and services. They are as follows:

- Micro-purchase procedures for purchases up to $2,500, many of which can be conducted using a government-issued credit card

- Simplified acquisition procedures for purchases up to $100,000.

Because of the cost savings achieved by these expedited approval and ordering procedures, the government is working to get the dollar thresholds raised even higher so that the simplified procedures can be used to an even greater extent. Review FAR Part 13 to determine if your product or service can be purchased using these methods.

15. Are there any websites that are particularly useful for government procurements?

The government is developing a website called FirstGov (http://firstgov.gov) that will allow citizens to search all on-line government documents. This site will have the ability to search one billion documents in less than one-quarter of a second, and it will be able to handle at least 100 million searches a day. This will make it much easier for citizens to find government information and services. In addition, it will allow agencies to determine whether they are duplicating the efforts of other government agencies. Armed with this information, the agencies can then ensure that the data are consistent or streamline their processes so that only one agency provides the data.

In addition, the FAR Council issued a proposed amendment to the FAR to designate "FedBizOpps" (formerly known as the Electronic Posting System) as the single point of universal public access to government-wide procurement opportunities. FedBizOpps is accessible online at www.fedbizopps .gov. The proposed rule requires COs to post each contract action that is expected to exceed $25,000, along with the place of contract performance and set-aside status.

Under the proposed rule, agencies had until October 21, 2001, to begin posting all applicable actions on the FedBizOpps website. The Office of Federal Procurement Policy (OFPP) expects that FedBizOpps will create a central point for electronic access to acquisition information; create an index of all business information at one Internet location for searching and downloading; provide access through adaptable, interface-friendly electronic tools with widespread commercial acceptance; and allow potential companies and service providers to access and download information through a variety of commercial electronic means and business applications, including web-based technology, bulk data feeds, and electronic mail. FedBizOpps also offers an automatic e-mail notification feature, which will provide information about contracting opportunities for specific supplies or services or specified agencies. Finally, FedBizOpps will be linked to the Procurement Marketing and Access Network ("PRO-Net"), an Internet database of small businesses managed by the SBA. This link will increase small business awareness of government procurement opportunities.

16. What is the HUBZone program?

The HUBZone—Historically Underutilized Business Zones—Empowerment Contracting program was specifically called for in the Small Business Reauthorization Act of 1997. Federal agencies were able to solicit contract offers under the new guidelines starting on January 4, 1999. The program encourages economic development and creates job opportunities in distressed rural and urban areas. These areas are classified as distressed based on specific unemployment or low-income criteria. The program provides a contracting preference to small companies located within the geographic boundaries of these areas, as well as companies that hire employees who live within those areas.

A HUBZone is an area that is located in (a) a qualified census tract (as defined by Section 42(d)(5)(C)(i)(1) of the Internal Revenue Code of 1986) and/or (b) a qualified "nonmetropolitan county" that is not located in a metropolitan statistical area (as defined by Section 143(k)(2)(b) of the Internal Revenue Code of 1986) and in which the median household income is less than 80 percent of the nonmetropolitan state median, or the unemployment rate is at least 140 percent percent of the state average. To help contractors determine whether geographic areas meet these criteria, the SBA, at http://map.sba.gov/hubzone/init/asp, identifies which parts of a state are classified as HUBZones and even allows you to input a specific address to determine its HUBZone status.

More than 7000 urban census tracts and 900 rural counties, in addition to every Native American reservation, currently qualify for HUBZone status. These HUBZones may change annually since the statistics used by the departments of Labor and Commerce as qualification criteria for the HUBZone program are updated annually.

For a company to qualify under the program, a small business must meet the following requirements as outlined by FAR Part 19:

1. Its principal office must be physically located within a HUBZone.

2. It must be wholly owned and controlled by U.S. citizens.

3. A minimum of 35 percent of its employees must permanently reside with a HUBZone (although it does not have to be the one in which the company is located).

The small business must also be certified by the SBA as a qualified HUBZone business.

Once qualified as a HUBZone, a small business can be awarded contracts on a sole-source basis, competitively procured through a HUBZone set-aside procurement, or under full and open competition in which it will be given a price evaluation preference. This price evaluation preference means that other non-HUBZone *and other non-small business* companies will have 10 percent added to their prices as part of the price evaluation. Manufacturing HUBZone businesses are eligible for sole source contract awards up to $5 million and $3 million for other businesses.

17. What is the Javits-Wagner-O'Day (JWOD) Act and how does it apply to procurement?

The Javits-Wagner-O'Day Act of 1971, Public Law 92-28 (41 U.S.C. 46–48c), was designed as a follow-on to the Wagner-O'Day Act enacted in 1938. The Wagner-O'Day Act promoted the use of the products provided by blind people in federal procurement. The JWOD Act helped meet socioeconomic goals and established the Committee on Purchases of Blind-Made Products. The committee's role was to define and establish long-term employment opportunities for blind people by mandating that all federal agencies purchase specified supplies made in nonprofit organizations employing blind individuals.

Senator Jacob Javits believed that the original law did not go far enough. He sought to amend the original Wagner O'Day Act to permit other nonprofit organizations serving people with other severe disabilities to participate in the program. The JWOD Act also authorized nonprofit organizations to sell services, as well as products, to the federal government.

The committee administering this program is now known as the Committee for Purchase from People Who Are Blind or Severely Disabled. Its charter is to determine which products and services should be purchased by the federal government under the JWOD program. In addition, the committee determines the fair market price for supplies and services based on changing market conditions. The committee has designated two central nonprofit agencies: National Industries for the Blind and National Industries for the Severely Disabled to facilitate the distribution of orders among nonprofit organizations participating in the JWOD program.

Individual Participant Benefits of JWOD

The goal of the program is to increase employment and training opportunities for people who are severely challenged and help, if possible, prepare them for other employment opportunities. In addition, it gives challenged people a way to earn an income, support themselves, and enjoy the benefits of full-time employment. JWOD program participants may lead more productive, independent lives.

Government Procurement Benefits of JWOD

The JWOD items are available to government activities only through GSA, the Defense Logistics Agency, or specific contractors authorized to order from GSA. The JWOD program benefits the federal government by providing it the following:

- A standard source for certain products and services

- A source committed to quality in product and service delivery

- Fair market prices

- Reduced procurement paperwork

- Low pre- and post-award management costs

- A feasible way to improve progress in meeting socioeconomic goals.

18. What are some of the policies that the government has in place to ensure integrity throughout the procurement process?

The U.S. government works hard to ensure that all citizens are treated equally. That policy holds true for business dealings with the government as well. The government has a whole host of regulations and standards that apply to people working with or within the government, covering federal employees, contractors, and subcontractors. While not all acts might be illegal in the nongovernment world, people working with government business are required to refrain from any activities that even have the appearance of being improper or questionable. The responsibility is placed on both government personnel and contractors. For example, a CO may not accept a bribe because it is illegal, but a company offering a bribe is also an illegal act.

FAR Part 3

FAR Part 3 covers "Improper Business Practices and Personal Conflicts of Interest." Government personnel and contractors must be aware of and comply with all the regulations outlined in FAR Part 3.

Office of Government Ethics

The Office of Government Ethics establishes an objective and comprehensive set of ethical conduct standards for government officials. These standards address issues such as gifts, conflict of interest, conflicting financial interests, employment outside the government, and other employment issues within the government. It also applies to work being performed on behalf of the government.

Procurement Integrity Act

FAR Part 3.104 establishes the requirements of the Procurement Integrity Act of 1998. Violations of this act could result in up to five years of imprisonment or a fine of up to $100,000. A contractor organization can be fined up to $1 million. This act has two main focuses:

1. It sets forth strict restrictions on federal procurement personnel and contractors. This act applies when a government, contractor, or subcontractor employee works on any activity related to a procurement and, for government personnel, up to two years after the procurement. This includes developing requirements, preparing purchase requests, or drafting a solicitation for a proposal or information. These regulations apply to all procurements including sole source (which is a procurement method used when there is only one provider of a product or service).

2. The Act sets forth direction on protecting proprietary information. Companies or individuals competing for

a government contract award must provide a Certificate of Procurement Integrity if they are the successful offeror on a contract valued above the simplified acquisition threshold. Subcontractors, while not required to submit a certificate to the government, are required to submit one to the prime contractor.

The bottom line is that all business conducted with the government should be carried out according to these rules and regulations and remain above reproach.

Chapter 3
Commercial Item Contracting and GSA Schedule Contracts

Over the years, the government has gradually shifted from military specifications and standards to commercial item acquisitions. Commercial item acquisitions help reduce government operating expenses and enable more contractors to enter government contracting. Through the use of General Services Administration (GSA) schedule contracts, any government agency receives similar prices, terms, and conditions from a whole host of federal contractors.

19. What is the historical perspective to commercial item contracting?

In the beginning of recent procurement history, from about 1940 to 1980, the government worked with relatively few suppliers for the products and services it needed. Why? Because the government set stringent requirements for many of the products and services it needed and few companies were interested in redesigning their products, retooling their machines, or taking the time to understand the federal procurement process. In addition, the government's extensive requirements raised the price of the products.

The cost of getting into the market was high, and few companies could afford the risk. The companies already conducting business with the government at that time did quite well—with only limited competition, these companies could charge whatever price they wanted. The government entered into "sole source" relationships with these companies because they were the "only game in town" and no one else could provide the products and services needed by the contracting agency. Requirements were written with an eye on what the company could actually do because the government knew so much about each company with which it worked. The companies, therefore, had no incentive to try innovative approaches or to reduce costs. Because the relationship between the agency and the few contractors supporting it was extremely close, it was difficult for new companies to break into the government market.

Granted, not *all* items that the government procured during this period were government-unique items, but the regulations were applied to all purchases of products and services. Thus, there were instances of hammers that cost $50 and toilet seats that cost $200. The government had detailed specifications and rigorous procurement regulations for everything, and frustrated contractors responded with higher prices to cover the costs of conducting business with the government.

To sum up this period in procurement history:

- There was a close relationship between the government agency and the contractor. The contractor could provide the exact products and services required because they worked so closely together.

- The procurement process was simple. The government wrote the requirements, and a few terms and conditions, and the contract was signed. Negotiations were minor.

- A one-to-one relationship existed. There was typically one government program to one contractor, so it tended to be easy to manage.

- This limited supplier base resulted in high prices for the government.

- There was little incentive for existing contractors to innovate or to reduce prices.

- There were high barriers to entry for all other companies, so competition was not maximized.

- The government was committed to using one company. If that company went out of business, the government was at risk.

- Many companies refused to get into the government marketplace because it was so complex and tightly regulated.

20. What did the Competition in Contracting Act do for federal procurement?

The Competition in Contracting Act (CICA) of 1984 came about to change the existing system. Basically, the government was being overcharged by the few contractors that were doing federal business; new contractors who could not get a "piece of the pie" leveled accusations about the exorbitant prices of the favored contractors. Since taxpayers, too, were upset about the rising costs to government agencies as they procured these expensive goods and services, the federal government decided to do something about the problems.

CICA encouraged all contractors to pursue federal government business and leveled as many barriers as it could so that companies would enter the federal market. It forced agencies to develop new contracting sources. CICA had significant ramifications for government procurement, including:

- The contracting method was changed to encourage full and open competition and not sole source.

- Sources had to be actively sought out so the government could learn new ways that might be used to solve its problems. In addition, the government needed to teach these new contractors the complex world of federal procurement and military specifications.

- Requests for proposals now had to be distributed to a wider audience. Frequently the contractors would question the way things were handled and suggest new and, sometimes, improved ways. The government then had to build in time to answer the contractors' questions as part of the procurement cycle.

- Source selection procedures had to be developed to help the government select who the winner would be. This wasn't as important before when there was just one company that could do the work, one company bidding, and that same company selected. Now the government was getting proposals from many large and medium-sized companies.

- The SBA was formed and the government began receiving proposals from small companies as well.

- Protests showered the government. With the additional contractors now interested in procurements, many contractors became upset because of the time and resources they spent fruitlessly pursuing government business. Protesting was a way to question the government's source selection process in the hopes of overturning the award decision and making it more favorable to the protester. These protests took a lot of time and effort for the government to resolve, causing procedures to be created to handle this inundation of protest activity.

While the concept of increasing competition was excellent, the approach still contained flaws that bogged down the federal procurement process. For example, if there is only one supplier of a widget, the government basically buys what the company has to offer as long as it meets the minimum criteria for widgets. As more and more widget suppliers get interested in the government's requirements for widgets, the government now has to set up detailed specifications and source selection plans to determine how it will select the widget contract winner. Further, it has to set up laboratories and procedures to test the widgets to ensure that they are meeting the appropriate standards. In addition, the government needs a whole host of acceptance, quality, and inspection terms and conditions established in the contract, as well as people on both the government and contractor sides to ensure that the widgets remain at the same standards. And of course, because there are now so many contractors interested in selling widgets to the government and only a few of them will actually win the contracts to do so, there are more protests. All these extra government efforts drive up the price of a widget from the price it would command in the commercial marketplace.

To sum up the period of our procurement history from the 1980s until 1994:

- More companies than ever were interested in and pursuing government business.

- The government was able to take advantage of the new ideas, innovations, and lower prices that competition affords.

- The government now had multiple sources it could use to meet requirements so its risk was reduced.

- Many people outside the procurement were now able to see into the federal procurement process. The government had to do everything fairly and above reproach using the new competition procedures.

- Detailed specifications had to be written for everything. In addition, with so many companies, detailed testing procedures had to be established to ensure that products and services were provided or performed as required.

- Contractors now had the "protest tool" if they didn't like the way the government handled a source selection. This process became expensive and timely for the government.

21. What did the Federal Acquisition Streamlining Act do for commercial item contracting?

There have been, and still are, many movements afoot within the government to contract out as much as possible. Les Davison, a procurement analyst in the Office of Acquisition Policy of GSA, stated the following in his article, "A GSA Primer for Commercial Items," published in the October 1996 *Contract Management*:

> With the passage of the Federal Acquisition Streamlining Act (FASA) in 1994, Congress signaled a dramatic shift in the course of procurement policy for the federal government. Arguably, FASA is the most far-reaching procurement reform in the last 50 years. Central to the FASA reforms are the mandates to maximize the use of acquisition of commercial items and to acquire those items in a manner similar to that used by the commercial sector.

This sums up much of what the procurement environment dealt with and is continuing to deal with in the federal marketplace. David Barram, when he was the director of GSA, joked in his speeches that "this isn't your father's GSA" to signal how drastically GSA has had to adapt to the changing procurement environment. Now, virtually *all* items procured by GSA are commercial items. FASA fundamentally changed the way the government does business. How much of an impact did FASA make in the procurement world? FASA alone altered around 250 previous procurement laws and regulations.

There was so much change because the government wanted to maximize the use of commercial items. It's always been understood that the federal government is unique because of the *types* and quantities of items it buys. While the quantity is still unique, now the *types* of things that the government buys are just like those that average consumers buy.

Further, the government wants to buy these commercial items just like commercial companies do. In doing so, it is getting rid of the "comfort blanket" of its tried-and-true government procurement practices and moving to commercial procurement practices. So, after much thought and deliberation from both the government and industry, Federal Acquisition Circular 90-32 implemented the new commercial items rules in Federal Acquisition Regulation (FAR) Part 12 in 1995.

22. What makes something a "commercial item"?

A commercial item can be defined as an item that saves the government and the vendor the time and expense of designing and making the first item.

During the procurement reform of the 1990s, Congress wanted to make it easier for the government to buy the same items that a consumer could easily buy. For example, when consumers go to a hardware store to buy a hammer, they don't give the hardware store a multi-page specification describing the hammer. They simply look at the hammers that are available and buy the one they need. The hammer is an example of a commercial item. So Congress made it easy for the government to buy anything that qualifies as a commercial item. It defined a commercial item broadly: "Any item other than real property that is of a type customarily used by the general public or by nongovernmental entities for purposes other than governmental purposes and one has been sold to the general public or has been offered for sale to the general public." How eager Congress was for the government to use commercial items can be seen in this second part of the definition: "Something is a commercial item as long as it had been offered for sale even though nobody bought it!"

As one court said, "One of the purposes of a solicitation requirement for a commercial product is to avoid the design and engineering risks associated with new equipment by procuring a commercially proven item. New equipment like [a protester's] proposed test station, which may only become commercially available as a result of the instant procurement, clearly does not satisfy the RFP requirement for commercial off-the-shelf (existing) equipment." *Chant Engineering Co. v. United States,* the Court of Federal Claims No. 06-282C, January 10, 2007.

23. How did FAR Part 12 change commercial item acquisitions?

When FAR Part 12 was initially revised in late 1995, it primarily focused on products with very few services. The changes in FAR Part 12 focused on two main aspects:

- Increased discretion for the CO in buying commercial items

- Increased use of market research in buying commercial items.

Increased Discretion for the CO

FAR Part 12 allowed COs a great deal of flexibility in buying commercial items. For commercial item acquisitions to be successful, COs had to be able to purchase in a manner similar to a commercial company. The regulation-laden approach that the FAR had prescribed for all these years did not work with this new type of acquisition process. In addition, COs were told to be creative and innovative in their contracting approaches when procuring commercial items. The FAR was still around for guidance, but the overriding theme was to apply the best commercial practices to obtain optimum products and services at the lowest overall price.

Although the government has the ability to use discretion in implementing commercial item acquisitions, one thing has not changed: the government employees' responsibility to the taxpayer to ensure that goods and services are purchased at the best value to the government customer to save the taxpayer money. COs are expected to request volume discounts and to leverage other industry best practices to ensure they get the best price from the contractor.

When a solicitation involves commercial items, the CO is *required* to use the procedures and policies stated in FAR Part 12. In addition, the CO *may* use the simplified acquisition procedures in FAR Part 13, the sealed bidding procedures in FAR Part 14, or the negotiation procedures in FAR Part 15. The decision as to which contracting procedure should be used—simplified acquisition, sealed bidding, or negotiated procurement—still resides with the CO. If there is any discrepancy between FAR Part 12 and any other parts of the FAR used in the procurement, FAR Part 12 takes precedence.

Increased Use of Market Research

A practice that has been used by commercial business for years is to develop subject matter experts responsible for buying similar products and services. For example, having one person buy all computers for the company allows that person to focus on the computer industry and understand its trends—and thus make better buying decisions. Since the government cannot have one person buy all the computers for the government, it has instituted the next best thing, which is market research.

The government CO responsible for buying computers for his or her organization is required to conduct market research so that he or she can make more informed buying decisions. The government has a whole host of websites that are available to its employees who are conducting market research so that much of the leg work can be done once and used across the entire government. Market research is just one more way the government is trying to leverage industry's best practices for its commercial item acquisitions.

24. What does the government look for in market research?

Market research is designed to key in on specifications and terms and conditions.

Specifications

The government conducts market research early in the procurement to determine if any commercially available items will meet the government's specifications. By determining this up front in the procurement, the government can minimize its dependence on government-unique items to meet its requirements. For some agencies, like GSA, most of the items procured are commercially available. Other agencies, such as DoD or NASA, still need many government-unique items.

Terms and Conditions

The government must also use market research to determine which terms and conditions should be used to procure the necessary goods and services. The general rule of thumb is that agencies should use the terms and conditions that are typically used in commercial contracting for a particular product or service. In addition, they should add only those terms and conditions necessary to meet provisions of law or executive orders. In fact, FAR 12.302(c) prohibits the CO from adding terms and conditions that would violate commercial practice:

> The contracting officer shall not tailor any clause or otherwise include any additional terms or conditions in a solicitation or contract for commercial items in a manner that is inconsistent with customary commercial practice for the item being acquired unless a waiver is approved in accordance with agency procedures.

25. Does the uniform contract format still apply?

While the uniform contract format is still used for other types of acquisitions, it does not work for commercial item acquisitions. The uniform contract format has standard sections A through M, which contain specific types of information in each section (for example, Section C: Statement of Work, Section L: Proposal Preparation Instructions, and Section M: Evaluation Criteria). It does not work with SF 1449, which is used to establish a contract between the government and the contractor. The theory is that commercial item acquisitions can have much shorter contracts and you don't need all the parts of the uniform contract format as you did in the past.

26. Can the contractor negotiate terms and conditions once they are established in the RFP?

Yes. Just because a particular term or condition is an industry customary practice does not mean that every company within that industry uses the practice. Therefore, the government could easily fashion a solicitation that included terms and conditions that were unacceptable to a particular company. To level the playing field, the government may decide to designate which terms and conditions are non-negotiable and which ones may be subject to negotiation.

27. Can the government still use best value techniques in a commercial item acquisition?

Yes, of course. Say, for example, the government issues an RFP for a product and two companies submit bids. One offers a higher price with a longer warranty, and one a lower price with a shorter warranty. Even in a commercial item acquisition, the government may still get two different bids that must be carefully evaluated against its source selection plan to determine the company that represents the best overall value to the government. Commercial item acquisition does not change that.

28. Can the government unilaterally change the terms of a commercial item contract?

No. The government cannot unilaterally change the terms of a commercial item contract since the contract requires that modifications be agreed to mutually.

In non-commercial contracts, the government puts the usual changes clause into its contracts, which lets the government unilaterally change the contract. But because the government tries to adopt business rules when it enters into a commercial item contract, it adopts the "deal is a deal" concept of business. If the government wants to change the terms of a commercial item contract, it must get the contractor's approval.

29. What are GSA multiple award schedule contracts?

GSA acts as a buyer for the entire government on a worldwide basis. GSA provides three basic services:

- *Federal Supply Service*—which helps federal agencies procure supplies, equipment, vehicles, etc.

- *Public Buildings Service*—which develops, builds, and manages federally owned and leased buildings

- *Federal Technology Service*—which procures information technology products and services.

GSA works with companies to put products and services on a GSA schedule. These schedule contracts are either deadline-based (meaning all proposals in response to an RFP are due by a certain date and time) or open-ended (meaning that a company can submit a proposal and work with GSA to negotiate it at any point). COs reviewing companies' GSA proposals are looking at their historical data, current contract information, market research, prices, product offerings, and discounts available to the company's most favored customers. Upon successful negotiation, the contractor is awarded a GSA schedule contract and can sell to any U.S. government agency worldwide. Schedules are typically for one to five years; however, the Evergreen program, sponsored by GSA, allows companies to hold schedules for an initial period of five years, and then to have three five-year option periods. This could potentially make for an unprecedented contract length of 20 years.

GSA schedule contracts, coupled with the broader government-wide access contracts (GWACs), represent a shift in federal buying and contracting patterns. Prior to these contract vehicles, an agency, division, or command would buy only the products or services needed for its organization. This "agency-centric" view of procurement was expensive to maintain since many agencies were going off to procure similar items, causing redundant efforts. Moreover, the government was not able to leverage the vast buying power in the industry to allow it steep company discounts. Finally, each organization negotiated its own contract with each company, which meant that one organization could get a significant discount and favorable terms and conditions from a company that another organization might not be able to obtain.

The "new" procurement approach is a "government-centric," or enterprise-wide view. In GSA schedule contracts and GWACs, one procurement agency negotiates the contract with the company and the prices, terms, and conditions are available for use anywhere in the government. This means that a customer working for the Veterans Administration in Hines, Illinois, can get the same products and services as a customer working for the U.S. Army in Fort Meade, Maryland. In addition, GSA used to buy more products from companies through schedule contracts; now it is buying more services through those contracts. So a company can have instant access to all government buyers for any product or service that it sells on the schedule contract.

In addition to the already-discounted prices available on the schedule, a government buyer may request, and sometimes be granted, a further price reduction when placing the actual order. The contractor has to explain why a discount was granted in the particular situation (for example, large-quantity buy); otherwise, the government will expect similar discounts on all future orders.

Procurement becomes a matter of the CO reviewing the various GSA MAS contracts to locate the products and services required, determine the companies providing those products and services, and run a "mini" competition among three or more of those companies to determine the winner. Contracting becomes a simple matter of issuing a delivery order against a pre-existing contract vehicle by shopping, comparing prices, and contracting—all accomplished online.

30. What are some of the tools GSA has available for contractors on multiple award schedule contracts?

The GSA MAS contracts have continued to become many contracting officers' "vehicle of choice" for procuring products and services. In fact, schedule sales have gone from $4.1 billion in FY96 up to approximately $13.7 billion in FY00. These numbers were presented by Bill Gormley, the assistant commissioner officer of acquisition for GSA, at the National Contract Management Association meeting held September 26, 2000. To help facilitate government purchases through the schedule contracts, GSA has provided the following services:

GSA Advantage! System

The GSA Advantage! system is an electronic tool used by contractors and government buyers. Contractors put their products, services, prices, terms and conditions in the system and government buyers from around the world can "shop online." The buyer can then select three or four vendors that it is most interested in, send them the requirements, and receive proposals back. After evaluation, the buyer can make an award decision and the winning contractor provides the products and services.

E-Buy

Currently, it is optional for a contractor to put its contract information into the GSA Advantage! system. Soon, however, GSA will require its schedule holder contractors to put their products, services, and prices on the GSA Advantage! system. This system paves the way for the e-Buy program, which will allow government procurement officials to solicit price quotes instantaneously from competing product and service providers.

In today's procurement environment, the government buyer may solicit quotes from three to four providers. In the e-Buy arena, companies will be categorized according to Dunn and Bradstreet's Universal Standard Products and Services Classification (UNSPSC). When a buyer needs something, it will select the appropriate UNSPSC category and all companies within that category will be sent notification about the request for quote. Once the request for quote time is closed, the buyer may select the company that represents the best overall value to the government and issue an order to that company. This ensures that all companies holding schedules and listed in the GSA Advantage! system will be able to bid on a request for quote.

Corporate Contracts

Companies are able to bid on and win multiple GSA schedule contracts. GSA is encouraging companies with multiple schedules to develop corporate contracts that would consolidate all their schedule products and services into one contract. The benefit to the company is that rather than managing multiple schedule contracts with varying prices, terms, conditions, durations, etc., the corporate contract would allow the company to manage one unified contract. Of course, whether migrating to a corporate contract is a good business decision for the company depends on the prices, terms, and conditions currently negotiated on the various schedule contracts.

31. When can a simplified acquisition use multiple awards?

Congress made one procurement streamlining change in the 1990s that made it easier for the government to use simplified acquisitions. Another change was to let the government make multiple awards of contracts when it made sense to do so. Although the FAR gives a contracting officer help in deciding when to make multiple awards in sealed bids or negotiated procurements, the FAR does not give any guidance on when the government should use simplified acquisitions. GAO gave some helpful guidance. It looked at the FAR's guidance in sealed bids and negotiated procurements and said that the "FAR advises that IFBs are to provide for multiple awards where the contracting officer determines that multiple awards 'might be made if doing so is economically advantageous to the Government.' Section 14.201-8(c) of the FAR adds that after the receipt of bids, '[t]he contracting officer shall assume, for the purpose of making multiple awards, that $500 would be the administrative cost to the Government for issuing and administering each contract awarded under a solicitation,' and that '[i]ndividual awards shall be for the items or combinations of items that result in the lowest aggregate cost to the Government, including the assumed administrative costs." *Para Scientific Company,* B-299046.2, February 13, 2007.

32. Are there any significant terms and conditions in the GSA MAS process that a contractor should be aware of?

Contractors, too, welcome the GSA MAS contracts because they can go through the contracting process a fewer number of times and, once awarded, can sell to anyone within the government procurement community. Their products and services are publicized through many of the GSA marketing tools, thus providing wider access and exposure for the MAS contract. Presumably, this access and exposure can lead to more sales for the contractor. However, the GSA MAS contracts are not without problems.

For starters, GSA is not the only agency that can issue GWACs. Deidre Lee, then-Administrator of OFPP, in her address to the 2000 National Contract Management Association's World Congress, talked about her initiative to get information about all the GWACs available to all COs on their desktop computers. It seems that in the current environment, the company is making recommendations about which GWAC the government should use to secure the company's products or services, rather than the CO determining which GWAC offers the government the best value for its money. By receiving information about all the schedules, products, services, terms, conditions, and prices, the CO can make an informed decision regarding which contract vehicle is best to use from the government's perspective, not the contractor's perspective.

In addition, the GWACs, and in particular, the GSA MAS contracts, are still indefinite delivery/indefinite quantity type contracts, which means that a contractor could go through all the effort to get awarded the contract and never see any business resulting from it. In addition, most contracts under the GSA schedule are competed among three or more companies. This means that the contractor is always in the competition mode, even after it has been awarded the schedule contract. These efforts to secure delivery orders can range from quick responses to full proposal efforts. Closely tied to this issue is that the government is encouraged to seek further price reductions from contractors even lower than the published GSA schedule prices. And of course, if one government agency is successful in negotiating a lower price, all subsequent procuring agencies expect the same lower price.

A third area of concern for the parties stems from several of the clauses used to manage the GSA MAS contracts. These clauses and GSA Regulations (GSAR) citations are Price Reduction (GSAR 552.238-76), Examination of Records (GSAR 552.205-71), and Price Adjustment (GSAR 552.215-72).

In the price reduction clause, the government is granted the right to most favored customer pricing wherever and whenever it occurs. So if a company has a long-standing commercial customer who buys a lot of its products and services in return for discounted prices, the contractor must provide that same level of discount to its government customers, regardless of the quantity purchased. This means that the contractor must maintain constant vigilance over the prices being used *anywhere* throughout its company to ensure that the government receives prices at or below them.

In the examination of records clause, the government retains the right to audit preaward and postaward data. In fact, the GSAR allows preaward data to be audited postaward if approved by the senior procurement executive.

In the price adjustment clause, the CO can lower the price of a contract if he or she determines after award that the price negotiated was increased by a significant amount because the contract failed to provide necessary information; to submit current, accurate, and complete information; or to disclose changes in its prices and pricing policies that occurred after the original submission and prior to the negotiations.

Several of these clauses were addressed by the Government Electronics Industry Association (GEIA). GEIA commented on the FAR's treatment of commercial items that require the government to include only the contract clauses that are required to implement provisions of a law or executive order or be consistent with standard commercial practice. GEIA also commented on the government's ability to examine records as being inconsistent with the Clinger-Cohen Act of 1996 because the Act removed certain government audit rights with respect to purchasing commercial items.

OFPP upheld the validity of the postaward audit clause and the price adjustment clause by stating that GSA (and the Veterans Administration) seek to maximize company choice and allow contractors onto the schedules without requiring the contractors to engage in competition to receive the contracts. Basically, since the government allows for numerous contractors to supply products and services to its buyers, the government needs the protection that these clauses provide. This buying situation is different from commercial practice because typically a commercial company would deal with only a few companies that may or may not have competed for the contract.

The bottom line is that for the short term, these clauses are not going away. It is the company's responsibility to stay abreast of further modifications to the GSA MAS program and make a business decision about whether the benefits outweigh the work involved in complying with the requirements.

33. How does a contractor secure a GSA schedule?

GSA has two types of RFPs: dated RFPs and open RFPs. In a dated RFP, GSA puts out the requirements and all interested companies must submit a proposal by the specified date and time. These RFPs are like the typical competitive environment in which all competitors are vying for one or several contract schedule openings. In an open RFP, the requirements are available to industry and a company can decide to submit a proposal at any time. These RFPs allow a company to submit a list of its products and services, demonstrate the commercial availability of those products and services, and submit competitive prices. Either type of RFP can result in a contract that allows for additional products to be added later.

To submit a proposal to GSA, a contractor should review the contracting opportunities available on the GSA web page as well as the FedBizOpps website. Instructions for proposal submission are found in the RFP. Upon careful review and evaluation by GSA, the company may be awarded a contract. If it is, it must put all its products, services, and prices on the GSA Advantage! system. A customer, if it so chooses, may order products and services directly off the GSA schedule prices listed in Advantage!

In today's competitive task order environment, the company works with various government agencies to learn of upcoming program opportunities. Since the government agency selects the three or four companies it wishes to receive proposals from, the company's goal is to be included as one of the soliciting companies. If the company receives the RFP, it will then have a minimum amount of time to submit a proposal to the procuring agency. This proposal will include a solution developed from the products, services, and prices contained on the company's GSA schedule. In addition, the government may request, and the company may offer, a discount off the GSA prices to secure the business. However, the company should be aware that these discounts may be required on future business opportunities.

When e-Buy is fully implemented, the procuring government official (located anywhere in the world) can put requirements on e-Buy and the companies with the required products and services on their schedule contracts will be sent electronic notification of the solicitation. In this way, all contractors who have the required products and services on their schedule contracts will be sent notification of future pending requirements. This is in contrast to the way things are done today, when the company must seek out future requirements that have been generated anywhere in the world.

34. Are agencies required to use the Federal Supply Schedule?

No. Even though the FAR refers to the Federal Supply Schedule (FSS) as a "mandatory source," agencies are not required to use it. FAR 8.002 states that agencies "shall" get the supplies and services they need from a list of sources. The list includes what the FAR calls "mandatory" federal supply schedules and "optional use" federal supply schedules. But "mandatory" does not really mean mandatory, according to GAO. "Under a mandatory FSS contract, an agency generally must order its requirements under that FSS if its minimum needs will be met by the products or services listed in the schedule. However, as conceded by the protester, its FSS contract is not mandatory; thus an agency's use of that contract is voluntary. There is nothing else in the FAR or elsewhere that compels the agency here to meet its requirements under the protester's FSS contract." GSA, which administers the FSS, agreed with GAO's "voluntary" interpretation of mandatory schedules: Unless a statute or regulation explicitly makes a particular FSS contract mandatory, using the schedule is voluntary. *Murray-Benjamin Electric Company, L.P.,* B-298,481, September 7, 2006.

35. What are the standards for disabled access? What are the Section 508 compliance issues?

The government has a responsibility to its employees and constituents using government systems to ensure that people who have a visual, hearing, manual dexterity, or mobility impairment are granted the same access to computer technology as employees who are not impaired. Section 508 requires accommodations for disabilities in equipment procured on government contracts and task orders signed after June 21, 2001. Further, these regulations give impaired persons the right to sue if there is a lack of compliance. The underlying premise of Section 508 is that companies must make computer technology accessible through multiple senses or abilities.

These standards do not apply to existing systems but to all future purchases. Section 508 applies both to systems for use by government employees and to government systems for use by citizens. Currently, it does not apply to commercial or private systems. Section 508 includes hardware, software, systems, and services. Any company that sells directly to the government or acts as a third party reseller to the government is affected by this legislation.

Currently, companies are required to self-certify their compliance with Section 508 standards. The government fully expects the requirements for this program to continue to become more stringent over time, requiring a third-party certification process. Some of the current requirements include:

- Using alternatives to color to indicate important information

- Using the keyboard and mouse as ways to control the program

- Using text equivalents for every nontext element

- Using synchronized captioning techniques for audio portions

- Using warning methods if the program is about to time out

- Allowing volume control features

- Accommodating screen readers and Braille displays.

To comply with the legal standard, a company must demonstrate a "good faith" effort to provide "reasonable accommodation" for disabled people to use the systems. Definitive guidelines and further information can be obtained at http://section508.gov.

36. If a contractor is not getting a fair share of task orders, what can the contractor do?

While Congress likes competition, enough is enough. Once an umbrella contract has been competed among a number of companies, and the winner (or winners under a multiple award contract) determined, the need for full and open competition for the task orders for specific work under the contract is reduced. Any winning company of a contract using task orders is entitled simply to "a fair share" of the task orders issued under that contract.

So when Congress considered how much competition there should be prior to issuing task orders, Congress not only demanded a lower level of competition, but also limited the ability of disappointed companies to file protests over any task order the company was not awarded.

In fact, Congress prohibited protests of task orders except in three limited circumstances. Task orders could be protested only on the grounds that the order increased the scope, period, or maximum value of the contract under which the order was issued. After that prohibition, there's not much left to protest.

37. How can task orders be protested?

GAO has found some other ways task orders can be protested. Some protests have succeeded.

Beyond-Scope Task Orders

An agency had an indefinite delivery/indefinite quantity (ID/IQ) contract for "noncomplex systems integration services" involving integrating commercially available off-the-shelf hardware and software. Under this hardware-software contract, the agency ordered management services that involved activities such as assisting in publicity; identifying federal, state, and private opportunities for potential collaboration/partnership with the Army; and monitoring, tracking, and overseeing the execution of new initiatives. The task order was for a "warm body," not for hardware or software.

In finding that the task order was beyond the scope of the contract, GAO laid down some guidelines for how to determine whether a task order is beyond the scope. "In determining whether a task order is beyond the scope of the original contract, this Office considers whether there is a material difference between the task order and that contract. Evidence of such a material difference is found by reviewing the circumstances attending the procurement that was conducted; examining any changes in the type of work, performance period, and costs between the contract as awarded and as modified by the task order; and considering whether the original contract solicitation adequately advised companies of the potential for the type of task order issued. The overall inquiry is whether the modification is of a nature which potential companies would reasonably have anticipated." (*Floro and Asso.*, B-285451.3, B-285451.4, October 25, 2000.)

This task order, according to GAO, was beyond the scope. While it involved computers, it did so only vaguely and certainly did not involve integration of hardware and software.

GAO-Fashioned Protestable Task Orders

GAO decisions have added protestable issues that do not directly involve the "scope, period, or maximum value" of an ID/IQ contract, but still involve variations of them.

In one case, a protest of a task order was allowed because the protest really involved the underlying solicitation that led to the task order contract. After a task order for travel was not issued to a small business, the task order was protested on the basis that the task order and the solicitation for the underlying contract violated the small business set-aside requirements. GAO saw the protest as one addressed to the solicitation and not the task order issued under it and handled the protest. Its rationale was that GAO always has authority to handle protests involving violations of law or regulations, such as the small business set-aside requirements.

In a similar case, GAO heard a protest involving a task order for environmental remediation at a closing military base because the underlying solicitation and contract violated the laws and regulations giving local businesses preference in the award of such contracts and task orders.

GAO has found other exceptions involving the violation of laws and regulations. It has considered task orders when an agency was attempting to circumvent the law and regulations by, for example, using a nonappropriated fund instrumentality or using a cooperative agreement or grant instead of a contract.

38. Can the failure to get a task order be challenged as a claim?

If protests complaining about not getting enough task orders rarely work, then a claim may be a better approach for a vendor that is denied a fair opportunity to be considered for task orders. The only alternatives a vendor may have are filing a claim under the multiple award contract with the contracting officer and filing an appeal with the appropriate board of contract appeals. For example, the Armed Services Board of Contract Appeals (ASBCA) concluded that it would hear claims from a vendor arguing that the government was not giving it a fair opportunity to compete. The Board noted that vendors can file a claim for damages for breach of the awarding orders clause of the contract, distinguishing between protests and claims: "These are separate and distinct forms of relief with 'protests' governed by FAR Subpart 33.1 and 'claims' by FAR Subpart 33.2. The statute, regulation and contract clause prohibit only protests." The Board also cited a decision that showed what a breach looks like: "In Community Consulting International, . . . we held that we had jurisdiction over a claim for breach of a fair opportunity to compete clause in a multiple award indefinite quantity contract where the contractor was given the opportunity to bid on only 26 of the 51 orders awarded." *L-3 Communications Corp.*, ASBCA 54920, 06-2 BCA P 33374.

39. Can losing a blanket purchase agreement be protested?

Another contract vehicle that uses task orders is a blanket purchase agreement (BPA). When that is set up, no contract is established until an order is placed against it. If a firm loses a BPA, it can protest that loss to GAO. In *Labat-Anderson Inc. v. United States,* 50 Fed.Cl. 99 (2001), the government issued a solicitation for a fixed-price BPA to a contractor already holding an FSS contract. The government decided to use negotiation procedures more typical of a FAR Part 15 acquisition. After Labat lost, it protested to the U.S. Court of Federal Claims. The government asked the court to dismiss the case but the court refused because a BPA, not a task order, was involved. The BPA, according to a later court decision, "is not a task order itself, but rather a vehicle against which task orders will be placed." Further, the court agreed with the holding in *Severn Cos., Inc.,* 97-1 Comp. Gen. ¶ 181, n. 1, 1997 WL 270342 (1997), which reasoned that the task order protest bar ". . . was not intended to preclude protests with respect to the placement of BPAs against GSA FSS contracts." *Group Seven Associates, LLC v. The United States,* 68 Fed.Cl. 28 (2005).

Chapter 4
Subcontracting

In view of the complex nature of some government procurements, a company may decide to take on subcontractors in order to complete the work. This chapter focuses on some of the considerations that subcontractors and prime contractors should take into account when entering into a subcontract agreement.

40. Why should a company subcontract?

Subcontracting occurs because of several situations. A prime contractor could decide to use a subcontractor because it wants to go after a certain business opportunity and realizes it cannot do it alone because it doesn't have the capability or the bandwidth. A subcontractor may decide to work with a prime contractor because it wants to pursue new business opportunities but needs the infrastructure, backing or capability of a prime contractor. In addition, the government places requirements on federal prime contractors to subcontract out part of the contract work. By subcontracting work to small and small disadvantaged businesses, the prime contractor meets the government's requirements.

41. What should a prime contractor consider when determining whether to subcontract?

When a prime contractor is determining if it should subcontract some of its work, it explores a lot of data. Some factors that a prime contractor should consider when deciding whether to subcontract include:

- Capability analysis

- Cost-effective solution

- Contract risk/reward

- Competitive position

- Customer preference

- Quantity discounts

- Final analysis.

Capability Analysis

A company needs to assess its internal capabilities to determine if subcontracting is a necessary alternative. The company may not have the capabilities needed to conduct a program by itself. Sometimes the company may have the needed capabilities, but the skill level required by the customer is greater than what the company possesses. For example, a customer requires 25 programmers and a company has only 10. Another scenario is that the company has 25 programmers, but because of when the program will occur, the company will not be able to fulfill the customer's requirements and meet the company's commitments to existing customers. If any of these situations exist, the company should seriously consider a subcontractor relationship so that it can pursue a contract.

Another situation can exist as the government moves to consolidate many of its operations across agencies. For example, say the government has multiple locations with multiple contractors doing similar work and wants to consolidate the efforts into one regional facility. A small company that was the incumbent on one of the previous contracts may be asked by a larger company to partner. The small company brings a wealth of information and expertise from its previous client work, and the larger company has the infrastructure and bandwidth to handle the larger contract.

Cost-Effective Solution

Sometimes a company selects a subcontractor because the subcontractor can provide a more cost-effective solution to some of the contract requirements than the company can. For example, a contract has numerous requirements for training. The company cannot handle the requirements internally unless it pulls people from existing contracts that are generating revenue. The company decides to bring in a subcontractor to share the training requirements because the company was able to negotiate a rate with the subcontractor that is less expensive than using internal people and still secure a profit for the work performed. Because the company was able to work with a subcontractor, it could work on the contract without sacrificing profit potential on that contract or the other contracts it was working on.

Contract Risk/Reward

A subcontractor, by taking on some of the terms and conditions that the prime contractor must meet, shares some of the contract risk. As compensation for sharing the risk, the prime contractor shares some of the contract reward or profit with the subcontractor.

Contract risk/reward is an important analysis for a prime contractor to conduct because some customers' contract terms and conditions could render a program not worthy of bidding on by a prime contractor. If a subcontractor is willing to accept the terms and conditions that the prime contractor cannot meet, then the prime contractor can bid the program because it knows if the subcontractor does not perform, the prime contractor has contractual remedies built into the subcontract.

As part of this analysis, a prime contractor will ascertain whether it retains enough of the contract business to make it worthwhile to bid. A contractor may find that if it subcontracts too much of the work out, it is left with a great deal of risk in managing so many subcontractors but not much of the profit. In this situation, It may not be worthwhile to assume the risk from a business perspective.

Competitive Position

Another analysis that the company should complete when deciding if it should work with a subcontractor is whether the subcontractor adds anything to the company's competitive position. If the prospective subcontractor has an existing business relationship with the customer that the customer perceives as positive, then the subcontractor could bring competitive strength to the company's team. In such a case, the subcontractor would also have a wealth of customer knowledge it can share with the team to help win the contract.

Typically, a subcontractor that is well positioned and can help improve a team's competitive edge will have many teams pursuing it. When this is the case, the desirable subcontractor may play off one team against another to secure the best terms and conditions or it will enter into subcontract relationships with all the teams, knowing that at least one will win and the subcontractor will have the business regardless of who wins. If this is the case, the company will need to conduct further analysis to determine if the subcontractor's improved terms and conditions or the fact that the subcontractor's talents are no longer a discriminator because it is on every team outweigh the benefit it brings to the team.

Customer Preference

Sometimes a prime contractor chooses a subcontractor because the customer either directly or indirectly states a preference for a particular company. Sometimes the customer hints strongly about including certain subcontractors on the team because of their expertise, product line, or technical talent. Other times, a customer prefers a subcontractor because of the customer's existing environment. For example, the customer may have a lot of the subcontractor's products currently installed or the customer has worked with the subcontractor in the past. In such situations, the subcontractor may have a stronger say in the subcontract relationship than normally expected because the subcontractor has the inside track with the customer.

Quantity Discounts

Another strategy that companies often employ is to work with one subcontractor on multiple contracts to secure quantity discounts. The prime contractor usually can negotiate a lower price with a subcontractor by offering it increased sales. This strategy also works well if the company needs to buy the subcontractor's products and services for internal use, because it helps to solidify the relationship.

Final Analysis

Finally, a prime contractor must review all the factors to determine if working with a subcontractor is the right business decision. Often it is. However, remember that a subcontractor relationship could cause a winning team to lose the contract if the prime contractor does not conduct the analysis properly. For example, poor analysis could cause the contractor to miss learning about a subcontractor's poor-performance track record or to miscalculate the subcontractor's discount. These types of situations could cause the prime contractor to lose the contract or to win an unprofitable contract (because the profit ends up in legal fees needed to get the subcontractor to perform).

42. What should a subcontractor consider when determining whether to subcontract?

Some companies find subcontractor relationships attractive because they allow companies to work on contracts that they might not have been able to work on alone. For example, if a company is small or if it provides a product that the government or a commercial entity would not typically release an entire contract for, working with another company allows the first company to work on larger programs and sell greater quantities. Other benefits to the subcontractor include the following:

- Cost-competitive solution

- Contract risk/reward

- Learning opportunity

- Capitalizing on an existing relationship

- Program requirements

- Competing on multiple contracts simultaneously.

Cost-Competitive Solution

When a company works alone, it is responsible for providing all components of a solution. A small company, or a company providing only one small piece of the overall solution, may not have the leverage to provide a cost-competitive solution like a large company that provides the bulk of the solution internally. In such cases, working with another company would allow the small company to provide greater quantities and work on contracts that it normally could not work on. Likewise, a large company may subcontract as a way of trying out new business lines without fully committing its resources.

Contract Risk/Reward

By subcontracting, a company shares the reward that it receives on the contract but it also mitigates some of its risk by sharing it with the prime contractor. The amount of risk and reward (or profit) a company gets by subcontracting depends on what each side negotiates.

Learning Opportunity

Subcontracting gives the subcontractor the ability to learn the details of the business in a relatively risk-free environment. By working with other companies, the subcontractor can learn new ways to conduct business from each new subcontracting opportunity. Because the subcontractor needs to worry only about the requirements, terms, and conditions in the subcontract, the subcontractor can take the time to observe the company with which it is working.

Capitalizing on an Existing Relationship

Subcontracting allows a well-performing subcontractor to capitalize on its existing relationships to grow its business. For example, a subcontractor works for a prime contractor on a commercial contract. The contract is up for re-compete. The subcontractor is courted by other contractors interested in the business. By entering into nonexclusive relationships with each of them (meaning that the subcontractor works with multiple prime contractors on the bidding process), the subcontractor improves its chances of winning the re-compete work with a minimum amount of additional effort.

This situation can also be triggered by the customer. The customer could tell a prime contractor to work with a particular subcontractor if the contractor wants to secure the business. This is known as a *directed subcontract*. Technically, the federal government cannot offer directed subcontracts; however, sometimes prime contractors get very strong "indications" from the government about working with a particular subcontractor. The government can direct a subcontract if there is a national crisis or emergency or if there is a compelling business reason to do so.

Program Requirements

A subcontractor may not be able to meet all the program requirements, but it may be able to provide a cost-effective solution. Often, a small company cannot take on the risk and exposure of meeting all the contractual obligations; if it did accept the risk and could not meet the contract requirements, the company could go out of business. Subcontracting gives companies the ability to provide a piece of the solution without having to meet all the requirements, terms, and conditions imposed by the customer contract.

Competing on Multiple Contracts Simultaneously

Depending on the subcontracts, a company may be able to sell its product through multiple contracts at one time. Obviously, spreading a company's resources too thin doesn't do either party any good. However, through careful planning and management, a company can increase its chances at business because it has increased the number of contracts being pursued. This works best in situations in which the subcontractor is selling its product to multiple prime contractors.

43. How can a company find a prime contractor to work with?

Finding a company with which to bid can be a challenge for a subcontracting company. If the subcontracting company wishes to pursue this route, there are several things it can do to enhance its chances of locating a large company with which to do business.

The subcontracting company can begin by establishing itself as a reputable contractor on its existing contracts. Nothing speaks louder than a stellar track record of solid performance. The subcontractor's contract performance may be in federal contracts or commercial business.

Next, the subcontracting company should understand its own capabilities and be able to clearly articulate them to a potential prime company. Often, a subcontracting company becomes enamored with the thought of becoming a contracting partner, but it cannot define the specifics of its own offering.

Finally, the subcontracting company must understand the marketplace and know which customers have money for the goods and services the company offers. By targeting specific customers and prime contractors, the subcontracting company can channel its resources to those opportunities that represent the biggest potential market.

Recent contract announcements in the *Washington Post* or the *Wall Street Journal* are a potential avenue for subcontracting companies. Likewise, the company can review the classified employment section to determine what skills the winning contractor requires. A subcontracting company with a niche product offering can work with the prime contractor of an existing contract to add its product to the prime contract's offering. Finally, marketing directly to the customer may generate a need for the subcontracting company's product. In this situation, the customer may help the subcontracting company determine an appropriate contract vehicle through which to sell its products.

What is important to keep in mind is the structure of a large company. Often the person running one major program in a company has no idea what another person running a different major program is doing or what needs they might have for subcontractors. Therefore, the up-front work that the subcontractor does can help to target the subcontractor at the right piece of prime contractor business. For example, a subcontractor should determine the programs the large company is pursuing, learn who is responsible for those programs, and assess how they might be able to help the team succeed.

44. What does a prime contractor need to consider before entering into a subcontractor relationship?

The prime contractor needs to review the following aspects of subcontractor management.

Amount of Subcontractor Involvement

The company acting as prime contractor has overall responsibility for all the steps in the review process. But like an orchestra conductor, the company must direct a team of internal and external sources to produce a solution that is harmonious with the customer's environment. To do that, the company must decide how to achieve the delicate balance between prime contractor and subcontractor that leads to a winning performance, in this case, a contract. The balance is delicate because there is always more at stake than just winning the contract. Many subcontractors and prime contractors work together on future opportunities.

Subcontractor Prices

The company must determine how much of the business to keep for itself and how much to subcontract. Part of this decision is made using a make-or-buy analysis: If the company does not have the internal capability to provide the product or service, it must subcontract the work to another company. However, the company must realize that the price it can offer the customer for a subcontracted product or service may be higher than the price proposed by a company that provides the product or service internally.

Revenue Sharing

Another issue arising for the company is whether there is enough work that can be done internally to motivate the company to prime the deal. Marketing and proposal development can be expensive propositions. If the company must subcontract out a large portion of the contract, then the company must also give away a large part of its profit from the contract. There is a certain point at which the company may decide that the investment to prime the deal is not worth the contract risk or minimal revenue after award.

Company Value

The company has to be very clear about the value that it brings to the customer through the contract. A prime contractor that subcontracts out all the work and tacks on an exorbitant program-management fee just to run the contract will probably have to answer some customer questions about what the customer is getting in return for paying the program-management fee. Just as a prime contractor examines the value a subcontractor brings to the team, the customer is looking for the value the prime contractor brings to the team. A company, acting as prime contractor, must clearly articulate the products or the meaningful services it will provide on the contract. Otherwise, the customer may decide to contract directly with the subcontractor and write out the prime contractor all together.

Other Deals in the Pipeline

The company is not making a decision to bid on a particular program in a vacuum. A company typically reviews multiple deals at any point in time. However, this does not mean that the company will always have many great contracts to bid on. The company may experience lean years in which it bids on contracts that it would never have considered during more prosperous times. Either way, the company must cultivate relationships with potential subcontractors early in the process in case the company decides to bid; however, do not string along the subcontractor if the company decides not to pursue a contract.

Subcontractor Involvement

The company must decide how much it wants a subcontractor to be involved in the marketing and proposal development process. Sometimes a subcontractor brings fresh ideas, innovative approaches, and genuinely better ways to do things. Other times, a subcontractor does not have the expertise that the company is looking for. Also, each subcontractor that the company uses will not typically have the same level of input on the prime contractor team. The company will determine each subcontractor's level of involvement based on the subcontractor's level of expertise.

Partners Today; Competitors Tomorrow

The reason a prime contractor has such a challenge in determining how much involvement it should allow the subcontractor to have is that a subcontractor could be working with you on a program today and competing against you on another program tomorrow. Some of the tasks that could be shared with the subcontractor could expose a great deal of information about the company's business, which would be extremely useful to a competitor. The more areas that the subcontractor is involved in, the more of a chance it has to garner the company's secrets, which it may (but shouldn't because of the nondisclosure agreement) use in its own repertoire of competitive tools.

Partners Today; Competitors Today

Another problem that complicates the prime contractor-subcontractor relationship is that the subcontractor can be a supplier selling to the company and its competitors on the same deal. Although every prime contractor wants an exclusive subcontractor relationship to help its competitive position, sometimes a subcontractor works with multiple prime-contractor teams pursuing the same deal to improve its chances at winning. If a subcontractor is working with multiple prime contractors, the company acting as prime contractor must decide how involved it wants the subcontractor to be in the proposal process. The prime contractor needs to protect its own competitive position, so it may not be able to let the subcontractor get too involved in the program for fear that its strategy may be leaked to competitors.

Break Out Work among Subcontractors

Another key issue for the company is to decide how work will be divided among subcontractors, particularly if two or more subcontractors can provide the same type of product or service. This decision can be difficult because each subcontractor is trying to get as much of the program as it can so it can grow its own business base. The best approach is for the company to define the roles and responsibilities early on in the relationships so that each party knows what it is responsible for providing. It also helps if the company does not make promises it cannot keep.

For example, on an indefinite delivery/indefinite quantity contract, a prime contractor should not promise 60 percent of the training work to one company and 40 percent to another when the customer has total flexibility with regard to when it wants classes scheduled. In such cases, the prime contractor wants to make sure its subcontractors are each prepared to provide training as soon as possible; that way, if one cannot provide the training, the other subcontractor will. It does not make sense to promise one subcontractor 60 percent of the training if it cannot provide the training at a particular time and the other company can. In addition, if the subcontractor that was promised 60 percent of the training repeatedly cannot deliver the training at designated customer times, it could potentially harm the relationship the prime contractor has with the customer.

Unfortunately, subcontractors push to get percentages from prime contractors as part of their contract to improve their internal business case. If the company's subcontractor requires percentages, the company should mitigate its risks by including in its agreement alternative courses of action in the event that the subcontractor cannot meet the customer's requirements.

Effect of Strategic Alliances

In today's marketplace, companies frequently form strategic alliances for just about anything: product development, services, research, distribution, and marketing, to name just a few. These alliances are usually developed because they benefit both companies. However, sometimes strategic alliances force the company to do things "in the interest of good will in the alliance" instead of acting on what is best for the program that the company is working on. Strategic alliances tend to be rather all-encompassing, and the proposal team may be forced to work with the strategically aligned company even if it is not in the team's best interest to do so.

Interrelationship of Programs

Another area that a prime contractor must consider when working with a subcontractor is the relationship the subcontractor has with the company on other programs. To help secure a solid competitive position, the prime contractor may merge the requirements from multiple programs and work with only one subcontractor for all the programs. In return for this larger business potential, the subcontractor should provide greater discounted prices or more advantageous terms and conditions.

45. What should a prime contractor keep in mind when working with subcontractors?

A prime contractor should consider several key factors when working with subcontractors.

Time Required

A prime contractor needs to keep in mind how much time it takes to work with subcontractors. A great deal of time is involved in the marketing, discussion, negotiation, instruction, follow-up, and buy-in that the prime contractor must commit to each subcontractor. If a subcontractor is new to the business, the contractor will need to provide even more detailed instructions. Too often, a prime contractor assumes that a subcontractor does business in a similar fashion only to find out later that there are major discrepancies. The value of clear communication cannot be overstated. The contractor needs to communicate clear instructions to the subcontractor on how the customer or the company wants something done. If the subcontractor delivers an end product that does not satisfy the customer's or company's request, the company should consider the following explanations:

- The instructions were not clear.

- The instructions were given to someone who was not doing the work, and that person did not clearly communicate the instructions.

- The subcontractor does things a certain way regardless of how others want the work done.

- People doing the work are not familiar with the program requirements.

- The subcontractor had other priorities so it could meet only the minimum requirement.

- Multiple people on the proposal team are providing direction to multiple people on the subcontractor's team.

- The subcontractor made a strategic decision to support the program at a minimum level, believing the prime company gave it too much work to do on the program.

- The usual problems occurred: human error, technology glitches, and personality conflicts.

Commitments about Subcontractors' Products or Services

The prime contractor takes a great risk if it makes promises to the customer about the subcontractor's product without verifying the information with the subcontractor. On the surface, this prospect seems odd: Why would a prime contractor commit on behalf of its subcontractor? However, this often happens when the prime contractor prepares for negotiations or final proposal revision and tries to do everything in its power to secure the contract. Timeframes are tight, contract details are complex, and the subcontractor isn't always available when the prime contractor needs it, so the prime contractor gets sloppy in good subcontract management techniques.

When this scenario occurs, the prime contractor risks having to perform the agreed-upon task for the customer. This could be a dire situation if the contractor does not have the capability to perform the task. In such cases, it needs the subcontractor. The subcontractor may comply with the new requirements at no extra cost; it may comply with the new requirements but charge the prime contractor a higher price; or it may be unable to comply with the new requirements.

If the subcontractor cannot comply, the prime contractor must either renegotiate with the customer (which is an unlikely scenario) or try to secure the products or services from another subcontractor.

Level of Subcontractor Involvement

Once again the prime contractor needs to decide how involved it wants its subcontractor to be. The subcontractor knows its product or service best and, therefore, it can demonstrate, negotiate, or market it better than anyone. However, during proposal-submission activities, the prime contractor and the subcontractor spend a great deal of time developing pricing strategies and negotiating, which involve revealing highly sensitive data. The prime contractor is in a vulnerable position because the subcontractor could be a competitor tomorrow, so the prime contractor may want to limit the subcontractor's involvement.

Short Timeframe for Negotiations

There is typically a brief period for negotiations, usually two weeks from the time a call for final proposal revision is made until it is due. For a prime contractor working with many subcontractors, it must develop its strategies early and negotiate with each subcontractor quickly to ensure the final proposal revision is completed on time. A strategy that most companies use is to negotiate with the highest dollar value subcontractors first because price reductions here can greatly enhance the team's competitive position.

Negotiation Timing

The best time to conduct negotiations differs for the prime contractor and the subcontractor. The best time for the prime contractor is before contract award so it knows its risk. When the prime contractor submits its final proposal revision, it may decide to trim its overall price to win the contract. To do this, the prime contractor must know exactly how much a subcontractor is willing to lower its prices so that the prime contractor knows exactly how low a price it can bid and how much support it will get from the subcontractor.

On the other hand, the best time for a subcontractor to negotiate, particularly one that is working on multiple prime contractor teams, is after contract award so that it has to negotiate with only the winning contractor. In addition, the subcontractor is in a better position after the prime contractor submits the final proposal revision because the prime contractor is basically committed to using the subcontractor on the program. Consequently, the subcontractor's negotiation power is stronger after award. The solution that most prime contractors and subcontractors reach is to negotiate prices and price-affecting terms and conditions before final proposal revision submission and negotiate any other terms and conditions after award without changing prices.

Prime Contractor: Single Point of Contact

Before initial proposal submission, the company can initiate conversations with the customer. Once the initial proposal is submitted and during the after-submission activities, the prime contractor becomes the single point of contact with the customer for questions, live test demonstrations, discussions/negotiations, pre-award visits, amendments, and best and final offer call. The prime contractor decides how much information it should share with the subcontractor. Any questions that the subcontractor has must go through the prime contractor. Basically, the prime contractor is the conduit of information because it must funnel information from the government customer or commercial customer to the subcontractor and from the subcontractor back to the customer. If the communication process breaks down, the program is in jeopardy.

Prime Contractor: Single Point of Accountability

The prime contractor is responsible for doing whatever it takes to win the program. Its company and its subcontractors are depending on it to do so. As the single point of accountability, the prime contractor must ensure that the decisions that it makes are for the good of the whole team. Similarly, it frequently must choose between its corporate interests and the goals of the procurement team. It also must ensure that any changes made to the program are communicated among the team members. Typically, any change has a "domino effect" within a program: one change necessitates several other changes throughout the process. The prime contractor must understand the program well enough to know who is affected by any changes and inform them so that they can take appropriate action.

46. What tasks do prime contractors and subcontractors work on during a proposal and subsequent contract effort?

The following list includes tasks that could be shared with subcontractors:

- Writing proposal sections

- Developing strategies

- Reviewing the proposal

- Sharing customer information

- Sharing competitor information

- Developing products

- Integration

- Technical or management services

- Advertising

- Marketing

- Producing the proposal

- Research and development

- Independent test and validation

- Involvement in other programs

- Demonstrating the product

- Oral proposals

- Pricing strategy

- Contract performance

- Add-on business

- Future program opportunities.

47. What should a subcontractor consider when working with a prime contractor?

Subcontracting is a wonderful option for companies interested in getting into a business area without all the risk associated with being a prime contractor. However, subcontracting is not without its own set of challenges that must be carefully evaluated before a company decides to subcontract. Some of those considerations include the following.

Deciding How Much the Business Is Worth

Just as the prime contractor must decide how much involvement it wishes to have from the subcontractor, the subcontractor needs to decide if it is willing to provide the level of support requested by the prime contractor. For example, a subcontractor may be working with a prime contractor that just wants generic product descriptions and prices or the contractor may want the subcontractor to be intimately involved every step of the way. In the first case, the cost of sale is minimal; in the second case, the cost of sale is much greater. To determine if the cost of sale is too great to even be considered, a company should conduct return-on-investment and opportunity-cost analyses. After these analyses are performed, the company can decide if this is the best opportunity for it to participate at that particular time.

Working on Multiple Prime Contractor Teams

Another issue a company needs to address arises when a subcontractor is involved in multiple prime contractor teams pursuing the same customer opportunity. These relationships can get tricky if they are not managed well. One method of managing the relationship is to ask the subcontractor to sign a nondisclosure agreement, which prohibits the subcontractor from sharing information from one prime contractor with another prime contractor. A subcontractor that has or is perceived to have shared inappropriate information with a competitor will probably be kicked off the team or, at a minimum, not be asked to pursue future business opportunities with the offended prime contractor.

To help segregate efforts on a prospective proposal, a subcontractor may have different people working on each team the subcontractor works with so that there is no perceived or real conflict of interest. Or the subcontractor may elect to offer the same products, terms, conditions, and prices to each prime contractor team to simplify the relationships. However, this approach does not bode well for prime contractors that are trying to differentiate themselves from their competitors.

Doing Things the Way the Prime Contractor Wants Them Done

A subcontractor is often used by the prime contractor to supplement some of the skills the prime contractor is deficient in. The opposite situation can exist as well: the subcontractor could have a great deal more experience in developing business opportunities or proposals, so the prime contractor stands to gain the most from the subcontract relationship. The bottom line, however, remains the same: the subcontractor must abide by the way the prime contractor wants to run the program. Some prime contractors need a lot of help and they are willing accept their subcontractor's help; some prime contractors don't need or want any help from their subcontractors. This can present a frustrating experience for the subcontractor, particularly if the subcontractor has more experience than the prime contractor.

48. What does the subcontractor need to provide to the prime contractor?

The subcontractor must provide certain information to the prime contractor for the prime contractor to be able to submit a proposal to the customer.

Technical Solution Proposal Section

The subcontractor must provide the prime contractor with information about the technical solution that the subcontractor is proposing. This information can be submitted as a formal proposal or in a less formal manner. The prime contractor needs the technical solution to develop its proposal to the customer. The prime contractor will normally want something in writing, as opposed to a verbal submission, in case there is an issue after contract award about the subcontractor's performance.

Prices

The subcontractor must provide its price for providing its services or providing the product. These prices may be based on commercial list prices or General Services Administration schedule prices, or may be developed based solely on the terms and conditions of the program. Prices typically are given for the life of the contract unless other provisions have been made. Prices are given per product, service, or labor hour for each year of the contract and include any necessary escalations or discounts granted. For commercial contracts, the final price is all that is required. For government contracts, price buildup (e.g., cost, general and administrative, overhead, profit, fee) and supporting documentation may be required.

Integration Support

If the contract requires products to work together, the subcontractor may be asked to help develop a solution with the prime contractor. The subcontractor must do this because it best understands how the product works and how the service is supposed to be provided. Solution-development support could take the form of remote or local access to systems or technical expertise. The subcontractor may need to provide demo products or gratis licenses to products to ensure that all of the subcontractor's products work together as intended.

Draft Subcontract Revisions

A subcontract is not typically signed until after the prime contract has been negotiated. However, during the early stages of the process when the prime contractor submits a proposal to the customer, the prime contractor still needs a commitment from the subcontractor that it will provide the products and/or services as required. The subcontractor must demonstrate its willingness to accept the customer's requirements, and a draft subcontract is one way to do this.

A draft subcontract outlines all the terms, conditions, and requirements that the prime contractor wants the subcontractor to accept during contract performance. The subcontractor reviews the draft and indicates any revisions by marking up the document. The subcontractor submits its prices at about this time. Once this is done, the two can begin negotiations and either reach agreement in a subcontract that is ready to be signed or reach an impasse and have a list of open, non-agreed-upon issues. If they are not significant, these issues will be resolved after contract award. If they are significant, either one or both of the parties may decide to back out of the relationship.

Representations and Certifications

Representations and certifications are used by the customer to require the prime contractor to claim as true certain facts about itself. The prime contractor cannot make many of these representations and certifications unless it imposes the same requirements on its subcontractors. Representations are predominantly used in government contracts and seldom used in commercial contracts. Following are some typical representations and certifications that the prime contractor and the subcontractor may need to make:

- Has a drug-free workplace

- Is an equal opportunity employer

- Has procurement integrity

- Has small business certification

- Has 8(a) or small and disadvantaged business certification

- Abides by Buy America Act provisions

- Adheres to industry standards (e.g., ISO 9000, Software Engineering Institute Software Capability Maturity Model level).

Résumés

The subcontractor may be required to submit résumés of key individuals who will work on the program after award. Also, if the prime contractor flows down a key personnel clause to the subcontractor that requires that the customer approve a résumé before the individual begins work, the subcontractor needs to comply. If the clause also requires the key individuals to work on the contract for some period of time (e.g., 90 to 180 days), the subcontractor and the prime contractor are bound by this requirement.

Past Performance Citations

Customers that request past performance contract citations typically want them from the subcontractors as well. If the subcontractor has performed well on past contracts, this will not be a problem. However, if the subcontractor has not performed well, there is a great possibility that the subcontractor could lose the program for the prime contractor. To ensure that the subcontractor does not cause problems on a proposal, it should always provide excellent service on existing contracts. Consistent good work will also ensure the subcontractor future contracts.

Willingness to Answer the Customer's Questions

As discussions between the prime contract and the customer begin, there may be issues about the subcontractor's portion of the work. The prime contractor is in no position to make commitments on behalf of the subcontractor unless it is authorized by the subcontractor to do so. Therefore, the subcontractor must be willing to help the prime contractor answer any of the customer's questions about its offering and to help in any way it can to win the procurement.

49. What should a subcontractor keep in mind when working with prime contractors?

There are some aspects of contracting that a subcontractor should be aware of as it works with prime contractors. These aspects include the following.

Statement of Work Clearly Reflects the Subcontractor's Work

Both the prime contractor and the subcontractor should ensure that the subcontract statement of work continues to reflect the actual work that will be provided by the subcontractor. What sometimes happens is that the prime contractor and subcontractor develop an original statement of work that covers the work that the subcontractor will perform but then as proposal updates, amendments, and negotiations occur, the work that the subcontractor will do changes. Problems can occur when those changes are not reflected in an updated subcontract statement of work.

All the Products and Services the Subcontractor Is Selling Appear in the Statement of Work

The subcontractor also must ensure that the subcontract document reflects the actual products and services it believes it will sell under the contract. Ideally, the subcontractor would like to verify that the prime contractor's proposal contains descriptions of the products and services that the subcontractor will provide under the contract. Several issues can arise.

The sales discussions between the two companies don't mean anything until they are actually documented in the subcontract. The prime contractor could tell the subcontractor that many of its products will be proposed, but unless they are documented in the subcontract schedule, they are not covered by the subcontract. Similarly, the only products that the government can buy on a prime contract are those that are listed in the prime contract. If the subcontractor's products are not listed by name, they are not being proposed, and the only way the government could actually order them is for the prime contractor to go through a contract modification process after award. For a prime contractor to go through a modification, it must ensure that the government wants the modification, the government must find funding for the modification, and the modification must be negotiated before the government can buy the subcontractor's additional products or services. There are many points along this process that can result in a "No Go," with the initiative dropped and the subcontractor's products not added to the contract or purchase.

A certain amount of trust and business cooperation has to occur. Ideally, the subcontractor would like *all* of its products and services listed in the prime contract proposal. Unfortunately, this is not realistic because it would take the prime contractor's proposal out of the competitive range and nobody would get any revenue from the effort. The prime contractor has the ultimate decision authority (if the subcontractor wishes to stay on the team), and it may need to negotiate items out of the subcontract and resulting prime contract to lower the overall contract price. The point is to make sure that the subcontract and prime contract reflect the actual negotiations that have occurred between the prime contractor and subcontractor.

Ability to Negotiate for Additional Products and Services after Contract Award

Also important is how changes will be approached after contract award. First, the subcontractor must be aware that the prime contract must allow changes to be made to the contract through a changes clause in the prime contract. If the prime contract does not contain this clause, changes cannot be implemented throughout the life of the contract unless they are later negotiated into the prime contract. Typical change clauses grant product changes due to obsolescence or technology refreshment. The clauses typically carry the stipulation that the new product must be at the same or a lower price than those previously proposed to meet the requirement. The products proposed under these clauses must also comply with all the other prime contract terms and conditions unless new terms and conditions are negotiated and agreed upon.

As a subcontractor, you want to ensure that the prime contract has a changes clause and that the prime contractor will make every reasonable attempt to help you add new products and services to the prime contract. You want that agreement documented in your subcontract to protect yourself in the future. For example, clauses should provide for the right to swap out old, no longer manufactured products for newer products or to add products with new technology capabilities to the contract throughout its life. In addition, you want to ensure that competitors' products are not added to the contract without some sort of competition that you are eligible to participate in.

Prices

The prime contractor is under a lot of pressure to lower the contract price to remain competitive. A subcontractor must decide how competitively it can price its product to help the prime contractor win the business as well as to make a reasonable profit performing under the contract after award. As a basic rule of thumb and due to the competitive nature of government business, prices for the same products tend to be lower on government contracts than they would be on commercial contracts. If a company wants to retain high profit margins on its products and services, government contracting may not be a reasonable business strategy. If, however, a company wants a solid revenue stream from a customer who will pay its bills, the government business may be a reasonable business strategy. Some of the other considerations that the subcontractor must make include:

- *Future sales*—What is the value of future sales? How realistic are those future sales? If the subcontractor has a niche product and the future looks bright, it may be more willing to maintain its price at initial submission and then lower it as more competitors enter the field. A subcontractor who has a 'me too' solution may need to lower its price to help the prime contractor even get the business.

- *Future relationships*—The subcontractor may also consider future business relationships with the prime contractor to help determine how it should price its products. If future revenue streams look promising, the subcontractor may be more willing to cut its prices for each particular contract.

- *Ability to perform at the lower prices*—The subcontractor, regardless of any other considerations, must be willing and able to perform the contract with the product and services prices it negotiates. It doesn't do anyone any good for the subcontractor to come in with super low prices and the prime contractor to win the program only to find out that the subcontractor cannot operate at the prices quoted and must either default on the contract or go out of business. Therefore, the subcontractor must understand how much it actually costs to produce a product or provide a service, including its overhead and general and administrative costs, before it can determine a price that it can live with over the duration of the contract.

Do not assume that prices can be modified after contract award. This is particularly true on government business, but applies to commercial business as well. When a customer awards a contract, it usually does so based on some sort of competitive process. What incentive does the customer actually have to allow a prime contractor (and its subcontractors) to raise their prices after contract award? It doesn't make good business sense to do so. There is a contract with the stated prices and unless a case can be made that changes to the prime contract that result in higher prices actually produce some tangible *benefit* to the customer, the customer would not see any business value for allowing the change to occur. Yet, too often, prime contractors and subcontractors get into this very mindset: Go in with low prices now, win the business, and we'll deal with the low price issue after award.

50. How does a subcontractor determine if it is worth working as a subcontractor?

A subcontractor should consider return on investment and opportunity cost to determine if it is worth working as a subcontractor.

Return on Investment Analysis

A return on investment analysis consists of reviewing how much money the company will have to spend to get the business versus how much money the company can realistically expect to earn if the company and the prime contractor win the contract. When deciding how much money will be needed to win the program, the company should analyze its involvement in each stage of the process and look at how many people will be needed to do the work plus their salaries for that period of time. People that the company may need to consider include representatives from technical, management, business, legal, and other support organizations. Expenses for any travel, proposal duplication, producing the product, providing technical support, and other costs associated with turning in a proposal to the prime contractor and conducting the after-proposal submission activities must be included in the analysis.

The company then needs to compare these expenses with how much it can reasonably hope to make on the program. The company does this by analyzing the revenue, expenses, profit, contract type, prime contractor's business case, and subcontract terms and conditions. It then factors that number by a win factor.

A *win factor* is the percentage the company assigns to the win probability. For example, if the prime contractor is the incumbent, has a great relationship with the customer because of stellar contract performance, and is typically the low-cost provider, the company might assign a win probability factor of 90 percent (i.e., the company is 90 percent sure that it will win the contract). However, if the prime contractor is trying to get its first contract with the customer and entered the marketplace within the last few years, the company would set its win probability at a much lower percentage.

After the company figures out how much it will cost to bid the program and how much it can reasonably expect to make, the company needs to assess factors other than financial ones. For example:

- How will the deal help the company's overall marketplace growth?

- How will this subcontract relationship affect the other subcontract relationships the company has with the prime contractor?

- Are the company's employees currently fully used? If they are not and the company is paying them anyway, the company should take advantage of the opportunity to work on the program.

- How does the program help the company meet its other goals and objectives?

Opportunity Cost Assessment

Another part of the equation is the opportunity cost assessment. An *opportunity cost* is basically an analysis that answers the question: If I wasn't pursuing this opportunity, what opportunity would I be pursuing and which opportunity has the greatest benefit to me? To answer this question, the company compares the return on investment analyses for multiple deals to determine which deal has the greatest payoff in terms of financial and strategic benefits.

Another factor that should be considered in the opportunity cost assessment is how much training the company needs in the marketplace. When a subcontractor is heavily involved in helping a prime contractor with a program, the subcontractor:

- Makes customer contacts

- Makes prime contractor contacts, from which it learns processes and procedures and technical strategies

- Meets other subcontractors, which provide it with more program contacts, and learns processes and procedures and technical strategies at the subcontractor level

- Acquires a detailed understanding of how the program will run after contract award

- Learns competitor information.

The company can use the information it learns to pursue future business opportunities. In addition, a proposal effort can help get the company's team members up to speed quickly on contracting and the marketplace at minimal expense. Finally, if the company demonstrates strong abilities through its greater program involvement, it can gain other business opportunities. The key is to decide if the benefits outweigh the risks.

Subcontracting is an excellent way for companies to work together to meet the government's requirements and share the contract risks and rewards. By paying careful attention to the issues discussed in this chapter, the two companies can increase their potential for a fruitful relationship.

CHAPTER 5
Marketing

During the marketing phase, a contractor tries to gather as much information as possible about the customer, subcontractors, and the competition. With an in-depth understanding of these three components—coupled with a solid understanding of the industry and the company's own capabilities—a company management team can make a valid bid decision, that is, whether to pursue a particular piece of government business.

51. What are the overall steps to conducting marketing?

Marketing involves a number of important steps.

Understand Capabilities

The company must have an overall understanding of its product offering, customers' environments, competitive environment, objectives, programs, projects, schedules, and resources. The company must then determine how to leverage that information to select one or more programs to pursue. A company may decide to pursue a vertical market, taking its product or service that meets a certain niche and attempting to sell it to the specific government agencies in need of it. An example would be missile guidance systems that are primarily sold to DoD. Alternatively, a company may have a product or service that meets the needs of a wide variety of industries rather than just a specific one, for example, software applications for managing projects.

Target the Appropriate Government Customers

The first step in selling to a customer is to determine which company product or service should be targeted to which customer. A prime contractor needs to determine which customers it should pursue; a subcontractor needs to determine which prime contractor team(s) it should secure a position on. Although the customer does not require a company to develop a marketing plan, the customer does expect the company to analyze contracting opportunities and pursue those for which the company believes it is qualified. When the company is identifying customers that can help it meet its strategic plan, the company should consider the customer's need, the customer's budget, the timeframe, the cost of sale, and the competitive environment. As a general rule of thumb, it costs less to obtain repeat business from existing customers than it does to secure business with a brand new customer.

Develop a Marketing Plan for a Particular Program

The process of developing a marketing plan is a good way for a company to evaluate market conditions, competition, the needs of the customer, and the company's strengths and weaknesses to determine where its marketing efforts should be directed. As part of the marketing plan, the company develops specific strategies for pursuing a contract program within a customer organization.

Assign a Program Manager and Salesperson to Pursue the Program

Both prime contractors and subcontractors assign program managers and salespeople to pursue the program. The prime contractor's program manager begins developing solutions by defining the acquisition strategy and by determining potential subcontractors. The subcontractor program manager begins meeting with prime contractors to secure the best opportunity. The salespeople from both organizations gather marketing information for the marketing plan and try to determine how the two companies might work together. The program manager and salespeople from each company work together to identify the internal team members, analyze and shape the RFP, and work to secure a positive bid decision. It is important at this stage that nondisclosure agreements are in place between the prime contractor and the potential subcontractors because a subcontractor could be talking with other prime contractors about a business relationship.

Gather Marketing Information

The team needs solid market research data to use as a basis for the marketing plan. (Later questions will address what types of information are needed, tools that can be used to get the data, and potential uses for the market research data after they are collected.)

Learn of New Program Opportunities

While market research gives a company overall information about its customers and competitors, it is still necessary to learn about changes in strategies and new program opportunities. Some of the ways to obtain these data include:

- Meet regularly with current customers to determine if they have any upcoming requirements.

- Subscribe to the "push" feature of FedBizOpps so that new opportunities will be sent to you via email.

- Read industry journals to learn of agencies' strategic directions and to determine if the company can help them obtain their goals. Then schedule a meeting with a company to talk about how your products and services might be incorporated into its strategic direction.

- Meet with subcontractors to determine if they are aware of new opportunities that they could work on with the company.

- Network with people at various levels to discover what is going on with a particular customer.

- Attend trade shows to learn what companies or agencies are offering and how they are permeating the marketplace. Identify areas where your company can play a part and convince them that you will add value to their team.

- Do an outstanding job on current contracts. Existing customers often provide valuable marketing for contractors who provide outstanding work and service.

Analyze the Program Requirements

After the company has analyzed the information and determined its position, the company reviews the program requirements to determine if it has the capability to bid. The prime contractor reviews the requirements in the customer's RFP. The subcontractor reviews the prime contractor's requirements in the prime contractor's RFP, which is usually a subset of the customer's RFP.

The requirements of commercial companies and federal agencies may vary in how they inform companies about their requirements. One difference, for example, is that the federal environment has more restrictions. A commercial company is not obligated to allow any company to bid on its program. It can select whomever it wishes to work with using whatever evaluation criteria it decides. The federal government must either accept proposals from all companies wishing to bid on the program or accept nonbiased criteria for the number of companies it will allow to bid on the program so that it can conduct an efficient competition.

Shape the RFP

Shaping the RFP is an industry colloquialism used to describe the process of a prospective contractor suggesting changes to the customer's draft RFP requirements. Shaping helps both the competing companies and the customer. The shaping process can include position papers, marketing meetings, draft document responses, and bidders' conference suggestions. Typically it takes the form of a company outlining the specific RFP requirement with which it has an issue; stating why it has the issue; and then providing recommended language to replace the existing requirement. The government reviews each of these draft document responses from all the contractors interested in the procurement; makes its decisions about which language changes it endorses; and reissues the RFP with the revised language along with the list of questions and answers submitted by all the potential contractors.

Develop a Budget

A bid and proposal (B&P) budget is a key factor in the company's bid decision. The company has to decide how much a program costs to pursue and if the potential revenue justifies the expense. B&P money is the most sought-after money in an organization, particularly in the government division of a company. This is because it represents the budget allotted for work to be done on a government proposal effort. It covers costs for all activities—from pre-RFP marketing to contract award. This budget must take into consideration the work required for the initial proposal submission; post- submission activities (like responding to clarifications); live test demonstrations; audits; oral presentations; and best and final offer submission.

Understand the Competition

The purpose of a competition analysis is for a company to gain a competitive advantage by analyzing specific teams competing for the same government program. The information from this analysis helps the company determine strategies for winning and a proposed price. The company should also examine conditions within the customer environment and industry to determine if they present an opportunity for the company or its competitors to exploit.

Make an Initial Bid Decision

A milestone in the marketing process is the initial bid decision. The purpose of the bid decision process is to gather information germane to a particular program, evaluate the information, and decide to either bid or not bid the program. Both prime contractors and subcontractors make bid decisions. The company makes this decision by assessing the company's internal capabilities, market conditions, customer understanding, and win probability.

The company can make its bid decision at any point during a procurement effort. The company needs to make a careful and thoughtful decision, because if the company decides to not bid a program after it completed significant B&P efforts, the company suffers a loss. Some companies reevaluate their decisions periodically as changes occur in the status of the following dimensions: customer program, internal capabilities, market conditions, customer understanding, win probability, team attributes, and competitors' attributes.

52. What kind of data are useful for market research?

Types of data that the team will have to gather fall into three basic areas: product offerings, customers' environments, and the competition.

Understand Your Product Offering

The first step in gathering data is to determine the company's product and service offerings. Typically, a company starts off with a basic product. The company eventually adds complementary products to the product line. It then offers services to help provide the necessary customer support once the products are purchased. The company modifies products and services as new customer requirements, internal considerations, and competitive requirements emerge. Sometimes it stops developing certain features and providing support for some products and services because the company can no longer produce them competitively or because it can obtain higher profit margins with an alternative product strategy. The team must review and understand the company's current products and service offerings at the initial planning stages so that the team can determine what it has to work with.

Understand Your Customer's Environment

It doesn't matter how good the company's product or service is if the company doesn't have a customer base. For this reason, the planning team must consider the next step in the planning process: the customer environment. An analysis of the customer's environment allows the company to answer the following questions:

- Who are our current competitors?

- How does the customer use our product or service?

- What would make our product or service more useful to the customer?

- Why isn't the customer using the product or service today?

- What budget does the customer have for this product or service?

Once the company understands the customer's environment, the company can then make some realistic assumptions about its own product line, marketing strategy, research and development, and product implementation.

Understand Your Competition

The final step in this data gathering process is understanding the competition. In today's environment of mergers, acquisitions, and bankruptcies, it is hard to keep track of who is in the market, who has teamed together, and who is out of the market altogether. Given the teaming agreements and strategic alliances that are formed between two companies pursuing a certain market, the team will quickly find that understanding the competition can be a full-time job because the competitive makeup changes so frequently.

However, understanding who the dominant players are and, more important, why they are the dominant players, can yield great benefits in determining the company's strategy. Companies are constantly looking for new and efficient ways to offer their products and services without sacrificing and, hopefully, enlarging market share. By capitalizing on the trials and errors of some of the company's competitors, the company can see how certain strategies could be implemented, as well as the strengths and weaknesses of implementing them.

This industry-watching allows the company to gain the benefit of seeing how new strategies would work without the risk associated with actually trying the strategies. Then the company can select the best parts of several competitor strategies to develop its own, and hopefully less risky, strategy. Therefore, it is imperative that the company keep track of the changes that occur in the marketplace with regard to how products and services are being offered so that the company can update or modify its own strategy if necessary.

53. What are some of the methods to obtain marketing information?

After the team determines what data it needs, the team must figure out where to get the data. Much information is available in the public domain. In addition, the government makes a lot of data available to contractors. These sources include:

- *Trade journals*—Industry and government magazines that deal specifically with an industry are a good source of marketing information.

- *Marketing intelligence*—Information can be gained from customer visits and marketing meetings.

- *Congress*—Members of various congressional committees assess the effect of new regulations and appropriations. These actions can significantly affect the program's success.

- *FedBizOpps*—This website publishes many government solicitations.

- *Agency's website*—Basic information about an agency, its organization, and its plans are available from the agency's website. Some of these websites have a "push" feature service that allows you to be added to a distribution list for new information that is posted.

- *Agency-published program documents*—Many planning documents are created during the procurement process, some of which are made available to contractors. These are often included on the website or as part of an electronic RFP release.

- *Government-wide documents*—Many agencies such as OMB, DOL, and OFPP publish documents, agency budgets, and acquisition plans on their websites.

- *Freedom of Information Act (FOIA) process*—FOIA allows a company to query an agency for previously collected information. This strategy may or may not be effective depending on how much information the original contractor is willing to release and how diligent a contracting officer is in reviewing any waivers for release of information. When a company submits a proposal in response to an RFP, it may also submit a redacted proposal, meaning that it blacks out certain information that it considers proprietary. Some companies "black out" all the information because they feel all the data is proprietary. In situations like this, the contracting officer may push for a document that allows all but a minimum amount of truly proprietary data. If the company allows most of its information to be seen under FOIA or the contracting officer questions and requires the company to release more data, then the contractor requesting the data, under FOIA, may get useful information.

- *Bidders conferences, presentations by government personnel, and customer site visits*—These meetings provide a lot of operational detail about the customer's environment and help answer the contracting community's questions about the particular solicitation or future plans.

- *Industry seminars/conferences*—These provide information about potential teaming partners and competitors, and future directions and product lines that each may be offering on an upcoming opportunity.

- *Market research agencies*—There are companies that conduct research on programs or competitors for a fee (for example, Gartner Group).

- *Small Business Administration*—SBA holds seminars and offers industry experts and detailed information on how to develop a marketing plan and where a small company can go for assistance.

- *Internet*—People can quickly scan for information on an industry or browse a company's homepage.

Some of the tools that a company can use to obtain the information include:

- *An on-line database or database service*—makes the research function easier and is helpful in quickly determining marketing statistics or trend data.

- *An automated system or method that provides facts about the company's current contracts*—can help in preparing customer briefings or in answering customer queries, for example, a past performance database.

- *A database or method of tracking customer contacts*—helps ensure that the customer receives a consistent message from the company by allowing the company to determine which salespeople are talking to which customers. It will also ensure that one customer is not bombarded by sales calls.

- *Any industry information service*—provides monthly analyses of available products and services and the pros and cons of each, which will help in the competition analysis area (e.g., Gartner Group, Datapro).

- *Universities*—often have excellent seminars available to help companies break into the federal or commercial marketplaces.

- *Professional organizations*—conduct lectures, develop federal procurement guidebooks, and provide excellent networking opportunities for companies pursuing federal business. For example, the National Contract Management Association (NCMA) sponsors national education seminars that bring industry and government experts together to discuss current procurement trends. Industry-specific organizations, such as the Government Electronic Industries Association and the Information Technology Association of America, are useful in providing lists of companies and contact points within the industry.

- *Agency competition advocates*—are responsible for ensuring that adequate competition exists for each program. Competition advocates can provide information on how to conduct business with a particular agency if the company decides to pursue federal business.

54. How does a company use marketing information?

Once the company has collected all the information it needs, it uses the data in a variety of ways:

- *Marketing plan*—The information can be used to develop the following sections of the marketing plan: internal conditions, external conditions, assumptions, objectives, and programs/projects.

- *Bid decision*—The information can be used as a basis for deciding whether to bid on a program.

- *Competition files*—Data collected on competitors become the company's competition files, which are used across multiple program efforts.

- *Company files*—Data collected on companies can be used to identify potential teaming partners and subcontractors on current or future programs.

- *Marketing strategy*—The information that is collected and analyzed is used to develop the corporate marketing strategy, which includes advertising, trade booths, corporate capabilities statements, position papers, marketing meetings, and industry briefings.

- *Customer files*—Information collected on a commercial company or an agency helps the company understand the customer better for current or future programs.

- *Technology files*—Information collected on technology that is applicable to the industry can help the company determine which technologies it should employ to win new business.

- *Proposal*—The information gained through these various sources can help the company write a proposal that demonstrates its understanding of the customer environment, highlights the company's strengths that are important to the customer, and allows the company to distinguish itself from the competition.

55. What are some of the benefits of shaping the procurement for the competing companies?

Shaping is useful to a company because it gives the company a better chance at winning by attempting to make the requirements more favorable to its own solution. Shaping can help a company gain a competitive advantage by suggesting changes to the requirements that help distinguish its solution from the competitors' solutions. By suggesting that the customer add certain requirements to the solicitation document or modify existing requirements, the company may have an opportunity to introduce its latest technology and, perhaps, gain a competitive advantage.

Whereas a commercial company can make whatever changes it deems necessary to the RFP document, the governmental customer must document the change and explain how the change helps the government meet its requirements more effectively. If the changes do not excessively limit competition, the government may decide to accept the suggested changes.

Shaping can also help the company render a positive bid decision on a procurement. If the draft RFP language has terms and conditions that would prevent the company's management team from pursuing the piece of business, the company could suggest language changes that, if accepted, would allow the company to compete for the procurement. For example, a term that might preclude a company from competing might be extensive downtime credits awarded to the customer if the contractor's products fail to work as specified.

Shaping is extremely useful in the subcontracting process for a number of reasons. For the shaping process to begin, the customer must provide some information about the program. This information can take the form of a draft RFP document, a bidders' conference, or one-on-one discussions with selected prime contractors. Once the prime contractor has this information, it has an idea of what the customer is looking for and it can begin discussions with potential subcontractors to work on the business. Likewise, subcontractors can begin to learn which prime contractors are competing for the program so they, in turn, can start marketing their products and services to the prime contractors with whom they would like to work.

If the contract is with the federal government, a large prime contractor will have to run competitions to select a subcontractor. The competition process can be time-consuming, although the use of automated tools is expediting the process. However, the prime contractor must pass a contractor purchasing system review, during which the government determines if the prime contractor selected the subcontractor that represented the best overall value to the government. Small companies have the competition process requirement waived. The shaping process helps companies competing for federal business by giving them a head start in completing the formalized subcontracting requirements.

56. What are the benefits of RFP shaping for the government customer?

Besides maximizing competition, the customer encourages companies to shape the procurement because the process allows the customer to understand specific company concerns and to fix problems early on to avoid or limit issues arising later in the procurement cycle. The customer needs to know the company's concerns because if there are clauses that make a program too risky for one company, chances are the clauses are too risky for other companies as well. This situation would not affect a commercial customer because it can begin negotiations if only one company submits a proposal. However, if a government customer does not get enough proposals, it may be forced to redesign the solicitation and re-compete the program. Thus, shaping the proposal helps the customer receive more responsive proposals from companies by eliminating problematic requirements. The shaping process also helps clarify potentially problematic terms, conditions, and specifications before any significant amount of contractor work has commenced.

Another reason that the customer encourages companies to shape the procurement is so that the companies can teach the customer about the industry and help it determine the products and services available in the commercial market. In addition, the customer can tap company expertise to determine if there is a new, better, or more effective way to meet the customer's requirements. This allows the customer time to analyze solutions immediately instead of spending time collecting data on what is available in the marketplace.

57. What should a company consider when developing a position paper or holding a marketing meeting as a way to shape an RFP?

One way that a company shapes an RFP is by presenting its opinions in a position paper that it sends to the customer or delivers during a marketing meeting with the customer's decision maker. Position papers are an effective way to suggest changes to the customer's RFP. Position papers should clearly present the issue, explain the company's position, explain the benefits of a proposed change, and suggest alternative language for rewriting the requirement. The customer is under no obligation to change the requirement, but if the company presents a good case, the customer may change its requirement.

Marketing meetings can be conducted at the customer location and may include a site visit and discussions with the actual users, or they may be conducted at the contractor location to illustrate the company's capabilities and facilities. Government customers typically limit these types of discussions to the period before the release of an actual RFP so that there is no violation, or perceived violation, of the Procurement Integrity Act. The Procurement Integrity Act prohibits any job offers, bribes, or source selection information from being offered or secured during a federal procurement.

The company must remember several key items and make many decisions when it prepares a position paper or marketing meeting. The issues include:

Determine who should submit or present the team's position— It may make sense for the prime contractor to submit the position paper or conduct the marketing meeting outlining the team's position. However, the prospective subcontractor may be better suited to do this if the issue falls within its area of expertise. Another option frequently used in the government marketplace is to use an industry or trade organization to provide an assessment of the impact that a particular program is having on the competitors.

*Determine to whom the paper should be submitted or presented—*The company should answer the following question: "Who has the authority to make a decision on the issue being raised?" If it is a technical item, the company should submit the paper to the program manager. If the issue stems from a contractual requirement, the contracts person should receive the paper.

*Provide information in a precise, accurate, easy-to-understand manner—*Break complex topics into easy-to-understand steps and keep explanations as simple as possible. By taking these precautions, the message has a much better chance of being understood, explained to others, and acted upon.

Remember that information will circulate—Present as much information as necessary to state the company's position, but remember that documents could end up in anyone's hands. Therefore, don't give away too much of the company's competitive edge.

Make specific recommendations—Present specific recommendations, including specific RFP language changes, when stating a position to the government. This way the customer can accept, reject, or modify the ideas presented based on the stated language and it does not have to spend time developing language that may or may not solve the problem being raised.

Raise an issue that can be resolved—Some requirements may seem totally erroneous to the company but because of FAR stipulations, the government is required to include them. Make sure the problem can be solved within the constraints imposed by the federal procurement process before submitting a change.

58. How does a company shape an RFP by responding to draft documents?

The government will sometimes issue draft RFPs, requests for information, and requests for comment as a way to begin solving complex program requirements before the final RFP is released. For large procurements that require a diverse mix of products and services, the customer may even issue several draft documents before it releases the actual RFP. For task order, labor, or commercial-off-the-shelf item procurements, the customer may not issue any draft documents because it has already done its market research and knows what is available commercially. Draft documents allow the contracting community a chance to see what is being requested and the customer to solicit feedback from the community about alternative approaches to meet its requirements.

The customer dictates whether the information that a company provides in the draft process review is shared with the rest of the interested companies. A governmental customer provides a document listing the questions asked by each company and the government's answer to each company. Because governmental customers release the questions and answers, the company must decide whether its questions could give its competitors an advantage. A commercial customer can either share questions and answers with the other companies or work with each company independently and not share the information with all the companies. The company must remember several key items when preparing a draft document response.

The customer may or may not issue the entire RFP. Although the company must use all the sections when making its bid decision, the customer may choose to issue only the technical statement of work or selected portions of the RFP.

The RFP is not contractually binding. The customer's draft document and a company's response to it are not contractually binding. This means that the customer's final RFP requirements can change quite substantially from the draft requirements.

Draft RFPs allows companies to get started. Up until the draft document stage, the company has had limited insight into the required solution. The draft document is the first time the company can see the solution as a whole. Armed with this information, the company can start lining up teaming partners, devising a solution, and preparing a program approach.

If interested, respond to the RFP. If the company is genuinely interested in the procurement, it should take the time to review and comment on the draft document. This is important because it lets the customer know that the company is interested in the procurement. The company's response is also important because if it fails to conduct a detailed analysis of the draft RFP then, the customer may be less willing to make requirement changes later.

Try to get rid of onerous terms and conditions. If the draft RFP contains clauses that represent significant risk for the company or that require a product that only one company can provide (thereby limiting competition), the company can suggest less restrictive alternative language to the customer. Often, the customer will evaluate the position offered and, if the problem affects more than one company, will change the requirement.

Draft documents represent the unadulterated version. Draft documents primarily come straight from the customer user community and, therefore, they represent the actual user requirements for the program. After this point, competing companies will suggest alternate language that will modify the original requirements. For this reason, the company should review the draft documents in detail to understand exactly what the customer is looking for in its solution.

Draft documents provide an opportunity to suggest new ways of approaching the problem. If the company has a new, better, and more efficient way to approach the customer's problem, it should suggest the alternate approaches in the draft stage. Once the customer moves into the final RFP stage, the customer is too far along in the approval cycle to consider other approaches. Many customers will not even entertain alternate solution proposals after the draft stage.

When the company receives a draft document, it should take several steps to ensure an adequate review of the document. These steps include the following:

- Create a team by selecting company members and subcontractors who have expertise in each of the major areas of the RFP (e.g., contracts, technical, management, maintenance, business, user assistance, training).

- Ask the team members to review the whole draft document so they understand all the requirements affecting their particular functional areas.

- Divide the RFP into sections based on the individual areas of expertise of the team members and ask the members to review the sections by answering the following questions:

  – Does it make good business sense to pursue the contract?

  – Are there any requirements that prevent the company from bidding on this procurement?

  – What risks will the company face if it bids on this procurement?

  – Can the company make a profit on the contract?

- Have the team review the draft document and suggest that each subject expert write his or her comments, questions, and areas of concern.

- Bring the team together and discuss the members' comments from each section.

- Conduct a management review to determine which comments should be included in the company's response to the proposal.

- Arrange the document in a format that makes it easy for the customer to understand the requested changes. To do this, the company restates the requirement and cites the paragraph number, states the company's interpretation of the requirement, states the reasons why the stated method may not be the best method, suggests alternatives, recommends a change, and substantiates the recommendation.

59. How can a contractor use bidders' conferences to shape an RFP?

Besides preparing position papers, attending marketing meetings, and responding to draft solicitations to shape an RFP, companies also should use bidders' conferences to shape an RFP. Bidders' conferences are customer-sponsored meetings designed to bring together all the companies interested in a customer's procurement for a general question-and-answer session. Bidders' conferences give the customer the opportunity to solicit input from the contractor community face-to-face. The conferences are good for companies because they can determine which other companies might be interested in a teaming relationship and which are potential competitors. Following are several key items that a company should remember when attending a bidders' conference:

Competitors—The company attending should be careful about how much of its solution it divulges at the bidders' conference because many of the other attendees will be competitors.

Not contractually binding—Items presented or statements made at the bidders' conference are not contractually binding. Therefore, companies still must wait until the actual RFP comes out to know the final customer requirements.

Sign-in sheet—The company can use the sign-in sheet as a resource because it will have the names of other companies that are interested in the procurement. The sheet also guarantees the company a spot on the customer's bidders' mailing list for the RFP. The company will remain on the bidders' mailing list until the company asks for its name to be removed or until the time of proposal submission.

One or multiple bidders' conferences—The customer may choose to have a bidders' conference before it releases the

RFP, after it releases the RFP, or before and after it receives the proposals. If the company is interested in the procurement, it should send one or more representatives to each conference.

Format—Bidders' conferences typically follow a standard format. The format for the conferences includes a brief customer description, an overall strategy for the procurement, a discussion on specific problem areas in the RFP, and an opportunity for companies to ask questions.

No matter what shaping method the company uses, the only way that it will know whether the customer accepted its suggestions for changes to the RFP is by reviewing the final RFP (or an RFP amendment if the RFP has already been released).

60. How are bid and proposal budgets different on commercial versus government programs?

On commercial contracts, a company may charge back to the customer the full amount of money needed to win the bid through a higher price. A company pursuing commercial business can determine its own rates and may change those rates for each program it works on. Similarly, commercial companies can charge whatever price they want to win business. Because the financial information is confidential, one customer would not likely find out what a company charged another customer for similar work.

On government contracts, financial information is allowed to circulate among government customers. Additionally, only a certain portion of the budget a company used to win federal business may be charged back to the government customer through its rate structure. Any additional money that the company needs to pursue the program is taken directly out of its profit.

The government determines what percentage of a company's federal government business base it will consider allowable. The dollar pool that is equivalent to the percentage allowed by the government is the company's total bid and proposal pool. The company can charge back that amount to the government in the form of overhead and general and administrative rates, provided the company disclosed this practice to the Defense Contract Audit Agency (DCAA). The company applies the overhead and G&A rates to all labor and material costs, and the company must use these same rates on every deal that it pursues during the applicable period of time. This information is documented in a Cost Accounting Standard (CAS) Disclosure statement for large companies as well.

The company can determine how to allocate these dollars across upcoming programs for the year. When proposal efforts exceed the budget because of poor planning or program slippage by the government, the company must decide to either continue bidding on all its desired programs and pay for the difference between budgeted and actual B&P expenses out of profit or not bid on other government programs.

61. What is included in a B&P budget and how is it determined?

A company develops a B&P budget for a proposal effort early on in the process, usually before the RFP is released. The budget normally includes costs for the following:

- Labor, including writers, editors, technical staff, management team, volume coordinators, production supervisor, and review team members

- Proposal space, office supplies, and equipment, such as computers, printers, and plotters

- Proposal production tasks, such as graphics, word processing, and duplication

- Temporary living expenses for writers coming from other locations to work on the proposal, visits to the customer site, and visits to company sites.

To determine what costs go into a B&P budget, the company's program manager, sales manager, and proposal manager first need to determine the likely schedule of events for the procurement effort. The proposal team then estimates the resources required for each stage of the procurement process. The B&P budget is then submitted to upper management, who may modify the budget. The approved budget and actual expenses incurred against the budget are managed by the proposal team's business manager.

Frequently, upper management will request a B&P status report to determine if the proposal team is progressing according to schedule and if the funds are being spent in direct proportion to the amount of work accomplished. If the team goes over budget, or if the program gets delayed, the company may decide to review its bid decision to determine if it still makes sense to pursue the program.

62. How does a company analyze its competitors for a particular program?

A company may not have the time, inclination, or resources to analyze every competitor on a program. The key is to select two or three competitors that represent the greatest threat to the company and focus on them. The company should address several areas when analyzing the competition:

- Determine what companies the competitor will team with:

  - What types of relationships does the competitor have with other companies?

  - Does the competitor have ownership/partnership/ marketing ties with other companies?

  - Does the customer have any preference toward the competitor's team?

  - What subcontractor is the competitor using for each component of the solution?

- Explore what products the competitor will propose:

  - Has the competitor competed for any similar deals recently? If it has, what was its product offering?

  - What is the competitor touting in its advertising, at conferences, and in its marketing literature?

  - Does any section of the RFP seem to favor one company?

- Determine how the competitor will position itself:

  - What win themes is it likely to use?

  - Will it emphasize low-cost or technical advancements?

  - What are its strengths and weaknesses?

- Analyze how the competitor will price its offering:

  - What are its contract revenues?

– What has its recent success record been?

– Has it decided to back out of other deals lately?

– What are its overhead and G&A rates?

– How will it price program management?

– How has it priced programs in the past?

– What are its labor rates?

– Where does it plan to run the program?

– Does it manufacture the products it offers?

– How will it price training and other support services? Can it develop the capability internally or does it hire subcontractors?

– What other contracts is it currently bidding?

- Determine the key players in the customer organization:

– What are their preferences?

– What companies have they worked with before?

– Are any of the former key customer players now working for the competitor?

– How do members of the customer evaluation board feel about the competitors?

– How will the customer evaluate the proposals (i.e., what is most important to it)?

- Identify significant events that are occurring within the customer organization that may affect this procurement:

  – Any procurement scandals?

  – Does the company or agency have small business (SB) or small and disadvantaged business (SDB) goals that it must meet? Are there other legislative goals?

  – Is this a best-value procurement?

- Assess what the company looks like to the competition:

  – What does the competition think the company will do in terms of a bidding strategy?

  – What weaknesses does the company have that the competition will try to exploit?

  – How can the company mitigate those weaknesses?

The goal of the competitive analysis is to determine the company's competitive position in relationship to the other companies bidding on the program. This will help the company determine if its product or service has captured a certain market niche or if its solution is no different from that of the competitors. The analysis will also help the company analyze the features, benefits, and discriminators of its solution, which the company will want to emphasize in the proposal. Finally, this analysis will help the company decide how to package its product/service offering. The company's decisions as to which products and services to offer, at what price, and what features to include (such as warranty, maintenance, training, or user support) will ultimately either win or lose the program for the company.

63. What areas of analysis are required prior to making a bid decision?

Before the company spends a lot of resources to win a program, it must decide whether the potential success warrants the expenditure. The company must analyze the following areas to make a bid decision: customer program, internal capabilities, market conditions, customer understanding, and win probability.

Customer Program

The customer program components that are critical in making a bid decision include:

- Technical statement of work

- Terms and conditions that will be imposed on the company

- Areas of potential risk to the company

- Regulations that the company must adhere to

- Estimated timeframes for the procurement

- Past contractor performance expectations

- Contract performance requirements.

Internal Capabilities

The internal capabilities that a company should consider when making a bid decision include:

- Technical capability

- Corporate resource availability

- Personnel availability for proposal development

- Personnel availability for contract performance

- Funds availability

- Potential revenue if the company wins

- Past performance

- Risk-mitigation plan

- Company's make or buy decision results.

Market Conditions

The market conditions are those items outside the company that may affect the company's success on a customer program, including:

- Raw material availability

- Labor availability, if required to hire externally

- Pricing strategy

- Economic trends.

Customer Understanding

The company must understand the customer environment in order to succeed. To understand the customer to a degree that will ensure success, the company must become knowledgeable of the following:

- Past performance with the customer

- Customer's degree of satisfaction with current contractor

- Customer's decision makers

- Customer's program objectives

- Pending legislation and budget considerations.

Win Probability

The probability of the company winning the program is based on two components: the attributes of the company's team and the attributes of the competitors' teams. Components that the company should consider in each of these areas include:

- Team attributes

  - Customer-perceived strengths

  - Customer-perceived weaknesses

  - Strategy for highlighting strengths

  - Strategy for mitigating weaknesses

  - Strategy for minimizing competitors' strengths

  - Strategy for highlighting competitors' weaknesses

  - Pricing strategies

– Strategy for minimizing risk areas

– Market position

– Past performance

– Subcontractors' or prime company's actual strengths and weaknesses

- Competitor's attributes

  – Customer-perceived strengths

  – Customer-perceived weaknesses

  – Pricing strategies

  – Market position

  – Past performance.

By comparing the attributes of the company's team against the attributes of the competitors' teams, the company can estimate its win probability. This win probability is tempered with the company's analysis of internal capabilities, market conditions, and customer understanding.

64. What work must be completed before making a bid decision?

The company should also finish other work before making the bid decision. This could include:

- Receiving letters of intent to bid from the major subcontractors or from the prime company

- Estimating potential revenue if the company wins the program

- Analyzing risks and determining how to mitigate them

- Developing a high-level technical approach for how to solve the customer's problem

- Developing a high-level management approach for how the contract will operate after award

- Developing high-level pricing strategies

- Identifying the proposal management team

- Determining key personnel to be used on the contract

- Developing the proposal schedule

- Developing the bid and proposal budget.

65. What are the implications of the bid decision process?

After the company completes the analyses and tasks described in the previous sections, it can make the bid decision. The number and types of people who determine whether the company should bid a customer program depend on the size of the company. For example, if a company is small and is owned by one person, the bid decision is made by one individual. If the company is a large corporation, many people may be involved in the decision. Regardless of the number of people involved in the bid decision, the company must consider the following implications of its decision with regard to the rest of its business base: technical abilities, financial security, contractual obligations, personnel resources, operational capabilities, engineering abilities, and marketing approach.

The company must consider many components when making a bid decision. Even though a lot of work is involved in making the decision, the important thing for the company to remember is that the more analysis that it does up front to determine exactly what the company is committing to, the better position it will be in to respond to changes in the procurement. Anyone can slap a bid together and send it to the customer to evaluate. However, companies that follow this practice may encounter problems with the contract if they win. For example, they may default on the contract or lose substantial money because they did not take the time to analyze the deal up front. The savvy bidder understands that a well-organized bid based on solid analysis presents the company in the best possible light and yields the greatest return on investment potential.

CHAPTER 6
Ethical Pitfalls

The government has to buy things honestly and fairly. To make sure this happens, Congress has passed a number of laws aimed at making the procurement process fair. For decades, Congress has imposed conflict of interest restrictions on government employees. These laws regulate and limit the involvement of government employees and former government employees in contracts with the government itself as well as in contracts with private companies.

More recently, in the late 1980s, Congress passed the procurement integrity laws, focusing solely on the integrity of the procurement process. As a result, anyone involved in government procurement must be concerned with not only the government-wide laws applicable to all government employees, but also laws applicable to those involved in procurement.

And in 2007 and 2008, the government made important and wide-ranging changes in the procurement rules. These rules now require contractors to disclose wrongdoing they know about on their contracts or face debarment and suspension. In addition, all contractors *should* have ethics programs and some contractors *must* have them.

66. What do these more recent changes require contractors to do?

These changes make two major modifications in contractor ethics. One deals with the contractor's duty of self-disclosure and the other deals with codes of business ethics.

Self-disclosure

As a result of the 2008 changes, all contractors and sub-contractors face debarment or suspension for failure to disclose illegal contract activities they know about.

FAR 3.1003(a)(2) makes a contractor subject to suspension and debarment for a "knowing failure by a principal to timely disclose to the Government, in connection with the award, performance, or closeout of a Government contract performed by the contractor or a subcontract awarded thereunder, credible evidence of a violation of Federal criminal law involving fraud, conflict of interest, bribery, or gratuity violations found in Title 18 of the United States Code or a violation of the civil False Claims Act."

This clause was carefully written. First, the self-disclosure rule applies only to a "principal" in a company. It is not the employees of a company who must report possible wrong-doing. It is only a company "principal," defined by FAR 2.101 as "an officer, director, owner, partner, or a person having primary management or supervisory responsibilities within a business entity (e.g., general manager; plant manager; head of a subsidiary, division, or business segment; and similar positions)." Second, the self-disclosure duty applies only if the company principal "knows" about the illegal conduct—it does not apply to what the principal "should have known." Third, the principal must have "credible evidence" of law-breaking. Unfortunately, the FAR does not define that term.

Contractor Ethics Programs

As a result of changes made in 2007 and expanded in 2008, all contractors are encouraged to have corporate ethics programs that include a code of business ethics; a business ethics awareness and compliance program that includes a training program; and an internal control system to monitor the contractor's compliance with its ethics program.

How much of an ethics program a contractor *must* have depends on the size of the contractor and the size of its contracts. Large business prime contractors with a contract valued over $5 million with a period of performance of 120 days or more must have a code of business ethics, a business ethics awareness and compliance program that includes a training program, and an internal control system with certain required components. Small business prime contractors with a contract over $5 million with a period of performance of 120 days or more must have only a code of business ethics but not a business ethics awareness and compliance program that includes a training program or an internal control system.

67. Procurement integrity has changed over the years. What does procurement integrity now require as a practical matter?

Procurement integrity certainly has changed over the past five to ten years. When the procurement integrity laws were first introduced, a number of NASA scientists quit before these laws became effective, believing that these laws made them unemployable. And while procurement integrity did not, it scared a lot of people. Eventually Congress addressed the concerns of government employees and contractors about what they perceived as the overly broad scope of the procurement integrity laws.

The recent trend has been to continue to emasculate these laws. Gone are the days when everyone remotely related to the procurement had to sign a certification that could theoretically send them to jail if the certification turned out to be false. Moreover, small dollar contracts were excluded from some of the procurement integrity laws.

68. What are the basic restrictions of the procurement integrity laws?

There are four basic restrictions in the procurement integrity laws, found at FAR 3.104. They are restrictions on (1) disclosing procurement information, (2) obtaining procurement information, (3) making employment overtures to government employees in the procurement process, and (4) former government procurement employees getting paid by companies.

69. Does the dollar value of the contract determine what parts of procurement integrity apply?

Yes.

One easy way to make sense of the procurement integrity laws and to deal with them easily is to look at the types of dollar values of the contracts involved. Different procurement integrity rules apply depending on the dollar values of a contract: (1) and (2) above apply to all competitive procurements; (3) above applies to all contracts over the simplified acquisition threshold of $100,000; and (4) applies to contracts over $10 million.

All Competitive Contracts

Procurement integrity puts restrictions on disclosing bid and proposal information or source selection information. Gone is the phrase "procurement official," with its prerequisite that the procurement official was personally and substantially involved in the procurement. Now, all current or former government employees and anyone who advised the government on a competitive procurement cannot disclose procurement information.

Not all procurements are covered—only competitive procurements are. So a sole source contract and contract modifications are not subject to procurement integrity. The restrictions end when the ink dries on the contract. In addition, the coverage does not come alive again when there is a modification.

Next, procurement integrity restricts what information anyone can get before award of the contract. Under the old law, it applied to "competing contractors." Now, the restriction is broader: It applies to "persons," a word used by Congress. The old law said that you could not knowingly solicit procurement information; now simply obtaining the information is wrong.

All Contracts over $100,000

Next, procurement integrity deals with employment contacts for those involved in government contracts over the simplified acquisition threshold, currently $100,000. These are overtures or job "feelers" by or to prospective employers involved in a procurement. Procurement integrity sets up a process for a government employee to report the contact and then either reject the offer or recuse himself or herself from the procurement.

All Contracts over $10 Million

Finally, procurement integrity deals with the revolving door, but only for a contract over $10 million. The old law had a two-year ban from negotiation or working on a contract that the former government employee had worked on as a civil servant. That was repealed. Now there is a one-year prohibition that applies only to contracts over $10 million. It bans any work on that contract. It applies only to government employees who were actively involved in that large contract.

70. What land mines are in the procurement integrity law?

The biggest land mine is the early-warning requirement. No contractor can raise a procurement integrity argument in a protest to GAO unless the government has received an early warning about it: 14 days after the alleged procurement integrity violation became known.

71. Does a violation automatically invalidate the procurement?

A violation doesn't automatically invalidate the procurement process or cause a company pursuing the contract to be barred from winning the contract. If there was a procurement integrity violation, but it had no impact on the procurement, the violation will not stop the procurement. For example, an employee of one company might discover during the solicitation the price of a competitor's offer, which is a violation of procurement integrity. But if the company that knows about the price doesn't use that information, for example, to raise or lower its price, there is no harm to the procurement process.

72. What is the difference between a personal conflict of interest and an organizational conflict of interest?

The difference between a personal conflict of interest and an organizational conflict of interest usually is whether the conflict of interest is on the part of a government employee (personal conflict of interest) or on the part of the contractor (organizational conflict of interest). When a CO awards a contract to a company that employees his or her spouse, the CO has a conflict of interest. When a company has completed work for an agency seeking related work, that company may have an organizational conflict of interest in a follow-on contract.

As defined by FAR 9.501, an organizational conflict of interest "means that because of other activities or relationships with other persons, a person is unable or potentially unable to render impartial assistance or advice to the government, or the person's objectivity in performing the contract work is or might be otherwise impaired, or a person has an unfair competitive advantage."

A classic example of a organizational conflict of interest is a contractor writing a specification and then being allowed to bid on the work called for by that specification. There is a natural bias on the part of the drafter of the specification to write it so that only its product can satisfy the specification.

73. What are the CO's responsibilities?

Many COs aren't aware of how important their responsibilities are under the FAR's organizational conflict of interest rules. FAR 9.504 makes the CO responsible, for each planned acquisition, for finding and mitigating organizational con flicts of interest.

Eliminating the organization from the competition is often not the best solution to an organizational conflict of interest. The procurement system tries to avoid a conflict of interest and increase competition at the same time. These goals of the procurement system merge successfully when a competitor with a conflict of interest successfully mitigates a conflict and remains in the competition.

74. What does being "debarred" mean and is it serious?

Debarment is the most serious sanction a government contractor can suffer short of a criminal conviction. Getting debarred means a contractor usually cannot get government work for three years. Related to debarment is a "suspension," which makes a contractor temporarily ineligible for government work pending government determination of whether the more serious sanction of debarment should be imposed. Suspensions give the government time to investigate possible wrongdoing by a government contractor.

On what grounds can the government debar a vendor? A contractor can be debarred for a criminal conviction or civil (monetary) judgment for a range of bad contracting practices, such as using fraud to get a government contract. One ground for debarment is breaking the law "in connection with obtaining, attempting to obtain, or performing" a government contract. Another ground for debarment is a contractor committing "any other offense indicating a lack of business integrity or business honesty that seriously and directly affects the present responsibility of a Government contractor or subcontractor." FAR 9.406-2.

What are the procedures for debarment? FAR 9.406-3 carefully describes the due process a contractor must get and the agency must provide to properly perform a debarment. Significantly, agencies must consider any "mitigating factors" bearing on debarment. These factors must take current facts and circumstances into account. Failure to consider mitigating factors may prevent the government from debarring a contractor. In one case, a federal court overturned an agency's decision to debar a vendor, finding that the agency did not consider all the mitigating facts and also did not follow the procedure. *Canales v. Paulson*, Civ.A. No. 06-1330 (GK), D.D.C. July 16, 2007.

CHAPTER 7
Proposal Development

In its response to a government request for proposals (RFP), a contractor submits a proposal that contains, at a minimum, technical, management, pricing, and contracts sections. In addition, the government may request that additional sections be included in the proposal. This chapter addresses the components of an RFP and some of the issues that a contractor must consider when developing its response.

75. Is there a standard RFP format?

In the past, all RFPs followed a standardized approach. Now, with streamlining of the acquisition process and commercial item acquisition, the standard format may or may not be used. Although a government agency may not use the exact format, the main components must still be present in the RFP.

A typical RFP includes the following sections: cover letter, cover sheet, list of supplies or services, statement of work, directions for packaging and marking, inspection and acceptance, delivery and performance, contract administration data, special contract clauses, FAR clauses, list of attachments, representations and certifications, proposal preparation requirements, and evaluation criteria.

Cover Letter

The cover letter to the RFP contains several pieces of useful information. Normally, it includes an overview of the procuring agency, a program overview, the proposal due date, the due date for submission of questions to the contracting officer (CO), the contract type(s) used on the procurement, and a brief description of the products and services procured. It also informs the contractor of any upcoming bidders' conferences and additional information the contractor needs to submit a compliant proposal.

Section A: Cover Sheet Standard Form 33

Section A consists of Standard Form 33, which is a cover sheet that provides the following information:

- Contract number/solicitation number

- Type of solicitation—RFP, draft RFP, request for information, etc.

- Number of proposal copies required

- Date, time, and location for proposal delivery

- Name of CO responsible for the solicitation

- List of sections that are provided in the solicitation (draft documents may contain only some of the sections).

In addition, either the government or the company will fill out, at a later date, sections of the cover sheet, which include:

- Length of time the offer is valid

- Discount amount the contractor will offer for prompt payment

- Amendment acknowledgement

- Name of contact person if information is needed

- Name and address of the company

- Name and title of the person authorized to sign the company's contract

- Information about where the contract will be administered

- Accounting and appropriation information.

Section B: Supplies/Services and Prices

Section B is the "menu" for the contract. It lists the supplies and services the government wishes to buy. Section B, when completed, becomes part of the company's price proposal to the government detailing the solution components and prices for each contract year. Section B will vary, depending on the program's particular requirements. Examples of the types of items that a contractor may be required to provide on a government contract include:

- Manufactured products

- Research and development items

- Hardware, including warranties, spares and repair parts, and documentation

- Software, including warranties and maintenance, software licenses, and documentation

- Program management, including planning, reporting, technical support, data management, security management, training, and field assistance

- Labor, which is supplied from the prime contractor and subcontractors

- Travel

- Other direct costs (ODCs), which include cost items that are required to perform the work and are not covered under another cost category

- Training, including management courses, user training, instructor training, course maintenance, revisions, reviews, and specialized training courses

- Maintenance

- Documentation

- Technical data

- Contract data requirements lists (CDRLs), which are status reports, test descriptions, security plans, or other contract deliverables.

In addition, when the government negotiates the final contract, this section will include the general and administrative rate, the overhead rate, the facilities capital cost of money (FCCOM) rate, and the profit/fee.

Section C: Statement of Work

Section C describes the requirements that the contractor must be prepared to meet during contract performance. Requirements listed in Section C are typically mandatory, and the contractor must propose a product or service that meets the requirements. Sometimes, the government will have optional requirements that allow a contractor to propose or not to propose the requirements. Companies must understand that all mandatory requirements must be addressed in the contractor solution for it to be compliant. Types of requirements found in Section C include product requirements, maintenance requirements, technology requirements, product parameters, environmental requirements, standards compliance, integration with existing government-furnished equipment, communication requirements, and maintainability parameters. As a result of the market research that is now mandatory because of the Federal Acquisition Reform Act (FARA) enactment, specifications contained in Section C can closely resemble, if not match, the product specifications available in the commercial marketplace. If the contractor is proposing a different solution, it should ensure that the government has a provision for accepting alternative proposals; otherwise, the contractor's proposal will not be evaluated.

In addition, Section C may require the contractor to perform certain management tasks, such as program planning, configuration management, information system security planning, management reporting, CDRLs, training, maintenance, user support, providing a help desk for government users, software licensing, technology refreshment, personnel requirements, program management, adhering to a documentation update plan, and field assistance.

Section D: Packaging and Marking

Section D provides all the requirements the contractor must meet to mark and ship its products to the government site(s). Types of packaging and marking requirements include:

- Commercial packaging requirements

- Responsible party (the contractor or the government) for all damage, deterioration, or losses incurred during shipment, handling, and installation

- Warranty start date and duration

- Contractor point of contact if supplies are defective

- Replacement and return procedures.

Section E: Inspection and Acceptance

Section E describes the inspection procedures and acceptance criteria the government plans to use on the contract. The FAR gives the CO the right to inspect products or services to assess contractor performance. Likewise, the government can develop the acceptance criteria that the contractor's product or service must meet before government acceptance. *Acceptance is required before the contractor can invoice for products or services rendered.*

Government inspection and acceptance clauses vary widely. For commercial items, for example, the government may choose not to inspect the contractor's facility on the premise that the conditions under which products are developed for commercial use are sufficient for government use. Using similar logic, commercial products may be accepted upon delivery after quick visual inspection. On the other extreme, the government could impose acceptance criteria for products as described below.

1. The RFP and resulting contract may state that products must be 99 percent operational for 90 days after delivery. This means that if the product is functional for 88 days, and nonfunctional for days 89 and 90, the 90-day clock begins again. The contractor cannot invoice the government until the product is 99 percent operational for 90 continuous days, and acceptance has been achieved.

2. Acceptance also may be based on the timeliness and quality of CDRLs or deliverables. For example, the government does not have to accept a contractor's deliverable; the government can require the contractor to make modifications before it will accept the document.

3. Another acceptance technique the government can use is qualification testing. In qualification testing, the government may require that each product be tested immediately after contract award to ensure that it still meets the requirements as confirmed in the contractor's proposal. Once the government tests and approves all products during qualification testing, at the time of delivery it will conduct a simple visual inspection and sign the acceptance document. Once the contractor receives the signed acceptance document, it can invoice the government.

The government may accept services at the time the services are provided; for example, each month the government may accept the services rendered the previous month, or at some predefined milestone in the project, such as after the first article test for services rendered up through the first article test.

Many government agencies use the standard form DD250 as the acceptance document. The contractor prepares the DD250 with a list of products and services delivered. The authorized government representative at the receiving site signs the document. The DD250 is then included with the company's invoice that is sent to the government's payment office. The DD250 may be signed by the contracting officer (CO) or the contracting officer's technical representative (COTR). COTRs are used primarily when the CO is not available to sign or if the CO is not located where the work is being performed.

The government is now mandating the use of earned value management systems (EVMS) on certain contract types. EVMS is a way for the government to assess if the amount of work performed by the contractor at any point in time is commensurate with the amount of labor hours and budget expended. For example, if the contractor has invoiced 50 percent of the costs for doing a job, it should have completed 50 percent of the work and the government should have received 50 percent of the value.

Section F: Delivery and Performance

The government uses Section F to stipulate how delivery and contract performance will occur after contract award. Many different types of information can be included here; for example, delivery order process, task order process, product delivery location, contract term, late or early delivery implications, special delivery requirements, and CDRL review process.

Section G: Contract Administration Data

Contract administration data, which appears in Section G, includes any information that explains how the government and the contractor will work together after contract award. This section may include requirements for invoicing, payment, subcontracting reports, socioeconomic status verification, and quality assurance requirements.

Note: The government now requires all contractors to register in the Central Contract Registration system before they can be awarded a contract. Go to www.ccr.gov for further details.

Section H: Special Contract Clauses

The government uses Section H to cover any contract clauses that are germane to the particular contract. Types of clauses that may be included are travel regulations, downtime credits, warranty issues, maintenance requirements, training requirements, software/technical data rights, qualifications for waiver, compliance to standards certification, and engineering change proposals requirements. Again, due to FARA, these clauses should closely mirror what is available commercially.

Section I: Federal Acquisition Regulation (FAR) Clauses

The program manager and CO determine the contract type that is appropriate for a program. This decision is based on the amount of risk involved in the contract, the amount of information the government has about the requirements, and whether the product or service is commercially available in the marketplace. For example, if the government needs a brand new research and development effort that has never been done before, it will probably use a cost type of contract. If the government wants to buy a product that is commercially available in the marketplace, it will probably use a fixed price contract.

Once this decision is made, the CO reviews the FAR to determine the types of contract clauses that apply to the selected contract type. These clauses are listed in Section I of the RFP. Only titles of the FAR clauses are listed in both the RFP and final contract, but the clauses are incorporated in their entirety in the resulting contract and performance. The government should ensure that it has the latest copy of the FAR. since it is updated routinely. The version of the FAR clause that is used is the one that is in place at the time of contract award, unless a contract modification is made.

Section J: List of Attachments

The government uses Section J to provide any additional information to the contractor. These attachments may include any type of information, such as lists of sites, standards, or CDRLs. Other information that may be provided to the contractor includes contractor personnel requirements, site plans, or engineering drawings.

Section K: Representations and Certifications

Section K includes all the representations and certifications that a prime contractor must make on behalf of its team. These representations and certifications may include Procurement Integrity, Buy American Act, Equal Employment Opportunity Employer, Drug-Free Workplace, Taxpayer Identification, Debarment Status, List of Authorized Negotiators, and Affirmative Action. Contractors may fill out and store these forms online in the Online Representation and Certification Application (ORCA), also found at www.ccr.gov.

Section L: Proposal Preparation Requirements

The government uses Section L to communicate to a company how it expects to see the proposal formatted. In it, the government usually includes:

- Number, title, and sections required in each proposal volume

- Description of how updates will be handled

- Page limitations

- Type size, margin width, paper size, and paper color

- Description of how questions will be handled

- Any other related procurement issues

- Solicitation provisions, such as solicitation amendments, late submissions, and proposal withdrawals or modifications.

The most important thing to remember about Section L is that it represents what the government expects to see in the final contractor proposal. This is because the proposal instructions in Section L are written in conjunction with the source selection plan. The source selection plan delineates each factor required and the points assigned to each factor. A synopsis of this plan is found in Section M, Evaluation Criteria. When a contractor organizes the data provided in a proposal differently than the government requests it, it is no longer easy to evaluate the contractor's proposal against the source selection plan.

Section M: Evaluation Criteria

The government uses Section M to communicate to the bidding contractors what solution components are most important during contract performance and the relative ranking of those components. This helps the contractor determine where the bulk of its time should be spent in solution development. The evaluation criteria are a subset of the source selection plan developed by the source selection authority during the procurement development process. Potential criteria for judging the proposal include:

- Contractor understanding of the requirements

- Results of a live test demonstration (LTD), if required

- Technical content

- Adequacy of the program management solution

- Corporate experience

- Price

- Personnel experience.

There should be a direct relationship between sections L and M. An offeror should understand how every part of the proposal it is developing is going to be evaluated. Confusion typically results when the government asks an offeror to provide data in the Section L requirements and does not mention how the data will be evaluated in Section M.

76. What is the difference between product and labor contracts?

The two main types of contracts are product contracts and labor contracts. When a customer needs products, a company must provide adequate descriptions in its proposal of the products it will provide and how those products meet the customer's requirements. The customer may require proof, such as testing or user documentation, to demonstrate that the company's products meet the requirements. In such cases, the bulk of the company's proposal tends to be product descriptions, explanations of how its products meet the customer's requirements, and proof that the products will work in the customer's environment.

Sometimes the customer needs to supplement its own staff with contracted resources. The customer may or may not know exactly how many people it needs or the length of time for which it needs them. Or, the customer may know what projects need to be accomplished but is unsure of how long these projects should take. Under these situations, the customer tends to rely on labor contracts.

In proposals for labor contracts, the company needs to provide the hourly rate for each labor category prescribed by the customer for each year of the contract. The bulk of the technical volume in a labor contract describes how the company will do the work, or it may simply be a compilation of the résumés of the people who will work on the contract. The customer may still require proof, such as interviews or a review of each person's résumé before they begin work on the contract, to determine if the proposed people meet the customer's requirements.

The government will frequently use contracts that require both labor and products. In these RFPs, the government will stipulate the requirements needed for each type of contract.

77. What is the difference between solicited and unsolicited proposals?

An inaccurate assumption made in the field is that the customer can solicit contractors to perform work or provide products only by releasing an RFP. However, prime contractors, with or without subcontractors, can submit unsolicited proposals to customers. A company creates an unsolicited proposal without the benefit of an RFP requirements document so it is more difficult for the proposal team to understand exactly the customer's requirements. However, unsolicited proposals are presented and evaluated without going through an active competition. This means that the customer could accept the proposal as is, or with modifications, and the actual requirement is never competed in the open market. Although commercial and government customers can accept unsolicited proposals, it is a little more difficult to get an unsolicited proposal accepted by the government due to the tight regulatory and competition requirements.

The use of unsolicited proposals is declining because the government has a requirement to conduct market research before it procures products or services. Market research requires the government to determine the available providers, estimated price, features, and level of interest in working with the government. Market research is the first step in ensuring that the government runs a fair and open competition.

However, small companies serving niche markets and agencies involved in the intelligence arena still provide and select a fair number of contractors using the unsolicited method.

78. What are some of the characteristics of a typical proposal effort?

A typical proposal effort has several key characteristics.

Proposals Have Finite and Short-Term Objectives

Proposal efforts have a specific task that must be accomplished (i.e., to complete a compliant, responsive, timely, and winning proposal). The amount of time typically available to complete the proposal is anywhere from 30 to 90 days. The amount of work to be accomplished and the short amount of time available do not provide team members the opportunity to develop into their positions. Candidates must be able to join the team, assimilate what needs to be done, and complete the work quickly.

Proposals Are Made Up of Quickly Assembled Teams That Work Together for a Short Period of Time

Proposal teams are put together quickly, and sometimes the team members have not worked together before. Often, a company working as a prime contractor will request support from its subcontractors to help on the proposal. When selecting team members, the company should select people who are knowledgeable in their fields, can handle diverse personalities, and will work as a team to get a project done under tight deadlines. The company and team members should remember that a proposal effort is fully staffed for only a short period of time. B&P costs skyrocket when many people are on the proposal effort for a long time.

The company must consider tasks to be accomplished, budget considerations, and the potential for losing critical personnel resources to other projects when determining how long people should remain on a proposal effort. If the company has many proposal efforts or short-term projects, it can rotate people between projects to contain costs.

Critical Decisions Are Made Quickly

The company must make decisions throughout the proposal process. Examples include selecting the companies, proposing products, and finalizing the terms and conditions of the proposal. Additionally, these decisions must not be made in a vacuum; the company must consider business, technical, and contractual implications. Often, these decisions are critical because they affect many sections of the proposal. Selected people must be able to quickly analyze a situation, make a good decision, and be able to operate in an evolving work environment.

Proposal Efforts May Have a Critical Shortage of Resources

The company probably will not have all the resources it would like to have for a proposal effort. Resource availability, budget constraints, or tight deadlines may result in a critical shortage of resources. People selected for the team must be able to work under less than optimum conditions and be willing to branch into areas outside their expertise to complete the job.

The Proposal Process Is Highly Interdependent

Proposal efforts move at a rapid pace and require close coordination between members because individual proposal tasks are highly interdependent. For example, the company must make technical decisions regarding a product's compliance before it can negotiate pricing and terms and conditions. Similarly, a company's high price may cause the technical team to choose a less expensive but still compliant product. A problem in one area could cause the team to miss the proposal due date, which could render all the team's hard work worthless, because the government cannot accept late proposal submissions. Therefore, the people selected for a proposal effort must be able to work well under pressure and understand the interdependent nature of their work. In addition, the government initiates changes to the RFP which must be communicated to all members so that the proposal can be updated accordingly.

People Branch Out Beyond Their Area of Expertise on a Proposal Effort

People are selected to work on a proposal effort because they bring a certain expertise to the team. However, although someone may be initially selected for his or her talent to develop the technical solution, that person will also be required to help resolve cost, contractual, and management issues. This broadening of skill sets may seem somewhat intimidating at first, but proposals are, for most people, one of the few working opportunities in which people feel pushed to their limit. It should also be cautioned that some people do not move out of their "boundaries" very easily. They were hired to do one job and may feel that they should not have to co-ordinate much with others to get it done. That attitude is not conducive to a successful proposal effort. Individuals selected must have the attitude of "doing whatever it takes to get the job done" for the team to have any chance of winning.

Customer Requirements Evolve

Finally, while all these challenges are going on internally, chances are that the customer is further refining its require-ments. The customer can submit changes to the require-ments any time during the procurement process. Customer changes require the team to regroup and reposition itself to meet the emerging requirements.

79. How many people should be involved in a proposal effort?

The size of the proposal team varies based on the com-pany's size, the size of the deal, how important the deal is to corporate objectives, and the role the company plays (e.g., subcontractor, prime contractor, teaming partner). A compa-ny working as a subcontractor may dedicate only one or two people to a proposal effort to assist the prime contractor. A prime contractor working on a large, strategic deal, however, may involve up to 100 employees to complete the proposal. Most proposal efforts have between 5 and 30 members.

However, the proposal team does not require all of its team members for the duration of the proposal effort. Typi-cally, a few people are involved in the beginning during the marketing and draft RFP analysis phase. After the customer releases the RFP, the bulk of the team members are added to develop the solution and to write the proposal. As the review process begins, team members are dismissed until only a few critical members remain. These members will remain with the proposal effort throughout the customer-questions process. The team is cut again so that only the members directly related to the best and final offer (BAFO) development (if a BAFO is required) remain. If the company wins the award, the team then quickly grows to begin work.

80. What are the key positions on a proposal effort?

Although companies vary in how they organize their proposal efforts, there are some standard functions that must be completed on every proposal effort. On smaller proposal efforts, one person may perform several or all of these tasks. On larger programs, some of these tasks may require multiple people to work on a single task. The company should keep in mind that this is how a *prime contract proposal team* functions. The prime contractor may ask subcontractors for help to fill some of the roles. Having the subcontractor involved in the process early on helps improve commitment to the program and allows the subcontractor to understand how the prime contractor will operate after receipt of the award. Similarly, the subcontractor may have a similar smaller organization set up within its own company to complete the tasks required by the prime contractor.

Program Manager

The program manager has overall responsibility for the proposal effort and may stay with the program after it is won as the account manager. In addition, the program manager:

- Manages all relationships outside proposal team (e.g., upper management, teaming partners, the customer)

- Directs overall program planning

- Chairs kickoff meeting

- Approves proposal process schedule

- Organizes total proposal review

- Monitors proposal budget

- Allocates personnel.

Salesperson

The salesperson has tracked the program since its early stages and understands the customer's needs and requirements. In addition, the salesperson:

- Makes customer visits to gain an understanding of the customer's environment

- Tracks the program by attending governmental agency briefings and reading agency web page announcements

- Reviews www.fedbizopps, which shows all the current and upcoming government contracting opportunities or amendments

- Identifies potential teaming partners and subcontractors for the program

- Gains internal management support for the program

- Helps develop win themes, discriminators, and benefits the customer derives from the solution.

Proposal Management Team

The proposal management team consists of the program manager and his or her direct reports. These direct reports include the technical manager, proposal manager, management volume manager, live test demonstration manager (if needed), and business manager. The proposal management team also includes representatives from the support organizations, such as marketing, contracts, engineering, and purchasing.

Proposal Production Team

The proposal production team is managed by the proposal manager and consists of an editor, production coordinator, system administrator, word processing specialist, documentation specialist, and graphics specialist. The proposal management team's responsibility is to produce a compliant proposal that addresses customer requirements and presents the company in the best manner possible.

Proposal Manager

The proposal manager leads the proposal team on a daily basis and completes the following tasks:

- Guides the development of customer issues and discriminators

- Assists in the solicitation process for products and services to be subcontracted out on the contract effort

- Monitors the development of detailed outlines

- Integrates the tasks of the various functional areas

- Develops a compliant, responsive proposal that reflects the company's offering to meet the government requirements

- Provides logistics support by coordinating information flow with suppliers and remote-site personnel

- Manages the production team to produce the proposal

- Develops and manages the proposal schedule

- Manages writing assignments from team members

- Conducts proposal review sessions

- Educates team members on the proposal process

- Reviews draft text and graphics.

Editor

The editor works with the proposal team and:

- Ensures that the proposal is written in a clear and concise manner

- Develops a list of standards that will be used throughout the proposal

- Edits and proofs text for grammar, style, content, and theme

- Ensures writing styles and formats are consistent throughout the proposal.

Production Coordinator

The production coordinator has overall responsibility for producing the proposal and completes the following tasks:

- Sets up tracking procedures for text and graphics

- Works as a liaison between the graphics, word processing, and writing teams

- Ensures the proposal meets quality assurance standards

- Schedules and oversees the production process

- Coordinates proposal packing and delivery.

System Administrator

The system administrator ensures that the writers' computers and local area network, if used, stay operational throughout the proposal process. In addition, the system administrator:

- Creates proposal directories

- Provides system access to authorized users

- Archives backups

- Creates file and drive naming standards

- Creates electronic copies for submission

- Manages proposal version control.

Word Processing Specialist

The word-processing specialist is responsible for producing the text portion of the proposal. To do this, the word-processing specialist:

- Recommends a word-processing package to use that meets the government's requirements

- Trains writers in the use of the word-processing package, if necessary

- Works with the graphics specialists to merge text and graphics files to produce the proposal

- Types in data from writers or formats files received from writers

- Ensures that the proposal meets the government's format requirements.

Graphics Specialist

The graphics specialist is responsible for the graphics that will be used throughout the proposal. To accomplish this task, the graphics specialist:

- Recommends a graphics package to use that meets the government's requirements

- Trains proposal team members in the use of the graphics package, if necessary

- Works with the word processing specialists to merge text and graphics files to produce the proposal

- Works with writers to produce graphics

- Incorporates graphics into the final proposal.

Technical Team

The technical team consists of the technical manager and technical experts knowledgeable in each area of the solution. The technical team is responsible for developing a technically compliant solution and documenting the solution in the technical volume. If an LTD is required, many of the technical team members will assume positions on the LTD team. The technical team also works with other proposal teams, such as the business or contracts team, to provide the most cost-effective solution to the government. The technical team conducts the following tasks for each solution component:

- Reviews the government's requirements and develops a preliminary solution based on the draft RFP

- Determines suppliers for each component and evaluates proposals from potential companies to assess technical compliance

- Develops the technical solution that best meets the customer's requirements

- Develops technical section outlines and writes about the technical solution in the proposal

- Determines if all the components of the technical solution will work together

- Incorporates comments of the review team as appropriate

- Works with the business team to ensure that the technical solution is properly priced

- Works with the contracts and management teams to assess potential risks

- Helps identify components of the competitors' solutions

- Helps prepare for management and government briefings or demonstrations

- Answers any clarification or deficiency reports the government may issue on a section

- Makes technical changes to the proposal, if deemed appropriate

- Helps negotiate with companies for any product or service relevant to technical areas

- Helps develop strategies to reduce costs for the technical solution at the time of the best and final offer.

LTD Team

The LTD team is made up of the LTD manager, demonstration developers, presenters, and support personnel.

LTD Manager

The LTD manager may be the same person who was selected as the technical manager or may be a different person. The technical manager, having the responsibility to develop and document the solution, is in the best position to assume the LTD manager function of demonstrating a compliant technical solution. However, depending on the due dates for the technical proposal and the LTD, the technical manager may be unable to accomplish both tasks, so an LTD manager would need to be added to the team. The LTD manager:

- Manages the LTD team

- Understands the technical solution being offered by the team

- Understands the government requirements for the technical solution and the LTD

- Prepares any LTD plans required by the RFP

- Conducts any solution demonstrations or benchmarks

- Secures equipment, software, and resources to illustrate solution features.

Demonstration Developers

The demonstration developers conduct all the preparation work for the LTD. Specifically, the demonstration developers:

- Understand how each component of the solution meets the RFP requirements

- Determine what components of the solution should be demonstrated

- Prepare the solution for presentation

- Ensure that all solution components are integrated.

Demonstration Presenters

The demonstration presenters include many of the demonstration developers who will present the actual solution and others who will make presentations at the demonstration, such as corporate executives or technologists who may give overview presentations. The demonstration presenters:

- Understand the solution that is being proposed

- Understand the solution features and benefits

- Develop scripts for the presentation

- Develop any handouts or materials that will be provided to the evaluators

- Present their portion of the LTD and are prepared to answer any questions from the evaluators.

Business Team

The business team consists of the business manager and cost/price analysts. The business team works with companies to secure the best available pricing and develops the price volume of the proposal. Specifically, the business team:

- Develops the cost proposal

- Works with the business manager to collect and document costs

- Builds financial models based on costs provided from companies to get an accurate total lifecycle cost for each contract line item number (CLIN)

- Ensures that quotes from companies are for the same things so that accurate comparisons are made

- Evaluates cost proposals from potential companies

- Assists in management reviews and incorporates comments, as appropriate

- Ensures that cost-estimating techniques are applied in a consistent fashion for each price proposal component

- Finalizes the business solution, including pricing strategies

- Ensures that company products used in the technical solution are costed in the business solution

- Ensures that company quotes match what is in the cost model

- Works with the legal and management teams to assess potential risks and attribute a potential dollar value to that risk

- Manages changes to the cost proposal and answers any clarification or deficiency reports the government may issue on the cost section

- Helps negotiate with companies

- Helps develop strategies to reduce costs for BAFO

- Manages the B&P budget

- Develops the financial outlook to determine when the contract will become profitable

- Documents pricing assumptions and relevant data for audits.

Management Team

The management team comprises the management volume manager and other analysts. The team develops and documents the program management solution. The type of people needed for the management volume depends on the specific RFP requirements. For example, if the RFP requires a description of the training approach, the team will need a training specialist to develop the section. The management team:

- Reviews the government's requirements

- Reviews existing management approaches to determine if they are applicable to the current RFP requirements

- Develops the approach of how the contract will run after award and ensures that the solution meets the government requirements and program cost objectives

- Determines suppliers for each management solution component and evaluates proposals from potential companies to assess compliance

- Develops any necessary procedures or processes needed for managing the contract after award, such as user training, order processing, or management reporting

- Determines corporate experience citations that demonstrate the company's capabilities

- Selects people to meet personnel requirements and provides résumés, if necessary

- Develops management section outlines and writes about each functional area in the proposal

- Incorporates review team comments, as appropriate

- Finalizes management solution

- Ensures that products used in the management solution will work, as required

- Determines if all the components of the management and technical solutions will work together

- Works with the business team to ensure that the management solution is properly priced

- Works with legal and management teams to assess potential risks by understanding the RFP clauses

- Helps determine what each competitor's solution will be for the management section

- Helps prepare for management and government briefings or demonstrations

- Answers any clarification or deficiency reports the government may issue

- Helps negotiate with companies for any product or service required in the management volume

- Helps develop strategies to reduce costs for the management volume at the time of best and final offer.

Contracts, Audit, and Purchasing Team

This team comprises several different functional areas (audit, contracts, and purchasing) that must work closely together to ensure that the company protects itself contractually in its relationship with the government, passes government audits, and enters into mutually agreeable subcontracts with suppliers. This team is also responsible for developing the contracts volume.

Government Regulation Compliance Representative

The government regulation compliance representative or audit representative helps to ensure that the company passes any government-initiated audit. Because the audits are varied, this person:

- Helps ensure that contractor purchasing system review (CPSR) requirements are addressed

- Validates that the proposal team is doing everything according to regulation

- Helps the proposal team prepare for audits

- Insists on getting dated, written quotes from companies

- Drives the solicitation process

- Drives the CPSR and other audit documentation efforts.

Contracts Representative

The contracts representative is primarily responsible for developing the contracts volume of the proposal. In addition, the contracts representative:

- Interfaces with the government CO to resolve contractual issues

- Works with the proposal team to develop solutions for issues

- Reviews the government's requirements

- Acts as the subject expert for contractual issues arising during contract pursuit and performance

- Develops the approach for how the contract will run after award with regard to contractual issues

- Ensures that the solution meets the specific government requirements

- Develops solicitation package components

- Evaluates company proposals to assess risk areas

- Collects representations and certifications from companies

- Reviews the proposal to determine the effect of commitments made

- Works with the business team to ensure that the management solution is properly priced according to government regulations

- Works with proposal management to assess potential risks

- Attends all government conferences, visits, and demonstrations

- Answers any clarification or deficiency reports the government may issue on the contract volume

- Ensures that changes to technical requirements or price-affecting terms are sent to companies

- Helps develop strategies to reduce costs at the time of best and final offer

- Negotiates the prime contract with the government

- Negotiates subcontracts with companies/partners

- Understands licensing requirements, maintenance options, and other requirements that affect costs.

Purchasing Representative

The purchasing representative helps the team identify suppliers for the goods and services required on the contract. Specifically, the purchasing representative:

- Helps ensure adequate competition for components being provided by outside companies

- Maintains company contacts

- Helps identify product sources

- Assists in the solicitation process

- Helps document the purchasing process for CPSR purposes.

81. What is the process for developing a proposal?

The proposal process is complex and highly integrated. It contains many steps that the proposal team must conduct to turn in a responsive, compliant proposal to the customer. The steps are as follows:

- Revisit bid decision

- Conduct high-level solution development

- Select internal team

- Establish external team

- Develop proposal outline

- Assign person to each outline section

- Prepare customer questions

- Develop and document technical and management solutions

- Develop and document any other proposal sections

- Develop oral proposal

- Develop price proposal

- Develop contracts volume

- Review proposal

- Produce and deliver proposal to customer.

Each of these tasks will be briefly described in this section. Further detail will be found in the supporting questions following this brief process section.

Revisit Bid Decision

The previous chapter discussed reviewing the draft statement of work. As an initial step in preparing a proposal, the team must carefully analyze the final statement of work. Because the customer can change as little or as much of the proposal as it wants between the draft and final stages, often companies will conduct another bid decision to ensure that they still wish to pursue the program. If the team's analysis results in continuing the bid decision, the team will continue its proposal development work. If the analysis directs the team to end the bid, all team members are notified and work on the effort ceases.

As the team reviews the draft RFP, it begins designing the solution and lining up potential subcontractors. When the final RFP is released, the team must determine if the changes in the customer's final RFP represent a significant enough change in requirements that the company is unwilling or unable to put together a responsive proposal in the time allotted.

Conduct High-Level Solution Development

The most time-consuming part of proposal development is developing a solution. This is because any RFP requirement may have multiple solutions available. Deciding on the best solution for the customer is a matter of insight and interpretation of the customer's needs. Which solutions the company chooses determines whether it wins or loses the contract. Therefore, the company usually goes through several iterations of the solution before it makes a final selection.

The key to solution development is that the solution be developed, reviewed, and approved *before* the proposal writing begins. However, the proposal team cannot sacrifice missing the proposal deadline as it searches for the perfect solution. The team must strike a balance between design iterations and choosing a solution so that it can begin writing the proposal and start production.

The term *solution* has several distinct aspects:

- The technical solution is developed in response to the customer's technical requirements and is documented in the proposal's technical volume.

- The management solution describes how a company will manage and operate the contract after award. It is documented in the management volume of the proposal.

- The business solution is the way in which a company prices each solution component. It is documented in the price volume of the proposal.

- The contractual solution describes a company's and its subcontractors' willingness to comply with a customer's terms and conditions. It is documented in the contracts volume of the proposal.

Each of these solutions is highly interrelated to the others. For example, the technical solution describes the products and services necessary to meet the technical requirements. The management solution describes how that technical solution will be delivered. The price volume provides prices for the technical and management solution components, and the contracts volume describes the terms and conditions under which the solution is offered.

Select the Internal Team

Selecting the appropriate people to handle the functions required in a proposal effort is key to proposal success. The abilities of the proposal team members can either make or break a procurement effort. When considering candidates for proposal positions, the company should remember the characteristics inherent in any proposal effort.

Establish the External Team

Early in the procurement process, the company deter-mines how much of the solution it can provide and how much of the solution must be contracted out. Often, the company decides that it is more cost-effective to contract out certain components rather than produce them or develop the capability to produce them in-house. After the company decides to bid on a program, its next task is to determine how much of the program requirements can be done using internal resources and how much of the program must be accomplished using external resources. Internal resources must be budgeted, allocated, and scheduled. If a company finds that it needs external sources, it can go to www.mysbx.com to find anotherr company that can work as a subcontractor on federal contracts. This site allows a company to search or post a contracting opportunity, see the profiles of the companies that might be interested in the opportunity, and discover ways to work more effectively on those opportunities.

Develop a Proposal Outline

Early on in the process, the proposal management team must finalize the proposal outline. In government RFPs, the outline is defined in Section L and the company should follow the outline prescribed. In commercial RFPs, the outline may or may not be defined. If it is, the proposal team should follow the customer's outline precisely because this is how the customer expects to see the information requested. If the contractor presents the information in a different manner, the customer may not be able to locate the data and the contractor's evaluation will suffer as a result. In the cases where the outline is not defined, the company must develop its own outline. This usually is a time-consuming exercise because every team member will have a different idea about how the requirements should be addressed. A basic rule of thumb is to present the proposal in the order of the statement of work. At least this way the customer can look back at its own document to determine approximately where in the company's proposal the information can be found.

Assign Someone to Each Outline Section

Once the outline is established, the proposal management team determines who has the expertise to complete each section. This person will typically analyze the requirements, research solutions, select the best solution given the requirements, test the solution (if possible), write about the solution, and prepare to modify or defend the solution if needed. The people responsible for the outline can be either the company's team members or potential subcontractors.

Prepare Customer Questions

The company and potential subcontractors work together throughout the proposal process to develop questions for the customer. Typically, the customer will allow a certain period during which it will entertain questions from potential contractors. It is important that the company team ask questions as soon as it has them during the procurement cycle so that it can get a better understanding of the customer requirements. Questions can cover technical, management, contractual, or business considerations. The customer then decides how it wishes to handle the answers. It can provide its answer to just the company requesting the information or to all the soliciting companies. The customer can choose any of the following options:

Discussion—The customer can elect to have a discussion with either the company submitting the question or with all the soliciting companies to answer the question. The discussion may be held at the customer's location or through a videoconference or teleconference.

Bidders' conference—Sometimes the customer decides to conduct a bidders' conference at which it answers all the questions submitted to date. The customer usually does not attribute the questions to the originators in hopes of preserving any competitive advantage a company may be trying to assert.

Formally documented—Governmental customers answer all questions and provide the answers in a written document to every company or post them on a website.

Develop and Document Technical Solutions and Management Solutions

When a company selects a subcontractor for its team, the subcontractor may work directly with the company to develop the proposal or it may submit its proposal to the company. The company then selects what it needs from the subcontractor's proposal to complete the prime contract proposal. The tasks outlined in the following chart are shared by the company and the subcontractor, and each party is responsible for its particular piece of the solution. The subcontractor may have representatives on both the technical and management teams. (See related question later in this chapter.)

Develop Oral Proposal

To expedite the proposal process, the customer may require the contractors to provide oral proposals in place of some or all of the written proposal. In an oral proposal, the customer issues an RFP as it normally would, but it allows the companies to submit either part or all of their proposals orally to the evaluation team. The customer records the oral presentation using either videotape or audiotape so that it can preserve each company's performance to help to resolve any disputes that occur during the evaluation and selection process.

The Federal Acquisition Streamlining Act (FASA) gave government evaluation teams the ability to conduct oral proposals. As more and more procurement officials get used to the new format and see the benefits of using the approach, more and more procurements will be conducted using this format.

Develop Price Proposal

The customer evaluates the companies' proposals to determine which company provides the products and services that represent the best overall value for the customer. To accomplish this task, the customer evaluates each company's solution in relation to its price. The technical proposal and management proposal contain the company's technical and management solutions, which are needed to develop the price proposal. In a product procurement, the price proposal must provide a price by year for each product or service that the company offers during the contract. In a labor procurement, the price proposal must include an hourly rate for each labor category the company proposes for each year of the contract.

Develop Contracts Volume

Customers require a company to submit a contracts proposal, which outlines the contractual obligations under which the company will provide the products or services. The customer wants the contracts proposal because the RFP, including the amendments and modifications made during the discussions phase, and the company's proposal, including proposal updates and responses to questions, will eventually become the contract. *Therefore, the customer uses the contracts proposal to ensure that the contractor understands that it is accepting the requirements of the RFP for the life of the contract.* Sometimes, the customer will include a draft contract for the company to mark up and sign as part of its original proposal submission. This is because sometimes the customer will issue an RFP, receive a company proposal, and immediately co-sign the contract, establishing a contractual relationship between the customer and the company. More typically, the customer will enter into question, discussion, and negotiation phases, but it is not obligated to do so.

Review Proposal

The company must ensure that it provided a solution for each requirement in the RFP. To accomplish that task, the company typically conducts a variety of reviews to ensure that:

- Each requirement is addressed

- The solution provided for each requirement will work

- Information is presented in the format outlined in the RFP

- Information is presented in a clear, understandable manner to help facilitate evaluation.

Produce and Deliver Proposal to Customer

The production team ensures that the documents written by the technical and management teams get incorporated into the final proposal that will be submitted to the government. The production team begins its work early in the proposal process by establishing standards and formats for the writers to make the production process as easy as possible.

82. How does a company develop technical and management solutions?

A company goes through similar processes in developing technical and management solutions. In addition to the steps listed in response to this question, team members developing a management solution have additional components that will be discussed in a follow-up question.

After carefully analyzing the customer's RFP, draft RFP, or design requirements and understanding how the customer will use the particular product or service, the team can design the technical and management solutions. All members of the solution design team must understand the customer's requirements and the overall solution design. As each component becomes workable, the team should continually validate it against the requirements and the rest of the solution to ensure a compliant end result. Solution development is evolutionary—the major components are determined, and the solution at the highest level is determined to be viable. Then, as each of the subcomponents is determined, each is validated against the evolving components from the other areas.

The subcontractor is key to the technical and management solution development process because it understands its product or service and how it can be used in the customer environment. The subcontractor also knows the competition for its solution component and can address the features of its solution that differentiate its product from the competitors' products and how the customer can benefit from those features.

The following steps are necessary to complete a technical or management solution.

Finalize Solution Components

A top-down approach to solution development works best if the team analyzes the business problem that the program is designed to solve. By breaking down the total solution into its components, a subject expert can develop a solution for his or her functional area and then ensure that his or her solution is integrated with the total solution. Finalizing solution components is easier if the customer released a draft RFP or request for information documents. The subcontractor is helpful in this process because it knows its product line, the capabilities of each product, and which product would be best suited to meet the customer's overall objectives. Multiple subcontractors may work with a prime contractor to figure out the best mix of products and services to offer the customer.

Validate Make-or-Buy Analysis

The next step for solution development is to validate the make-or-buy analysis for each solution, to determine when the company should produce the product or provide the service using internal or external sources. Once the RFP is actually released, the company may realize that it cannot meet the customer's requirements with internal resources and decide to work with a subcontractor. Or, the company may not be able to locate a subcontractor that it can work with so it may decide to do the work internally.

Another part of this decision process is whether the government has stated a requirement for small business or small disadvantaged business (SB/SDB) involvement. The government does this so that it can help companies with a certain socioeconomic status in the federal procurement process. When an RFP comes out, it can be under the "full and open" nomenclature, meaning that any company can bid on the work. Most government full and open RFPs have the requirement that if the prime contractor is a large company, it must locate and use small companies to conduct portions of the work. In the alternative case of SB and SDB set-aside programs, only SBs and SDBs can prime the contract and they must perform 51 percent of the work. The SB/SDB can subcontract out to large or small businesses to perform the rest. These government requirements also drive whether a company must work with other companies and what socio-economic title they hold.

Assess What Each Teaming Partner Will Bring to the Solution

If the company will have a teaming partner for the program, the company should determine early on what parts of the solution the partner will provide. This decision occurs before the solicitation process begins so that the team sends solicitations only for those goods and services the team requires.

Assign Each Component

The technical or management team manager assigns each component to a subject matter expert to develop the solution. The subcontractor may be responsible for the sections of the proposal pertaining to its solution components.

Gather Information to Develop a Solution

Many types of information are necessary to develop a solution, such as information about the customer, technology, competition, and past contract experiences.

Ensure That All Team Members Understand the Customer's Requirements and the Overall Solution Design

All members of the design team must have an overall understanding of the customer's requirements and how all the components fit together in the solution design. By understanding the big picture of the solution design, team members can develop individual solution components that are more closely integrated.

Conduct the Solicitation Process

The teams must evaluate company proposals for compliance as part of the solicitation process. The solicitation process helps determine which companies will provide the necessary products for the solution.

Test the Solution

Ideally, the team should test the solution before it submits the proposal. Although it is feasible for some components to be tested, time and resource levels do not usually permit the testing of every aspect of most solutions. However, the proposal team should feel confident that the solution will work as stated.

Finalize the Solution

The team must finalize the technical solution. Once this is done, the writers can begin writing the proposal. If the solution is not finalized, the writers will have to continually rewrite to accommodate product changes. If the solution continues to change up until the time of submission, the chance for submitting an inconsistent proposal becomes greater.

Manage Change to the Solution

Although a company strives to finalize the technical solution, outside influences will require changes to the technical solution. Any of these events could require changing the technical solution:

- Customer amendments that either add or change requirements

- Companies' products that cannot meet the government requirements

- Companies that are apparent winners as a result of the solicitation process but that are unable to reach a working agreement with the customer.

The team should monitor these areas and any others that may create change so it can prepare for any changes instead of being surprised by them.

Conduct Initial Reviews

The review process helps develop a better technical solution. The team should conduct multiple reviews as it develops the technical solution: one to ensure that the solution will work; one to review themes and discriminators; and one toward the end of the proposal process to ensure that each requirement has been addressed.

Write Proposal Sections

Once the solutions are defined, the team is prepared to begin writing the proposal sections.

83. How does a team write a proposal?

Outlined below are the steps involved in writing a proposal.

Provide Writing Assignments to the Proposal Writer

The writer could be either the technical team expert assigned to develop a solution component or a technical writer who is brought in to write a section and who has no involvement with developing a solution. The writer can begin preliminary data gathering and developing an outline, but he or she cannot complete the proposal until the solution is final.

Provide Information Packet to Writer

The proposal manager needs to give the writer an information packet that includes the following items:

- *Proposal outline*—The proposal outline illustrates how each section fits into the proposal.

- *Approximate page length for the section*—Page limits may be determined by the customer in the RFP or by the proposal manager. The proposal manager may determine how long a section should be based on the degree of importance it receives in the customer's evaluation criteria.

- *Proposal writing conventions and standards*—It is important the writers be given a style guide that contains proposal writing conventions and standards. The style guide should dictate the names the company intends to use throughout the proposal, such as the team name, product names, or version numbers. Providing a style guide will help ensure consistency throughout the sections of the proposal. A consistent proposal will help the evaluator understand what the company is proposing and limit the number of questions the contractor receives based on ambiguous data.

- *Format considerations*—The customer may dictate the format for the proposal in the RFP or the proposal manager may need to determine format standards, such as type font, margin width, headers, or footers.

- *Graphics guidelines*—The customer may dictate the format for the proposal in the style guide or the proposal manager may need to determine graphics guidelines, such as graphics size, shape, or font size.

Gather Additional Information

Besides the information the proposal manager provides, the writer needs general proposal information to write his or her section. This information includes:

- *Customer information*—Information about the customer's environment and requirements is necessary for the proposal writer to develop a compliant, responsive proposal.

- *Solution information*—Information about the solution components is necessary to highlight the solution features that are particularly relevant to the customer's environment.

- *Competitive information*—Information about the competitors is necessary to develop win themes and discriminators for the proposal.

- *RFP citations*—Information on which RFP sections contain requirements that must be addressed in a particular section of the proposal.

Develop a Section Strategy and Outline

A strategy and outline help the writer define the key components that should be discussed and make writing the proposal easier. In addition, during the review process, the strategy and outline also help ensure that consistent information is being provided across proposal sections to help sell the team's solution. Sometimes companies will develop proposal themes or win themes and emphasize them in their proposals. These themes are developed throughout the proposal so that a consistent message is portrayed. Each proposal section is used to develop or validate that theme.

The writer develops a strategy and outline for the section that includes:

- An understanding of the customer's requirements

- A detailed description of the technical solution proposed

- Customer issues and the specific features, benefits, and discriminators of the team's solution that address those issues

- Specific demonstrations of the proposal's strategies and themes (e.g., if commitment to quality is a proposal theme, the team needs specific measurements provided in this section to substantiate the proposal theme). Other approaches that may substantiate themes include:

  –Past contract successes

  – External validation of the company's solution

  – Results of product studies

– Reasons why alternative approaches will not work

– Description of the solution features and the benefits the customer receives from them

– Description of the items that discriminate or differentiate the team's product from its competitors' products

– Description of the proof for the section or how it can convince the customer to buy the solution (e.g., photographs, graphics, statistics, comparison charts, trend data).

A *customer issue* is any underlying want, desire, or need that drives an RFP requirement. For example, a previous contractor's shoddy workmanship might be a customer issue. This issue may drive the customer's requirement that a contractor "shall maintain a defect rate of 5 percent or less throughout the contract." The team's response could be to outline how quality measures will be implemented and to illustrate the features of its solution. Next, the team could provide a commitment to zero-defect manufacturing, which may be a key discriminator of the company's solution that distinguishes it from its competitors. Finally, the team may provide a description of how its quality measures decrease the defect rate and how having a zero-defect contractor will be beneficial to the customer.

Review Strategies and Outlines

The proposal outlines are reviewed by the management team to determine whether the order, content, logic, and strategy emphasis are appropriate. The team reviews the outline because it is easier to review than the detailed writing.

Complete Writing the Proposal

After the outlines are developed, reviewed, and approved by the appropriate team, the writer can finish writing the proposal section.

Conduct a Requirement Compliance Check

Before the proposal is produced in its final form, the team should review each requirement and response to ensure that the document is compliant. For example, if the proposal has gone through multiple reviews and rewrites, it is possible that responses to requirements were omitted. The team should review the document to ensure that all requirements are addressed and that they are addressed in the order suggested by the customer.

Turn Proposal over to the Production Team

Once the proposal is finished, the production team reviews the proposal for final edit, graphics, and production.

84. What are some of the unique components of the management solution?

Customers may have unique requirements that the company will have to include in the proposal. The customer may ask the management team to complete additional tasks as part of the proposal submission.

Select Appropriate Past Contract Experience

Sometimes customers will want proof that the company has done work that is similar in size and scope to the work the customer is requesting. In such cases, the company can use contract performance citations to highlight the specific details of work it successfully performed for another customer. Some companies keep their contract citations in databases so they can quickly and easily access the information for prospective customers. The degree of detail a customer will want to see in a contract citation varies; typically, governmental customers require more detail than most commercial customers. The proposal team will want to highlight its subcontractor's past contract experience as well to validate that it is capable of providing the products and services required.

Types of information that can be included in the contract citation include:

- Project name

- Contract term

- Contract value

- Customer name

- Contact information

- Summary of work performed

- Customer benefits

- Technology used.

Additional information sometimes requested on government contracts includes:

- Number of contract modifications issued

- Net fiscal result of the modifications, both positive and negative

- Effect of each contract modification on schedule or performance

- Number and type of engineering change proposals submitted

- Number of waivers and deviations requested

- Length of contract

- Number of late deliveries.

Select Appropriate Résumés

Another task that the management team may need to complete is providing résumés of the people assigned to work on the contract if it is awarded to the company. If the company will need to submit résumés, the team will need to select people with the skills that match the customer's or program's personnel requirements. The résumés will need to be formatted according to the customer's specifications. Each customer has its own format for how the résumés must be submitted. The company should develop a template based on the customer's requirements and ask each selected person to revise his or her résumé based on that format. The customer may request résumés from the subcontractors working on the contract as well.

If the RFP states a requirement for résumés, the company must first determine what type of résumé the customer is requesting. Sometimes the customer wants to evaluate only sample résumés, or examples of the types of skills possessed by the people in the labor category that the company is bidding on. When the company provides sample résumés, it does not need to guarantee to the customer that those specific people will be available to work on the program. More frequently, however, the customer may require the résumés of some or all of the key people who will be working on the contract. The customer may request that each person sign his or her résumé. By signing, the person agrees to work on the particular contract for the period of time stipulated, barring unforeseen circumstances.

The government, in particular, tends to be very specific about its required qualifications; thus, the team must be equally specific in providing people with the required skill sets or education levels. If the management team does not meet the government's requirements, the government may issue deficiency reports or deem the company's offer insufficient because the people the company is proposing do not have the necessary skill sets or education levels.

When it comes to resumes or any other part of the government's RFP document, it is important that the potential contractor not "give something for nothing." For example, if the government asks for a program manager who has an MBA and the contractor wants to propose a program manager who doesn't have that degree, the government cannot just ignore the fact that the requirement has not been met. The contractor must give the government something else that it feels is equivalent. In this case, a solution might be to propose a person who has many more years of experience than the government is looking for as a way to compensate the government for providing a person without an MBA. Alternatively, the contractor could propose the person without an MBA at a discounted rated to the government because it didn't meet the full personnel requirement. In either case, the government attaches a waiver document to its existing requirement and substantiates what it received from the contractor in lieu of the contractor not meeting the requirement.

Develop Detailed Plans, Processes, and Procedures

By providing details on how the team intends to manage every major component of work required under the contract, the company shows the customer that the company can perform the work if it is awarded the contract. Subcontractors and teaming partners may help determine plans, processes, and procedures because they may have some techniques that are particularly useful.

The types of processes that the company may include in the management volume are training, documentation, project reporting, subcontractor management, delivery order processing, deliverable development and production, task order development, maintenance, manufacturing, management reporting, and customer assistance.

For example, the following are some items that might be used in a section discussing a training approach:

- Introduce the training approach

- Provide success stories of previous training efforts, including customer, training objectives, results, and numbers of students

- Describe training issues important to the customer

- Describe how the company develops training courses

- Describe the media used to deliver the courses

- Provide résumés of key course developers and instructors

- Describe each course in the suggested curriculum

- Present course development and review cycle

- Explain quality assurance measures taken to ensure course effectiveness

- Present student feedback mechanisms employed

- Explain methods to keep the course current

- Describe the training materials available for the course

- Present sample materials

- Describe corporate training facilities.

Develop Work Breakdown Structure

The management team should begin working on a work breakdown structure (WBS) if the customer requires one, or if the company determines that a WBS is an appropriate method for capturing costs. A WBS hierarchically character-izes all the work that must be done on a program as well as the resources, schedules, and costs associated with complet-ing the tasks.

The first step in developing a WBS is to identify the major functional areas of the program. Then, within each func-tional area, the management team identifies the tasks that make up that function. Each subtask required to complete that task is then defined. The company can decide how many times tasks should be broken down and subtasks defined. The contract's complexity and the level at which the company chooses to manage costs drive the amount of detail in a WBS.

One benefit of a WBS is that it captures costs at the lowest level and can be used to estimate the next level of costs. Task details, including assigning resources, establishing depen-dencies between functions, and developing a schedule are tracked in a project management system. This level of detail allows a manager to budget costs across the contract in the proposal development phase and then ascertain at any time whether a function is being performed at, below, or above its designated costs.

A WBS also provides valuable input to the customer. The customer can determine the actual costs to perform a function and can easily decide whether it should continue to allow the contractor to perform the work or pursue other alternatives.

Develop the Contract Functional Organizational Chart and Staffing Levels

Most RFPs require companies to describe how they will set up the contract organization and explain where each function will reside in their organizations. Once the company has done this, the management team works with the other proposal team members to determine the resources required to run the contract after award. The management team also determines whether these resources will come from internal or external sources.

Gather Corporate Statistics

The customer may require information about the company's financial and personnel status. This information may include total revenue over the last defined period of years, percent of total revenue that is government business, annual turnover rate, lines of business currently being pursued, and other financial indicators to show corporate stability. The customer will want this information from the prime contractor as well as the subcontractor. This information is used to help the government determine whether the contractor is responsible as defined by the FAR.

Plan for Contract Deliverables

Contract deliverables are required throughout the life of the contract. Many deliverables are cyclical, such as monthly status reports or quarterly reviews, other deliverables, such as system test plans, are one-time only. Still others are driven by specific contract events. For example, an engineering change proposal may be necessary whenever a new product is considered for the contract. The customer may require deliverables as separate contract line items that have prices assigned to them, or the customer may require deliverable development as part of the program management costs associated with running the contract.

Not all customers require deliverables. If the customer does require deliverables, the company should determine the level of effort required to complete the deliverables. This level of effort, in terms of people and resources, gets translated into costs, which must be shown in the price proposal. In addition, if the company uses subcontractors to help complete the deliverables, their involvement must be stated in the statement of work in the subcontract. The company can estimate the level of resources required for completing a deliverable by doing the following:

- Reviewing other corporate contracts that have deliverables to understand the estimating techniques employed

- Requesting subcontractor input

- Analyzing the deliverable requirements and comparing the activity required to other similar corporate tasks to help determine an appropriate amount of time and resources (for example, if the deliverable is for preparing and delivering meeting notes, the company can just determine how long it typically takes to develop and disseminate meeting notes for internal corporate meetings.)

In some government RFPs, deliverables are referred to as CDRLs. The company must review two documents for each CDRL required: the standard CDRL form and the Data Item Description (DID) form. The standard CDRL form requires the following information: the CDRL name, delivery dates, recipients, and the corresponding DID number. The DID form details the specific data elements included in each CDRL delivery. Both of these documents must be reviewed to determine correct staffing levels for completing the CDRL. Copies of the deliverable and DID information are in the RFP or can be obtained through the Government Printing Office.

Establish Subcontracting Plan

Government RFPs will typically require two types of subcontract plans. One is contained in the contracts volume, and for it, the company must delineate specifically how much revenue is intended for each subcontractor, whether the subcontractor is a small business or a small and disadvantaged business, and what percentage of the deal each company receives. The other subcontracting plan may be required if the management volume addresses how subcontractors were selected to be on the team, what work they will perform on the contract, and how their performance will be measured. The company can get the information for this section by reviewing the justifications written up in the solicitation stage of the procurement and speaking with the subcontractors.

85. Why should customers use oral proposals?

Oral proposals minimize the amount of paperwork that is generated when producing a proposal and evaluating its contents. Written proposals can be a few pages long to thousands of pages long, depending on the size and type of procurement. Once the customer receives a company's proposal, the customer must evaluate the RFP and source selection plan requirements against each contractor's proposal to determine whether the proposed response is compliant. If the company neglects to provide certain information or if its response is ambiguous, the evaluator issues questions to the company to give it an opportunity to rectify the problem. If the company fails to answer the questions completely or further convolutes the issue, the customer may issue another round of questions or it may lower the proposal evaluation score because of the incomplete response. All this exchange of paper takes time and effort away from designing a better solution and determining the best price for the solution.

In traditional government procurements, the problem is heightened because the contractors may not speak with the evaluation team during the selection process so as to not violate the Procurement Integrity Act provisions. The Act prohibits contractors from obtaining and government officials from providing source selection information, contractors from offering or government officials from accepting bribes, and contractors from offering or government officials from accepting job offers. Because conversations between the government evaluation team and companies are nonexistent in traditional procurements, some of these issues can also serve as protest fodder after award if the issues are not handled appropriately.

Oral proposals minimize all the paperwork, time, resources, and confusion by putting the evaluation team in the same room with the people who will run the program after contract award. They give the customer an opportunity to see the people who will actually work on the contract, test their knowledge of the program and technology requirements, and have the contractor answer any questions immediately.

86. How does a company prepare for an oral proposal?

The overall process for preparing an oral proposal involves a number of steps.

Define the Solution

The company goes through many of the same steps when it develops the solution for an oral proposal as it does for a written proposal. However, once it develops a solution for an oral proposal, the company must determine how to best present the solution so that it meets the customer's requirements and illustrates the depth and breadth of the technical team's talents.

Understand the Customer's Requirements for Oral Proposals

Because of the varying requirements and enthusiasm for oral proposals among customers, the company must carefully evaluate the customer's RFP requirements to determine how much of the proposal must be submitted orally. Some customers are testing the oral-proposal format by requiring a written proposal to restate everything that was covered in the oral presentation. Other customers require that certain parts be presented orally and the remaining parts be provided in a written format. Some customers do not accept oral proposals. In a government RFP, Section L of the RFP will state specifically what the government expects to see and how it expects to see it.

Select the Presenters

The company must determine who the customer expects the company's presenters to be. Some customers will allow companies to use whomever they want to present the technical solution. However, more customers are requiring that companies use the people who will actually be working on the contract after award to present the oral proposal. This is important information because the company must not only decide who has the technical knowledge and management expertise to run the contract after award, but the company must also make sure that these people possess good communication and presentation skills. If necessary, the company must work with the person with solid technical knowledge and management expertise to help him or her refine and hone his or her communication and presentation skills. A company may also choose to use some of its subcontractors because they have expertise in a particular area. Typically, the government will not want high-level corporate presentations by either the president of the company or the salesperson on the deal unless they will be working daily on the contract.

Determine the Presentation Medium

Because of technological advances, the company has many different options for the oral presentation medium. However, before selecting a medium, the company should determine the customer's requirements. The customer may state that the oral presentation must be done in person at its location. If this is the case, the company can decide whether it wishes to use overhead slides or to give a multimedia computerized presentation. When the customer does not dictate how the oral proposal must be conducted, the company can select other options, such as interactive teleconferencing, real-time Internet-based chat rooms, or video technology.

Define Standard Presentation Formats

Unless formats are strictly defined by the customer, the company should define standard formats that each of its presenters must follow in making their presentations. The presentation formats should follow the customer's proposal instructions and evaluation criteria and consider the presentation medium. In addition, the customer may place time limits on the company's oral presentation.

Develop Draft Presentation and Script

As soon as possible in the proposal process, the proposal team should develop a draft presentation and script. A draft presentation and script help to fine-tune the solution and give presenters documents that they can begin reviewing and rehearsing.

A draft presentation and script provide the following benefits. They:

- Solidify the solution

- Illuminate holes in the solution

- Provide the review team with a preliminary presentation and allow the team to identify technical problems, presentation issues, and marketing opportunities

- Give the presenter a head start in working on his or her script by capturing the issues stated by the team during the preliminary presentation

- Highlight timing and topic transition issues

- Meet a customer deliverable if the customer requires copies of the presentation slides before the oral proposal presentation.

Review, Rehearse, Review, Rehearse

The company takes a lot at risk when it sends people in to make an oral proposal. The company basically gets one shot at getting it right. Evaluators try to ask questions that will expose problem areas and risk mitigation strategies. The evaluators have the benefit of surprise when evaluating the company's proposed solution because the presenter has no idea what the evaluators will ask, and the presenter may say something inadvertently that discredits the team. This is a great deal of pressure to put on a few people, especially if their previous positions have not provided them the training to do well in high-pressure situations.

There is hope, however. The proposal team must review the materials and help the presenters rehearse their presentation. These reviews must focus on technical, business, contractual, management, and marketing issues. The rehearsals help the presenters in two ways: by letting them fine-tune their presentation and by providing them with an opportunity to answer ad hoc questions from the review team to prepare for the actual government evaluation panel. Some companies use videotapes or outside presentation consultants to help identify presentation weaknesses.

Develop a Backup Plan

Even though the company may prepare its first-string presenters well, the company may lose its competitive position if the presenters cannot attend the oral presentation. For this reason, the company should have the presenters' scripts carefully detailed and develop a strategy for backup presenters.

Prepare Handouts and Additional Material

The company can prepare information to distribute at the oral proposal presentation. Product drawings, industry reports, trend analyses, and sample reports are all items that may be useful to the evaluators during the oral proposal. The company should limit the information to those topics that help the customer evaluate the company's performance on the particular program requirement. Additionally, the customer may require the company to provide copies of the presentation slides before the oral proposal presentation.

Coordinate Logistics

Once the customer informs the company that it has been invited to participate in an oral presentation of its proposal, the company needs to coordinate the logistics associated with the presentation. To do this, the company should finalize its list of attendees (which may be limited by the customer), transportation, equipment, and lodging.

Conduct Oral Presentation

The next step is for the company's presenters to conduct the oral presentation at the location that the customer deems appropriate. The presenters must limit themselves to the time designated by the customer. Government evaluators usually are adamant about time limits because they do not want to give one company an unfair advantage over another company.

Complete Follow-up Required by the Customer

After the oral presentation, the customer may require the company to submit information related to its oral proposal.

The customer may even issue questions that must be completed (either in writing or orally) by the company before the customer's evaluation. Additionally, the company may have to submit parts of the proposal (such as the price proposal or contracts volume) before or after the oral proposal presentation.

Information needed for an oral proposal presentation includes:

- Complete technical solution and management solution

- Any key personnel requirements from the RFP

- Any oral proposal presentation requirements from the RFP

- Presentation techniques

- List of the features and benefits of the proposed solutions

- Answers to questions likely to be asked by the evaluation team

- A solid understanding of the proposed solution so that presenters can answer ad hoc questions from the evaluators.

87. What are some of the contractual implications of the price proposal?

The price proposal is crucial because it articulates the products, services, and prices for each year of the contract. As such, it is important to remember that:

Assumptions made in the price proposal will drive decisions made on the account—The decisions the company makes for developing the price proposal will establish the budgetary guidelines under which the contract will operate. For example, if the company estimates that two people will be needed for the program and the contract requires three people to actually perform the contract work, the third person's salary will come directly from the company's profit, assuming it is a fixed price contract.

The solution and associated prices become the ordering menu for the contract—The prices the company bids for the products and services are the prices that the company is committed to for the duration of the contract. Although the contract modification process exists on contracts, the customer ultimately decides whether contract modifications will be accepted. Therefore, a company that offers steep discounts on product prices in its price proposals to win the procurement will be obligated to provide the products at those prices for the duration of the contract, or until a contract modification is made.

The accuracy of the costs will drive whether the account will become profitable—The more accurate the company's costs are in the price proposal, the better the chance that the account will operate profitably after contract award. This is why it is so critical that the company capture the price of all solution components described in the technical and management proposals in the price volume. Any solution component that is not priced must still be provided to the customer on a firm fixed price contract, but the customer will assume that the company is providing the component at no charge. This means that the cost for that item comes out of the company's profit. In a cost reimbursement contract, if the government agreed to the extra item, it would pay for the extra item.

88. Do cost and price refer to the same thing?

The terms *cost* and *price* seem to be used interchangeably in the government marketplace. However, they do mean two different things.

Cost, from the perspective of a company acting as the prime contractor, represents the dollars that the company must actually spend to provide the goods and services required. These costs can include subcontractors, products, raw materials, internal support group labor, and other direct charges. To determine *price*, the company first adds G&A, Facilities Capital Cost of Money (FCCOM), and overhead to these costs. Then the company adds its profit to these costs to determine the price for the goods or services it will provide to the customer.

From the perspective of a company acting as the subcontractor, *cost* represents the dollars that the company spends to purchase the raw materials to make its products or the salaries it must pay people on the program. Again, to determine price, the company acting as prime contractor first adds to these costs its G&A and overhead costs. Then it adds its profit to determine the price for goods or services it and the subcontractor will provide to the customer.

In summary, costs are the individual components of price. The price is what is turned in to the customer. For the prime contractor, the "customer" is the government. For the subcontractor, the "customer" is the prime contractor.

89. Can the government make an award decision based on the initial proposal submission?

Yes, the contractor's original proposal could be accepted as is. Many times the customer will decide that the original prices obtained through the initial proposal submission are too high or need modification. In these situations, the customer will ask the contractors that are still within the competitive range to submit a BAFO. (Since FASA, the term has been changed to *final proposal revision (FPR)*, but many people in industry still use *BAFO*.) The company should realize that both the commercial customer, through its desire to conduct an expeditious procurement, and the government, through its procurement reform and acquisition streamlining efforts, are moving toward a first and final offer. In such cases, a contractor will have only one chance to give the customer its best price. The company should keep this in mind when preparing its first price proposal submission, because the company may not get a chance to modify its proposal for a second chance at the program.

90. What is the overall process for developing a price proposal?

The overall process for developing the price proposal includes the following steps.

Understand What and How the Customer Is Buying

Team members must understand the technology and services that the customer is buying and the contract type the customer is using to procure the goods and services it needs. Pricing research and development programs is significantly different from pricing products. A research and development contract would typically be done as a cost-reimbursement type of contract because neither the government nor the contractor knows what it is going to take to get the contract accomplished. In pricing a product, the contractor can give a firm fixed price because it knows what it will pay to develop or purchase the product. Similarly, pricing a firm fixed price contract is different from pricing a cost-plus contract. In a firm fixed price contract, the contractor bears the burden of responsibility to determine everything required to get the contract accomplished and price it accordingly. Once it does that, it is bound to provide all the products and services on the contract at the price. Any overspending is the responsibility of the contractor. In a cost-plus contract, the contractor bids the estimated hours to complete the work, but if more hours are needed and the government agrees, more hours can be added to the contract at the government's expense.

Complete a Competitive Analysis

Before the company spends much time and effort on bidding the program, it must realistically assess how well it will do in the procurement. To do this, the company must determine how much its competitors are likely to bid versus how much its own prices are likely to be. The company must keep in mind that its own bid price must be high enough to manage the program after award yet low enough to win the procurement. If it looks as though the company cannot offer a competitive solution, it should not bid on the program.

Develop a Plan for Pursuing the Business

As the company prepares to make its bid decision, it must plan how to win the procurement. The plan may include special marketing arrangements or strategic alliances with other companies to enable the company to be more competitive. It is important that the business team members understand such relationships and the effect they have on program pricing. A teaming partner or subcontractor can play a critical role if it can provide competitive prices, because with its help the overall team has a better chance of winning the procurement. However, each teaming partner or subcontractor must decide for itself how much it can lower its prices to remain competitive while still retaining a high enough price to cover its costs and a profit.

Determine Components of the Solution and the Person Responsible for Each

The technical and management teams identify subject matter experts for each solution component. The business team needs to understand who is responsible for each component so the cost analyst responsible for a solution component knows whom to go to for technical clarifications.

Provide Cost Data for the Bid Decision

The management team needs financial information to make its bid decision. Often, the business team supplies B&P budgets, potential contract revenue estimates, and financial assessments of the risk required to win the contract as input to the bid-decision process. The team is basically trying to answer the question, "Knowing what our costs will be and our assumptions about what our competitors will bid, do we have a good chance at winning the program?" If the answer is no, the company should not bid on the program.

Gather Information to Cost the Solution

The business team must have the complete and current technical and management solutions for the price proposal and must work with the technical and management teams to understand the cost information that needs to be collected. The business team needs the following information: company name, product name, product version, product features, and unit prices by year for each solution component. Any extra services, such as training, maintenance, and documentation, are usually priced separately. Some companies keep this information in a database so that all proposal team members can have access to it. This becomes particularly critical if the solution changes frequently. On labor contracts, the company should provide hourly rates for each job category for each contract year.

The types of information typically needed to cost the solution include the following.

Subcontractor Data

Once the business team has the correct solutions from the technical and management teams, it needs to ensure that the appropriate cost data are available from the companies. A subcontractor will provide data about its products and services to help the company acting as prime contractor determine if it can conduct the program at a price that can win. Product literature helps the business team determine which features the subcontractor bundles in the product price. A governmental customer may also require commercial price lists from the proposal team. In addition, it can electronically obtain the contractor's GSA schedule prices. The government uses these price lists to determine if the price is reasonable. If the government requires these lists, the business team works with companies to obtain the necessary information. In addition, the subcontractor will know how the competitors in its particular field might bid a product, which will help the prime contractor determine its overall price strategy.

Market Studies, Industry Research, and Trend Analyses

The business team uses market studies, industry research, and trend analyses to determine pricing strategies. These analyses help the business team identify risks associated with pricing strategies as well as methods to mitigate those risks. Strategies used on previous programs also provide a valuable resource for determining pricing strategies.

Estimates

The business team uses estimates to project the costs over the life of the contract. Products or services obtained from subcontractors will normally be guaranteed through lifecycle contract pricing in the negotiated subcontracts. In such cases, the team uses the subcontracted prices as estimates for the contract. However, the business team must estimate other proposed items that are not covered in subcontracts, such as those provided by the prime contractor or products that will not be purchased in significant enough quantities to merit a subcontract relationship.

The business team should consider the following when establishing estimates:

- Everyone responsible for making estimates must use the same bases for estimates. For example, total number of labor hours in a year must be consistent throughout all estimates.

- Estimates must be time-phased over the life of the contract to support contractual requirements.

- The business team must document its estimating methodology, rationale, and assumptions for audit purposes.

Categories for cost estimating include:

- Labor (e.g., hours, skill level required, labor rates, task to be performed)

- Other direct charges to the contract (e.g., computer usage, packaging materials)

- Travel (e.g., air fare, per diem, car rental, number of days, number of people, location, purpose of trip)

- Subcontracted labor (e.g., hours, skill level required, labor rates, task to be performed)

- Product-related cost (e.g., research and development, cost of materials, cost of production, specifications).

Develop Cost Model or Understand How the Customer's Model Works

The *cost model* is the tool that drives the development of the price proposal. The cost model may be developed internally for a specific program, provided by the customer, or developed internally to handle all contracted programs. If the cost model needs to be developed, the business team should make sure it covers the following four areas:

- The model must be able to report the information in the format described in the RFP requirements because that is how the customer expects to see the price proposal.

- The model must be able to capture the data items required to adequately represent costs. For example, if the customer wants the contractor to offer quantity discounts, the cost model must show how the company acquired the discounts.

- The model must have the flexibility to run what-if scenarios. This feature becomes particularly useful when the company defines best and final offer targets for companies.

- Ideally, the model should interface with other corporate systems, such as the budgeting system, so that the costs to manage the program can be translated into the operating budget for the account after contract award. Also, if the customer requires the contractor to use a work breakdown structure for defining the work, the cost model should be able to feed cost-type information into that system so that the costs for each component of the work can be determined.

Not only is it important for the business team to review these main areas to identify all the requirements for the cost model, but it is imperative that the team understand the relationship between the data elements. Completing a data-flow diagram that outlines what data are needed for each calculation will not only help define the system, but will also help troubleshoot problems down the road. In addition, should the customer require changes to the price exhibits (which it frequently does), it will be easy for the team to add new modules to meet the new required functionality if the system is documented from the start.

The task of developing a cost model lessens significantly if the customer issues an electronic model that generates cost exhibits automatically. The business team must still validate the customer's model before keying in cost data to ensure that the model performs as expected. Everyone is capable of making a mistake, and evaluators are often required to complete a system quickly, so they may not have tested it thoroughly. The team should share any problems it identifies with the customer so that the problems can be resolved quickly.

In addition, if the company has developed a cost model for another program, the model may already have some of the capabilities built in. In this case, the business team may only need to add to the model the capability to report information the way the new customer expects to see it on the program.

Communicate to Subcontractor How Cost Data Should Be Provided

If the company will be working with a subcontractor, the company must inform the subcontractor of its costing requirements so that the subcontractor will provide pricing that is consistent with the customer's costing requirements; otherwise, the company's proposal will be evaluated as noncompliant. This is particularly important for a government program if the subcontractor submits its final price only to the company and its price buildup directly to the government. The company needs to work with each subcontractor to ensure that the company obtains the proper cost data so that the business team can prepare an acceptable price proposal.

As the procurement continues, the business team will need to know what specific details are required from each company so that the company can price its portion of the solution. The customer, for example, may require such unique terms and conditions that the subcontractor's commercial price for the product is no longer applicable. In this situation, the subcontractor would need to develop a price for its product on this program alone; however, through FARA, the government is trying to mirror commercial terms and conditions to the greatest extent possible, so it may not ask for unique conditions as much as it used to.

Participate in Solicitation Process by Evaluating Companies' Cost Proposals

The company acting as a prime contractor uses the solicitation process to ensure that the goods and services offered to the customer represent the best overall value. The business team evaluates the cost proposals submitted by the companies to help determine cost-competitiveness. For government programs, to comply with CPSR requirements, the business team must document why one company was selected over another company based on financial merits. Cost analyses, prices analyses, and price negotiation memoranda are all examples of the documentation that the team can use to substantiate its decision.

Conduct Risk Assessment

Most customer programs involve an element of risk for the contractor team. Adequate return on investment, parts availability, and poor-performing subcontractors are just some of the risks that a company acting as prime contractor must deal with to bid a program; however, the company can mitigate some of the risks. One way of doing this is by establishing a mitigation plan. The company does this by having the business team determine the dollar value associated with each.

To do this, the team gathers information, identifies what the risk components are, and determines methods to mitigate the risks so that the company can remain profitable. The inputs to this assessment include:

- Size and complexity of work

- Type of contract

- Effect of contract clauses, such as acceptance, liquidated damages, warranty, invoicing, payment, and insurance requirements

- Cost/risk area analysis, such as initial capital expenditures, minimum quantities, and avenues for future opportunities.

The company can also mitigate risks by using carefully worded subcontracts. A subcontractor that provides products or services is in the best position to ensure that those products and services meet the customer's requirements. If they do not, the subcontractor should be responsible for fixing the problem and suffering any associated financial loss.

To ensure that happens, the company should add a clause in the subcontractor's contract stating its work responsibilities and the financial repercussions of not meeting its responsibilities. Such a clause will not absolve the company, however, and it must accept the responsibility for fixing the problems that fall within its area of expertise, such as systems integration or program management.

Capture All Costs in the Cost Model

Although the business team conducts a competitive analysis early in the bidding process, the analysis is constantly reevaluated throughout the proposal process. As costs are accumulated, the business team captures them in the cost model. By having costs readily available in the cost model, the business team can quickly determine how close it is to the competitive range. Based on this information, the management team may need to reevaluate how it intends to deliver the solution required.

Develop All Parts of the Price Proposal Submission

To complete the price proposal, the business team must collect data about the direct costs incurred on a contract, such as:

- Direct labor

- Fee/profit

- Other direct costs, such as:

  - Subcontracted items

  - Standard commercial items, such as hardware, software, and maintenance

– Other costs, such as special tooling, travel, computer, or consultant services; packaging; and royalties.

In addition, for government programs, the company must obtain components of the price proposal from the disclosure statement the company submits to the Defense Contract Audit Agency (DCAA) for approval. These standard rates include:

- G&A costs

- Overhead

- Facilities capital cost of money.

Begin Developing Pricing Strategies

Pricing strategies help the business team meet the competitive range target. Strategies may be based on technology trends, assumptions, market studies, or customer information. These strategies may be applied across the entire solution or to selected components.

Help Model Competitors' Solutions

Sometimes, the proposal team will want to try to determine what the competitors will offer in their solutions. After the technical team determines the components of the competitors' solutions, the business team may be asked to model the competitors' solutions to help the proposal team know what price target needs to be beat.

As the business team gains more information about the company's competitors and the customer, the competitive range becomes a price target that the company strives to meet to have a good chance at winning the procurement.

The business team establishes a price target by analyzing the components of the solution and then making some assumptions as to what products the competitors will bid to meet the requirements.

After the products are defined, the team makes additional assumptions about the strategies competitors will use to price their product offerings. GSA schedules, Freedom of Information Act requests, and other pricing data are all useful tools in defining the prices that competitors will use. The business team adds these solution component prices to obtain the overall price target. Once the overall target for the program is established, each component of the solution must be assessed in terms of whether it can be provided for the cost allotted to it. The team reviews this process at the component level and at the whole program level to determine if and where the company wants to take risks to win the procurement.

The company should keep in mind that as it prepares a competitive analysis to determine a price target to beat, its competition is doing the same thing. As more data become available about the company and its teaming partners, the company's competitors are changing their targets to reflect the new information. Companies use as much information as they can get to help them price a procurement to win.

Find Out If the Team Made the Competitive Range

The process of gathering and validating cost information occurs continuously throughout the procurement process. The objective of collecting this information is to determine whether the company's team can provide the requested goods and services at a price that is within the competitive range for the procurement. A customer determines the competitive range for a procurement based on the following sources:

- The results of the should-cost analysis it conducts before it releases the RFP

- The market research it conducts during RFP development

- The historical contracted price for the same or similar items

- Contractor proposal prices

- The amount that the customer is authorized to spend on the procurement

- Results of the initial review of each contractor's technical and management solutions

- Results of industry analysis, government price schedules, commercial price lists, etc.

FARA's efficient competition clause has given the government the right to limit the number of contractors' proposals it should consider for award. The government can even limit the number of companies that actually receive the RFP if it expects a high volume of proposal responses.

It is difficult for the company to ascertain exactly what the competitive range will be on a procurement; however, based on its own industry analysis, the company can reasonably determine whether its price will be within the competitive range.

Manage Change to the Cost Model

As changes are made to the technical and management solutions, the business team will need to update the costs in the cost model to reflect the current solution. If a new company is added, the team will need to request a price proposal from the new company and to analyze it.

Conduct Reviews of the Cost Model Data

The business team needs to constantly review the cost model data to ensure that the appropriate components from companies' proposals are priced in the solution. If the company is working on a large deal with hundreds of products, it is easy for the company or the team to overlook a feature that is required for the solution to work.

Finalize the Application of All Pricing Strategies

Before the business team submits the price proposal, the team needs to review with upper management how the team will apply the pricing strategies to ensure support for the post-award pricing. The prices the team submits will be the prices that will be in effect on the contract. It is important that the team prices the contract appropriately and that everyone understands the potential risks to which the company is committing.

Review Technical and Management Proposals to Ensure That All Costs Have Been Captured

The business team should check one final time to make sure there is a corresponding price in the price proposal for every component listed in the technical and management volumes.

Begin Production

Once the review process is completed, the business team can print and verify the cost model reports. The price proposal is then turned over to the production team.

The following information is needed to develop the price proposal:

- Current technical and management solutions

- All parts of the price proposal submission

- Product literature and cost data from companies

- Market studies, industry research, and trend analyses

- Estimates

- Cost model

- Risk assessment

- Competitive range determination

- Cost or pricing data.

91. What is the overall process for developing a contracts volume?

The overall process for writing the contracts proposal is as follows.

Determine Type of Contract

The contracts team determines the type of contract the customer used to understand which clauses the company will need to comply with and to determine which clauses the company will need to pass down to the subcontractors. The contracts team also ensures that the subcontractors submit pricing based on the contract type. For example, pricing a firm fixed price commercial-items contract is different from pricing a cost-plus development effort.

Analyze Effect of FAR Requirements

On government programs, the contracts team must review the FAR requirements and explain the implications to the rest of the proposal team. The FAR requirements have significant implications for the success of the contract because they identify such items as allowable and unallowable charges; appropriate and inappropriate government contractor behavior; socioeconomic considerations; and contract type requirements.

Work with Proposal Team to Identify a Potential Subcontractor and Write Statements of Work

The contracts team works with the proposal team to identify a potential subcontractor. An important step in this process is to document the statement of work for the subcontractor. This will become the basis for the subcontract. The contracts team must then finalize which contract terms and conditions should be flowed down to the subcontractor. The clauses that should be flowed down are those that the prime contractor cannot meet without subcontractor support. All terms and conditions relevant to a subcontractor's product should be flowed down in the subcontract. Once the team has developed a specific subcontract, the team is ready to negotiate with companies.

The contracts team may ask other proposal team members to review the subcontract to ensure that it represents the understanding between the two parties. Oral agreements must be documented in the subcontract if they are to be contractually compliant. Additionally, the contracts team must relay information about the clauses that the subcontractor will not uphold so that the proposal team can estimate the risk associated with such exceptions.

Communicate Issues to the Customer and Work to Resolve Them

The contracts representative is a critical point of contact between the customer and the company. In that capacity, the representative communicates any issues the company has to the customer. The contracts representative often works with the customer to resolve open issues by gathering information on any outstanding issues from precedent set on previous contracts.

Write Contracts Volume

A commercial customer typically wants to see any exceptions and possibly a draft contract as part of its contracts-proposal requirement. The government tends to ask for more information, which a commercial customer could also request.

The contracts team compiles all the data and completes the contracts proposal by:

- Determining any exceptions to the customer's terms and conditions

- Collecting representations and certifications from companies if required by the customer

- Making representations and certifications on behalf of the prime contractor

- Completing a small business/small disadvantaged business (SB/SDB) plan with actual business base percentages for government contracts

- Completing the responsibility statement

- Completing the draft contract, if required.

Exceptions

The customer also requires the company to state in its contracts proposal whether it intends to take exception to any term or condition listed in the RFP. The customer evaluates any exceptions the company takes to the RFP requirements and determines the dollar effect of those exceptions. This dollar figure typically is added to the company's bid price. The customer then carefully evaluates all exceptions taken by all companies to determine which company, in light of all factors considered, represents the best overall value to the customer. The company should be wary of taking exceptions because doing so may eliminate it from the competition. Also, the company must fulfill any exceptions taken by the subcontractor in its proposal. It is often required that these exceptions be stated in a cover letter to the proposal in addition to being stated in the contracts volume.

Representations and Certifications

As part of contract performance, the government will expect the prime contractor and its subcontractor to abide by the representations and certifications they made during the proposal process. In addition, if the customer requires certification to ensure that products provided on the contract meet evolving government or industry standards, the contractor is expected to keep its product current so as to remain compliant.

Degree of Compliance with SB/SDB Plan

The government has small business and small and disadvantaged business goals that it must meet. It usually passes down those requirements to federal contractors. As part of the proposal evaluation process, the government reviews how close the company comes to meeting the goals set forth in the solicitation and to what lengths the company went to find qualified SB/SDBs.

Ways that companies can find SB/SDBs to work with include:

- Reviewing databases of small companies

- Working with the SBA

- Determining what companies are currently subcontracted to the agency

- Reviewing previous SB/SDB relationships

- Using companies that are part of the company's Mentor-Protégée program

- Evaluating capabilities listed on homepages on the Internet.

Responsibility Statement

The government reviews the responsibility statement provided by the company to determine the company's ability to perform the work. Later in the evaluation process, the government conducts a site visit to review the company's facilities, processes, organization, subcontract agreements, and so on.

Performance Risk

As part of the government's increased emphasis on a company's past performance record, the government has begun two initiatives to validate the company's competence in performing the required work. (See section outlining the types of information required on government past performance citations to determine components of a performance risk assessment.)

Draft Contract

The government may provide a draft contract in the RFP document that the contractor is required to sign as a part of its proposal submission. This is done so that the government can sign and execute the contract, should it decide to accept a contractor's initial proposal submission. Contractors should understand that anything they put in the original proposal submission can be accepted as-is and the contractor will be required to live up to fulfilling those requirements.

Prepare Transmittal Letter and Turn Over Contracts Proposal to the Production Team

The contracts team completes a transmittal letter that will be used as a cover letter to the customer. The letter includes the following information:

- Name of company submitting the proposal

- Volumes of the proposal provided at this time (in the event that there are different delivery dates for each volume of the proposal)

- Any exceptions taken

- Any other issue that the RFP says to address in the transmittal letter.

The transmittal letter is usually accompanied by a separate document stating the date and time that the proposal was delivered to the customer. This document acts as a receipt in the event that the proposal was hand-delivered to the customer site. By requesting a signature, date, and time stamp from the person receiving the proposal, the company has proof of the date and time that the proposal was delivered.

92. What is the overall process for reviewing proposals?

Most companies conduct many reviews of the proposal before it is submitted to the government. The company typically conducts the first set of reviews—individual, marketing, technical, management, live test demonstration, oral proposal, and pricing—as the proposal is being written and costs are being collected so that changes can be suggested and incorporated. The final reviews—internal proposal team and the total proposal—should be completed after the proposal is complete so that the proposal team can verify that all requirements have been addressed. These reviews do not have to occur as separate activities. Sometimes companies will merge marketing, technical, management, oral proposal, and pricing reviews and invite subject matter experts from each discipline to participate. On the flip side, a particularly difficult proposal may require multiple reviews before it can be considered compliant and responsive by the evaluation team.

At the conclusion of each of these reviews, the reviewers should meet with the proposal team representatives to discuss specific recommendations for a specific section of the proposal or for the entire proposal. The team should document the recommendations and list specific steps required to make the document more appealing. The team representatives should then determine which of the recommendations should be acted on based on the time remaining on the proposal effort and the amount of unfinished work at that point.

Conduct Individual Reviews of Each Section

The purpose of the individual reviews of each section is to prepare for the more formal reviews, which are discussed later. Throughout the proposal process, writers conduct individual reviews of their sections before the formal review to ensure that their sections meet the customer's requirements and the team's objectives. Writers may also review the sections with their manager before the review.

Conduct Marketing Review

The purpose of the marketing review is to determine if the proposal accurately covers the concerns that are most important to the customer. By ensuring that the customer's needs, wants, and desires are addressed, the proposal has a better chance at being deemed compliant and responsive during the evaluation. Even though the proposal can become a contractually binding document, it is still a sales document. Therefore, the company wants to present its goods and services in the best possible manner. Conducting a marketing review allows external proposal team members the opportunity to see the claims being made and to assess how the customer will receive them.

The typical participants in a marketing review include:

- Program manager

- Marketing manager

- Technical and management team writers

- Experts who understand the customer environment.

The process for a marketing review includes:

- Agreeing in advance on what the marketing themes should be for a particular proposal effort

- Communicating those themes to the section writers so that they can apply them in their sections

- Reviewing outlines or storyboards to see how the writers applied the themes

- Working with writers to make the themes stronger by providing statistics or other factual statements that lend credibility to the claims being made.

Conduct Technical or Management Proposal Review

The purpose of a technical or management review is to solicit input from outside sources regarding the validity, accuracy, and feasibility of the solution being designed. The goal is to ascertain whether the solution will work as intended for the customer's requirements. Typically, an internal review is conducted by proposal team members before an external review, which includes people who are not on the proposal team.

The participants in the internal review include the:

- Program manager

- Proposal manager

- Technical manager

- Subject matter experts/technical writers.

The participants in the external version include:

- All participants from the internal review

- Representatives from the teaming partner and subcontractor organizations

- Experts representing each area required in the RFP.

The process for a technical or management proposal review includes:

- Providing a program overview (if the review includes external people)

- Reviewing the customer's requirements for the volume

- Providing flow charts of each major process or functional area on the contract

- Providing descriptions of the overall solution

- Discussing each requirement and stating how the solution meets the requirements

- Reviewing the strategies and win themes that will be used throughout the proposal and provide the rationale for why the customer should pick the company

- Identifying open issues so that any of the experts can suggest alternative solutions

- Allowing the writer to work with the experts to get hands-on help with the open issues

- Conducting a reviewer assessment during which the reviewers provide their overall comments and suggestions to the proposal management team for improving those areas that may cut across multiple functional areas.

Conduct Price Proposal Review

The purpose of the price proposal review is to:

- Ensure that the company quotes collected represent the products and services used in the solution

- Validate that the correct company offering available to meet the requirement is used (for example, the minimum solution is used if the customer is emphasizing price in the evaluation criteria; or a more comprehensive solution if the customer is emphasizing a best value component in the evaluation)

- Ensure that the labor required to complete all services required on the contract is estimated

- Ensure that the cost model works as intended with the appropriate loads applied

- Ensure that the cost model provides the data required to meet the customer's submission requirements

- Assess if and how the company can make money on the contract after award.

The typical participants include the:

- Business team

- Business manager

- Technical team

- Technical manager

- Management team

- Management volume manager.

The process for a price proposal review includes:

- Providing technical and management writers with the costs that have been captured for their solution component

- Allowing the technical and management writers to validate these costs by reviewing the company quotes, estimate sheets, and assumptions

- Reviewing any discrepancy with the management team for resolution

- Requesting that the business team provide any additional quotes from the companies

- Incorporating changes into the technical, management, and price volumes as deemed appropriate.

Conduct Live Test Demonstration Review

The purpose of the live test demonstration review is to ensure that the team selected to conduct the presentation can accurately develop and demonstrate the solution, answer evaluation questions, and represent the company in the best possible light. Reviewers who meet the following qualifications should be selected:

- Know how to implement and present the solution, as well as those who do not know the solution so they can determine if it is being presented well

- Ask the types of questions the evaluators may ask to test whether the LTD presenters can answer them well

- Ensure that the LTD team members have good stage presence, word choice, knowledge, and presentation skills and can demonstrate the proposed solution effectively.

Conduct Oral Presentation Review

The purpose of the oral presentation review is to ensure that the team selected to conduct the presentation can accurately describe the solution, answer evaluation questions, and represent the company in the best possible light. Reviewers who meet the following qualifications should be selected:

- Know the solution and know if it is being presented accurately

- Do not know the solution so they can determine if it is being presented well

- Know what type of questions the evaluators may ask and can answer them well, and be good at answering questions on the spot

- Have good overall mannerisms, word choice, knowledge, and presentation skills and can project the marketing messages strongly.

Conduct Internal Proposal Team Reviews

The purpose of internal proposal team reviews is to:

- Correct any inconsistencies between sections and volumes. This effort alone will reduce the number of questions, clarifications, and deficiencies the customer issues to the team.

- Ensure that all managers understand how the program will run after contract award so that staffing and resource estimates are assigned appropriately.

- Ensure that what is described in the management and technical volumes is priced in the price proposal; otherwise, the company could lose money and never recoup its costs.

- Ensure that no required function to run the account is overlooked. Sometimes major topics can get overlooked because a writer thought that another writer was handling the topic in another section. The more experts the company has had review the proposal document, the better chance it has of providing a thorough document. It is also good to review the work against the work breakdown structure to ensure everything is addressed.

The participants in an internal review include:

- Managers representing each functional area

- Writers who are writing large portions of the proposal.

The typical process for the internal proposal team review includes:

- Providing copies of the entire proposal document to internal review team members

- Setting aside several hours to complete the review so that interruptions are minimized

- Allowing reviewers to keep an action-item list of tasks that need to be accomplished to make the document complete

- Reviewing the action item lists with the appropriate writers at the conclusion of the review

- Ensuring that changes are made to the proposal document before submission.

Conduct Total Proposal Review

The purpose of the total proposal review is to concentrate on how the evaluation team will perceive the proposal. At this point in the process, design issues are all resolved and the document is in near final form. The review should primarily focus on how each of the functional areas is represented and if all the customer's requirements are addressed. The total proposal review should be held while there is still time to make minor modifications to the proposal and should include many of the same individuals from the previous reviews. This continuity between review team members allows for an efficient review focused on the task at hand rather than on getting people up to speed on the approach.

The participants for the total proposal review include:

- All proposal tcam writers

- All proposal team management

- Review team members who provided useful feedback.

93. What are the production tasks required to submit a proposal to the government?

At this point in the process, the production team conducts the following tasks:

- *Make decisions about artwork to be used in the proposal.* The production team must decide if:

– Proposal and corporate logos will be used throughout the document

– Color or black-and-white artwork will be used

– Proposal covers and spines will contain artwork.

- *Orchestrate how the artwork will be completed after artwork decisions are made.*

- *Receive documents from the team members.* The production team receives electronic copies of the documents from each team member and formats the material as required by the RFP.

- *Produce graphics.* Any graphics required are submitted to the graphics department or to an outside company for development.

- *Send documents to editors.* Editors ensure that the document is grammatically correct and that formats are consistently applied to text and graphics. They also make sure that the proposal is within the required page limits.

- *Send edited copy back to writers for review.* Typically, the editors will have queries that need to be answered by the writers. In addition, the writers must review edits that have been made to ensure that the content has not been altered.

- *Merge text and graphics.* Once the text is finalized, graphics are incorporated into the document at the appropriate locations.

- *Send merged copy back to writers for review.* The writers should review the copy one last time to ensure that the graphics have been incorporated into the appropriate sections.

- *Order and receive all necessary supplies.* The supplies necessary for producing a proposal include paper, binders, tabs, packing boxes, tape, labels, and acetate sheets.

- *Prepare document for duplication.* Add a table of contents and list of exhibits to the camera-ready copy of the proposal. Ensure that headers, footers, and page numbers are correct on all pages. After reviewing the proposal for accuracy, duplicate and bind the document.

- *Conduct a quality review check of the entire proposal.* Once the proposal has been assembled, each copy should be quality checked to ensure that all pages are adequately duplicated and in the right order.

- *Assemble all documentation.* If the RFP requires various volumes of documentation, the production team must determine a method to label and catalogue these documents to make it easy for the evaluation team to refer to them.

- *Box and label all copies of the proposal and supporting documentation.* Each box should contain a list of the contents within the box and should be appropriately labeled.

- *Deliver or ship the proposal.* Proposals may be either hand-delivered or shipped via a commercial carrier. They must be at the designated government location by the date and time stated in the RFP or they will not be evaluated.

- *Maintain an electronic copy and hard copy of the proposal in a secure location.* It is important that the proposal team keep a copy of the proposal exactly as it was submitted to the government. This allows the proposal team to answer any questions posed by the government during the post-submission period.

- *Maintain an electronic copy in the organization's knowledge repository so that sections may be considered for use in future proposals.* This allows other people in the company to not "reinvent the wheel" but rather use what was already developed to contain costs on future proposal efforts.

The production team needs the following information:

- All technical volume sections

- All management volume sections

- All contracts volume sections

- All price volume sections

- Any other sections required by the RFP

- Any documentation required by the RFP

- Proposal preparation instructions.

94. What is the government's approach to contractor past performance?

FARA required government buyers to review contractor past performance information as part of the contract award process. With the government's emphasis on using contractor past performance as an indicator of future contract performance, agencies are requiring detailed information from companies with original proposal submission. This means that the contractor selects contracts similar in size and scope to the effort being contracted out and answers a host of questions about the contract, including size, term, contact information, statement of work, contract highlights, and variance analyses. The contractor then submits all this information to the procuring agency, which assigns government personnel to contact the program managers and contracting officers listed as contacts and either question them personally or request that they fill out an evaluation of the contractor's performance on the contract. The problems with this approach include:

- Contractors must continually submit past performance information, in varied formats, to any agency with which they wish to do business.

- Contractors can select only positive past performance to highlight in the proposal to improve their chances of winning the procurement.

- Government agencies have no centralized location to review contractor's past performance records.

- Government source selection requires a great deal of time and effort to collect, review, and evaluate past performance information.

- Some government customers are frustrated because they are asked to be references too many times, and some consequently refuse to act as a reference.

The government is currently in the process of changing its past performance approach. In January 1999, past performance was updated in FAR Part 12 and became a required factor in evaluation for all negotiated procurements valued at $100,000 or more. Further, FAR Part 15 requires that an agency discuss any negative past performance information (PPI) with any contractor within the competitive range or if the negative PPI will prevent the contractor from being included in the competitive range. Finally, FAR Part 42 requires that each agency review contractor performance on an ongoing, periodic basis during the contract and at the end of the contract. Once the contractor receives this information, it has 30 days to provide comments on the evaluations. If a discrepancy exists between the contracting officer and contractor over the past performance evaluation, it may be resolved at one level higher than the CO.

The past performance process is currently as follows:

- Past performance format is described in the RFP and the contractor responds with information and customer contact information.

- Either the Source Selection Evaluation Board (SSEB) or contractor sends out evaluations to customers, which are reviewed by the SSEB.

- A past performance score is assigned based on the level of risk/comfort the SSEB deems appropriate based on the contractor's past performance.

- Contractor may be allowed to explain a poor rating in clarification reports (CRs) and deficiency reports (DRs); however, the current trend is to have the contractor make any explanations in the original proposal in the event that CRs/DRs are not issued.

The overall plan from the Office of Federal Procurement Policy is to have a centralized database repository of contractor report cards. A report card would be given once a year to a contractor and include comments by the government program manager and CO. The report card format would be consistent across agencies and would therefore not require any further information from the contractor at the time of proposal submission.

While customer evaluations, either stored electronically or provided in the contractor's response, are one form the government uses to conduct the proposal evaluation, it is not the only method. The government can use any data it comes across to evaluate a contractor's potential to do the proposed work. This means that it can contact any government official for whom the contractor has worked; read any reports about the company on the Internet (provided they are from reputable sources); or ask the company for any additional data to illustrate performance on previous contracts.

95. What is the Past Performance Information Management System?

The Department of the Army has developed a central repository to collect past performance data on Department of Defense (DoD) contractors. The repository allows a current government customer to prepare and record contractors' performance reports and allows government buyers to retrieve past performance information on contractors for use in contract source selection decisions. The system is accessible by all DoD agencies. Future capability of the system will allow contractors direct access to their own information.

The database was developed and is maintained by the Office of the Secretary of the Army for Research, Development, Acquisition, Procurement Initiatives Directorate. Each service requiring access to PPIMS selects an administrator who will be responsible for the administering the system and obtaining passwords for individuals required to input information into the system. The CO must acquire a log on and access code to have the capability to input past performance information. Once the administrative data have been entered into the system, the CO or program manager can access the system to provide past performance information, including contractor ratings.

The evaluation system uses a five-color rating scale, ranging from blue for exceptional performance to red for unsatisfactory performance. Each color selected requires narratives describing the rationale for selecting a specific color. The information entered into the system and the definitions of the rating are forwarded to the contractor for review. If the contractor agrees with the performance report, the report is considered final and can be released for use in source selections.

If the contractor disagrees with the performance report, the assessor reviews the contractor's comments and, if warranted, makes appropriate changes. It is the assessor's responsibility to make reasonable efforts to reconcile the report and the contractor's comments. However, it is not necessary that they reach agreement on the report where doing so is clearly impracticable. In this case, the contractor's rebuttal or comments are made part of the performance report. The assessing official forwards the report, including the contractor's rebuttal and documentation supporting the assessor's position, to the designated reviewing official for an agency decision. The reviewing official documents the report, including the decision rationale. The decision of the reviewing official is final.

DoD has determined different contract dollar thresholds by business sector required for PPIMS performance reviews:

Business Sector	Dollar Threshold
Systems	$5,000,000
Operational Support	$5,000,000
Services	$1,000,000
Information Technology	$1,000,000
Construction	$500,000
Architect-Engineering Services	$25,000

The PPIMS is available at http//acqnet.sarda.army.mil.

96. What are oral proposals?

Oral proposals are an alternative way for the government to receive contractor proposals in response to an RFP. The other two ways are turning the proposal in as a traditional paper copy or submitting the proposal electronically. Oral proposals were advocated as part of acquisition reform to help streamline the procurement process. Oral proposals allow companies to present information verbally instead of, or in addition to, including it in their written proposal.

The Procurement Executive Association and Office of Federal Procurement Policy *Guidelines for the Use of Oral Presentations* of 1996 (PEA/OFPP) states that the primary purpose of oral presentations is to eliminate or reduce the need for written material by giving technical evaluators the opportunity to speak directly with a company that can verbally demonstrate its understanding of the work. However, some contracting officers feel uncomfortable relying solely upon the company's oral presentation and insist on a hard copy as backup.

Oral presentations have been used with increasing frequency over the past few years throughout government agencies. PEA/OFPP states that overall, government personnel report substantial savings of resources in both time and cost, thereby ensuring that oral presentations are here to stay in the government. According to PEA/OFPP, oral presentations should be used when a procurement can be defined in terms of a reasonably clear and complete requirement and the effort does not require highly complex technical or management information. When this is the case, the technical and management information may be more useful if submitted orally rather than in written form.

FAR Part 15.102 states that the government should consider the following when deciding if oral proposals should be used:

- Government's ability to adequately evaluate the information

- Need to incorporate any information into the resultant contract

- Impact on the efficiency of the acquisition

- Impact (including cost) on small businesses.

In considering the cost of oral presentations, contracting officers should also consider alternatives to on-site oral presentations (e.g., teleconferencing, video teleconferencing).

Many agencies use oral presentations to gauge an offeror's understanding of the requirement and how the proposed key personnel interact, present themselves, and communicate technical information to government personnel.

97. How does the government evaluate oral proposals?

Once it is determined that an oral proposal is appropriate for a particular procurement, the government must establish evaluation factors. It must ensure that the RFP contains instructions to companies stating how an oral proposal approach will be used to evaluate and select the contract winner. The solicitation must also describe the types of information that are to be presented orally, evaluation factors, qualifications of the personnel giving the presentation, and any limitations and/or prohibitions on the use of written material. Typical evaluation factors for oral presentations consist of technical and management factors, and how the offeror will approach accomplishment of the required tasks.

In addition, the FAR suggests that the solicitation state the location, date, and time of the presentations; any restrictions on the time permitted for presentations; and the scope and content of any exchanges that are permitted (FAR 15.210). The solicitation should also state format, content, whether the presentation will be recorded, and whether the presentation should address price or cost. Agencies that have used oral presentation techniques suggest that the oral presentations be scheduled as soon as possible after receipt of proposals (PEA/OFPP).

The government has to be careful in dealing with exchanges between the government and companies during the presentation. The solicitation should state whether the oral proposal constitutes discussions as defined in FAR 15.601 and 15.610. If the government plans to hold discussions, the decision of when and with whom to have oral proposals is critical. The government should allow sufficient time between presentations to permit the evaluators to meet and reach a consensus. It is also helpful if the solicitation states that briefing materials be received in advance of presentations. This will help the evaluators familiarize themselves with the company's proposed approach during the company's oral presentation.

When award without discussions is contemplated, the oral presentation process can become even more critical. Some government personnel have expressed concern that any exchange of information can constitute discussions. After completion of the offeror's oral presentation, the government may request clarification of any points addressed that are unclear. This type of exchange is allowed during oral presentations and does not constitute discussions in accordance with FAR 15.610.

One important point to remember when contemplating oral presentations is that FAR 15.102(f) states that "when oral presentations include information that the parties intend to include in the contract as material terms and conditions, the information shall be put in writing. Incorporation by reference is not permitted." So, if the government wants the company to include something in its proposal that was part of its oral presentation, a revised proposal with the desired term or condition from the company must be submitted in writing.

Oral presentations can significantly streamline and enhance the source selection process. However, they require planning, preparation, and coordination among procurement, technical, and legal personnel from the government to be successful. As time goes on, they will become a standard way of operating in the government procurement arena.

Sources:

Edwards, Vernon J. *Combining Oral Presentations with Discussions*, http:www.arnet.gov/Discussions/Water-Cooler/0400.html, online posting.

Federal Acquisition Regulation, Part 15, *Contracting by Negotiation*, January 1999.

Procurement Executive Association & Office of Federal Procurement Policy *Guidelines for the Use of Oral Presentations*, 1996.

CHAPTER 8
Cost Analysis

Once the government receives proposals, it evaluates the individual costs that make up each offeror's proposal.

Cost analysis gives the government a good picture of the contractor's costs but does not provide an assessment of market value. For that assessment, the government must conduct price analysis (see Chapter 9). Thus, the government performs both cost and price analysis on each offeror's proposal.

98. How does the government define contract costs on a submitted proposal?

The government considers three main components of contract costs: cash expenditure, expense accrual, and drawdown of inventory. Cash expenditure is the actual outlay or dollars in exchange for goods and services. Expense accrual is the expense recorded for accounting purposes when the obligation has occurred, regardless of when cash is paid out for the goods or services. Drawdown of inventory is the use of goods purchased and held in stock for production or direct sale to customers. The drawdown inventory can be expressed in either the number of units or the dollar amount of items drawn down.

99. What key factors does the government review in a submitted proposal?

The government conducts a cost analysis to review the separate cost elements and profit/fee in an offeror's proposal, and then applies appropriate judgment. The government is trying to determine if the offeror's costs are reasonable, allowable, and allocable based on the applicable accounting practices and standards, the applicable cost principles, and the terms of the contract. For example, a cost is determined to be reasonable if, in its nature and amount, it does not exceed the cost that would be incurred by a prudent person in the conduct of competitive business.

100. Why does the government review cost estimating systems?

The government reviews an offeror's cost estimating system in relation to the offeror's cost accounting system to ensure that costs are accurately estimated and accounted for over the life of a contract. The cost estimating system includes the policies, procedures, and practices for generating cost estimates and other data included in the cost proposal. These include organizational structure; established lines of authority, duties, and responsibilities; internal controls and managerial reviews; flow of work, coordination, and communication; and estimating methods and techniques.

101. What does the government look for in a contractor's financial systems?

The government reviews a contractor's cost estimating system, cost accounting system, and job order cost system. An acceptable estimating system establishes clear responsibility for the preparation, review, and approval of cost estimates. It provides a written description of organization and duties; detects and corrects errors; and protects against cost duplication and omissions. An acceptable cost accounting system integrates applicable information from a variety of company management systems.

Accounting systems include job order and process cost systems. An acceptable job order cost system allows the firm to account for output by specifically identifiable physical units. The costs for each job or contract are accumulated under separate job orders. In a process cost system, direct costs are charged to a process even though end-items for more than one contract are being run through the process at the same time. At the end of the accounting period, the costs incurred for that process are assigned to the units completed during that period and to the incomplete units still in process.

102. What type of estimating system does the government use?

When the government is reviewing an estimating system, it wants to ensure that the estimating method is equitable (that is, it produces fair and reasonable results) and that it is applied consistently. The government can use several different estimating methods. For example, a roundtable approach relies on experts in the field. In comparison estimating, costs for a new item are estimated using comparisons with the cost of completing similar tasks under past or current contracts. Detailed estimating provides a thorough review of all components, processes, and assemblies using detailed information.

103. What must the government include in the solicitation?

To obtain information for cost analysis, the solicitation must specify whether cost or pricing data are required. It must also specify that, when cost or pricing data are required, the offeror may submit a request for exception from the requirement to submit those data. Further, if cost or pricing data are not necessary, the RFP must state whether information other than cost or pricing data are required. The government will also state the format required for data submission and whether the government needs pre-award or post-award access to the offeror's records.

104. What is cost or pricing data?

The government considers cost or pricing data to include all facts that, as of the date of price agreement or, if applicable, an earlier date agreed upon between the parties that is as close as practicable to the date of agreement on price, prudent buyers and sellers would reasonably expect to affect price negotiations significantly. Cost or pricing data require certification of factual and verifiable information, including future cost projections. The government is trying to obtain a clear understanding of the information that the contractor is using to prepare the proposal so that the government is on equal footing with the contractor during negotiations.

105. What is information other than cost or pricing data?

The government considers information other than cost or pricing data to be any type of information that is required from the offeror to determine price reasonableness or cost realism but does not require the offeror to certify the data as accurate, complete, and current. This may include pricing, sales, or cost information.

106. What is the Truth in Negotiations Act?

The government makes the distinction between cost or pricing data and information other than cost or pricing data to comply with the Truth in Negotiations Act (TINA). Unless there is an exception, TINA requires a contracting officer to obtain cost or pricing data before taking any of the following actions when the price is expected to exceed the applicable cost or pricing threshold:

- Award of any negotiated contract

- Award of any subcontract at any tier

- Modification of a sealed bid or negotiated contract

The current threshold is $500,000 for both prime contracts and subcontracts.

107. When can the government grant an exception from TINA?

The government can grant an exception from TINA in four different situations:

1) If the agreed-upon price is based on adequate price competition

2) If the contracting officer determines that the item price is set by law or regulation

3) If the contracting officer determines that the solicitation is for acquiring a commercial item

4) If the head of contracting activity waives the requirement.

108. Which specific items must the contractor provide to the government?

The contractor must provide a cover sheet outlining basic information, such as:

- Solicitation, contract, or modification number

- Name and address of offeror

- Point of contact information

- Name of contract administration office

- Type of contract action

- Proposed cost, profit or fee, and total

- Any use of government property

- Whether the organization is subject to the Cost Accounting Standards (CAS)

- Statement allowing an examination by the government

- Date of submission

- Name, title, and signature of authorized representative

- Index of all cost or pricing information, including materials and services; direct labor; indirect labor; other costs; royalties; and facilities capital cost of money (FCCOM)

- Data that are verifiable and factual

- Relationship between contract line item number (CLIN) prices and total contract price

- Summary by CLIN

- Incurred costs for work performed before the contract

- Forward pricing rates (if agreed to by the government)

- Certificate of Current Cost or Pricing Data, which must use the exact wording from the FAR with the correct "as of" date. The contractor must affirm that the data are facts and not judgment.

109. What if the offeror submits false data?

If the offeror submits false data that it certifies as true and accurate, it has committed defective pricing. Defective pricing occurs when any price, including profit or fee, for any purchase action covered by a Certificate of Current Cost or Pricing Data is increased by any significant amount because the data were not accurate, complete, or current. In these situations the government is entitled to a price adjustment and interest on any overpayments, and it can also impose penalty amounts or contractual penalties.

110. When can the government request information other than cost or pricing data?

The government requires an offeror to submit cost information other than cost or pricing data when it expects that the offeror will be exempted from submitting certified cost or pricing data, as well as when the government needs cost information to determine price reasonableness or cost realism. For example, if the government is expecting only a single offer or if it is expecting significantly different technical responses from multiple offerors, it may require information other than cost or pricing data.

111. How does the government determine if the contractor's proposed costs are compliant?

The government must first determine if the contract is covered by CAS, which are issued by the Cost Accounting Standards Board (CASB). The CASB is made up of the Office of Federal Procurement Policy (OFPP) Administrator; a Department of Defense (DoD) representative; a General Services Administration (GSA) representative; and two private sector representatives, one representing the industry and another with specific knowledge about problem areas.

For contracts covered by CAS, costs are subject to the measurement, assignment, and allocability provisions contained in these CAS:

- Consistency in estimating, accumulating, and reporting costs

- Consistency in allocating costs incurred for the same purpose

- Allocation of home office expenses

- Capitalization of tangible assets

- Accounting for unallowables

- Cost accounting period

- Use of standard cost systems

- Accounting for paid absence

- Depreciation of tangible assets

- Allocation of business unit G&A

- Accounting for acquisition costs of materials

- Composition and measurement of pension costs

- Adjustment and allocation of pension costs

- Cost of money as an element of facilities capital

- Accounting for deferred compensation

- Accounting for insurance costs

- Cost of money of capital assets under construction

- Allocation of direct and indirect costs

- Accounting for IR&D/B&P.

If contracts are not covered by CAS, then the allocability provisions of FAR Part 31 apply. If the cost is not covered in FAR Part 31, then Generally Accepted Accounting Principles (GAAP) apply.

112. When does CAS coverage apply to contracts or subcontracts?

A contract can either be exempt from CAS coverage or CAS coverage applies and a disclosure statement must be submitted. Reasons that the government may exempt a contract or subcontract from CAS coverage include size of the business unit, dollar amount of contract award, small business concern, acquisition of commercial items, and method of pricing. Further, any contractor from a foreign country either in the United States or outside the United States may receive an exemption from CAS coverage.

A disclosure statement is required for any business unit that receives a contract in excess of $50 million or for any company that, together with its segments, received net CAS-covered contract awards exceeding $50 million in its previous accounting period. The government reviews the disclosure statement for adequacy and compliance.

113. Does the government look at individual cost elements?

Yes. When the government reviews an offeror's or contractor's proposal, it is trying to determine if the costs are allocable and allowable. To determine allocability, the government determines whether the costs were specifically incurred to meet a single cost objective or if the costs benefited the overall contract and other work allocated in a reasonable proportion to the benefit received. The government determines whether the cost is necessary to the overall operation of the business, although it is not directly related to any particular cost objective. As an example, let's say that you are a contractor that conducts both government and commercial business in a factory and the government is looking at the cost of your factory manager's salary. Let's keep it simple and say you do 50 percent government work and 50 percent commercial work. The government sees that the cost of the factory manager's salary is required on the contract. It also finds that the expense is not specifically incurred for a single cost objective but that it is split across two cost objectives: government and commercial business. Then the government checks to see if the cost of the factory manager's salary is split proportionally between each of these two cost objectives, that is, 50 percent to federal direct costs and 50 percent to commercial direct costs.

Next the government looks at several factors to determine whether the cost is allowable. This involves determining whether the cost is reasonable and whether it is allowable based on the FAR and the contract provisions. To determine reasonableness, the government ensures that this type of cost is generally recognized as necessary in conducting business. Specifically, the government assesses whether the cost is consistent with sound business practice, law and regulation, and established practices.

To determine if the cost is allowable based on contract terms, the government evaluates whether the cost is reasonable, that is, whether a prudent person looking at this cost would determine it to be reasonable. For example, is the contractor buying $1.49 ballpoint pens for contractor workers (reasonable) or $149 specialty pens for contractor workers (not reasonable)? The government also checks to ensure that the costs are properly measured, assigned, and allocated to the contract. Finally, the government determines whether the specific cost category is allowable according to either the contract or the FAR. For example, the cost of labor to perform the contract work is an allowable cost. The cost of alcohol is not an allowable cost. Some costs are allowable with restrictions, such as gains or losses on the disposition of property. Some costs are not specifically addressed and must be handled directly with the contracting officer before they are incurred. Some costs, such as patents, fall into multiple categories.

114. Does the government look at anything besides costs in cost analysis?

The government begins its cost analysis with market research prior to proposal receipt (just as it does in price analysis). In this market research the government looks at several items in particular: past contract files; audit and technical reports; the offeror's systems; and industry cost estimating guides and standards. First, the government looks at the offeror's past contract file to identify past problems or precedents. The government's purpose is to determine if the contractor has had any recurring problem that would present a future risk for the government. It is also trying to determine if any contracting situation differences are causing a discrepancy in the way that the offeror is bidding the deal.

Next the government examines relevant audits and technical reports. For example, if the government has developed a report on other proposals for identical or similar items or if the contractor has had its proposed forward-pricing rates and factors audited, the contracting officer will review these reports to identify any issues that could create risk for the procuring government agency.

The government typically reviews three offeror systems: purchasing, accounting, and estimating. The Contractor Purchasing System Review is a periodic review of purchasing records, policies, and procedures. This review allows the government to grant, withhold, or withdraw the contractor's purchasing approval. The Contractor Accounting System Review determines whether the firm's process for accumulating costs is adequate to support contract decisions that require accurate, complete, and current cost information. The Contractor Estimating System Review is used to reduce reviews on individual proposals; it checks to ensure that the overall estimating system captures costs accurately and produces reliable and consistent estimates. In this way it expedites the negotiations process and increases the reliability of an offeror's cost proposals.

The government will also examine cost estimating guides and standards relevant to the particular industry. These documents are developed by several organizations, including RAND, the Electronic Systems Command, U.S. Army, and the Naval Center for Cost Analysis.

115. Do the source selection authority and contracting officer ever request additional government expertise? Are these people qualified?

The acquisition team is made up of individuals with different types of expertise to handle the various aspects of the proposal evaluation. Different individuals or teams handle the cost analysis, technical analysis, audit, prime contract proposal analysis, subcontract proposal analysis, and form completion activities. For each of these activities, the government evaluation team must identify strengths, weaknesses, and any inconsistencies with the contractor's work and document them in a report. It also must identify inconsistencies between analyses, resolve any apparent weakness and inconsistencies, and check the reality of the evaluations.

116. How does the government evaluate the design of the work that the offeror proposes?

The government checks that the entire scope of work is broken down into work packages. These work packages describe short-term tasks and are distinct and distinguishable from other tasks. The government also wants to ensure that each of these work packages has assigned responsibility with start dates, end dates, and a budget. This approach tends to minimize work in progress because it establishes specific dates for objectives to be met rather than assuming that the whole program is a work in progress. These work packages are managed by a work breakdown structure (WBS), which is a hierarchy of tasks designed to decompose a major effort into smaller, more manageable tasks.

117. How does the government evaluate an offeror's planning assumptions?

Every assumption that the offeror makes in its proposal will drive business decisions made on the contract. Thus, the government wants to understand what assumptions the offeror is making to ensure that they are consistent with the government's view. For example, does the contractor assume that circumstances in the future will be the same or different from those in the past? Does the offeror assume that there are currently general performance problems with the way the government is doing the work either itself or through an incumbent contractor? Does the offeror assume that the status quo is required? Does the offeror assume that technology changes will be required? If so, what are those interruptions and shortages assumed to be? Does the offeror take a position on whether its assumptions are realistic and consistent? How do these assumptions affect the proposal?

118. Should the offeror include any contingency costs in its proposal?

The government wants to ensure that both it and the offeror are aware of any contingency costs included in the proposal. The first type of contingency costs arise from currently known and existing conditions. The impact of these contingency costs on contract costs can usually be forecasted within reasonable limits of accuracy. These costs should be included in the estimated costs.

The second type of contingency costs arise from currently known or unknown conditions. The contractor may be aware of some risk situations and budget a pool of money to deal with those specific contingencies. In addition, the contractor may want to include a pool of money for "just in case" items that it is unaware of at the time of submission but that "may" occur. The effects of these costs on contract costs cannot be forecasted precisely enough to provide equitable results to the offeror and the government. This type of contingency cost should be excluded in the costs and put into a separate document that outlines what the contingency is and how it will be handled during the life of the contract. The government wants these types of contingencies excluded because, although they may make the contractor feel more comfortable in bidding by ensuring that all potential risks are covered, if those contingencies do not occur, the government will be paying more to the contractor than necessary because the risks never materialized.

119. How does the should-cost analysis help the government evaluate an offeror's proposal?

The government uses the should-cost analysis that it completed during the pre-proposal phase to identify causes of inefficient or uneconomical performance in the offeror's proposal. These inefficiencies could be related to the methods used in contract performance or to the facilities or equipment used.

The should-cost analysis also helps the government determine the members of the multifunctional team who will evaluate the offeror's proposal. This team will evaluate the economy and efficiency of the contractor's existing workforce, methods, materials, facilities, operating systems, and management. This team may include 50–60 analysts on very large government programs. Even though that might seem like a lot of people and a costly undertaking, this approach should result in significant savings. If the government can identify inefficiencies in the proposal stage, it can promote short- and long-range improvements in the contractor's economy and efficiency.

120. How does the government evaluate and mitigate risk?

Risks should be analyzed, evaluated, and mitigated from both the offeror's and the government's perspectives. The offeror is concerned about investment risk, or the risk of recovering the money invested to perform the job. The offeror is also concerned about economic risk, or the risk of earning a reasonable profit. The government is primarily concerned about performance risk, that is, the risk associated with whether the contractor will successfully perform the work on the contract. The government can mitigate some of this risk by means of the contract type it chooses to use for the work. For example, a firm fixed price contract puts more risk on the contractor, whereas a cost-reimbursable contract puts more risk on the government. The government can also mitigate risk in the areas of clear technical requirements, government-furnished property, and contract terms and conditions.

The government can mitigate risk by writing clear technical requirements. Impossible-to-meet requirements, conflicting areas within requirements, and requirement ambiguity can all cause risk on a contract. The contractor should bring any of these conditions to the contracting officer's attention immediately for resolution.

The government can use government-furnished property (GFP) to mitigate risk. When the government provides GFP to the winning contractor, it assumes the investment risk because the contractor is not obligated to buy the equipment or products. In addition, it shifts any property loss to the government. If the contractor is concerned about the price of items rising during the contract term, the government can shift market risk by buying the materials and providing them to the contractor.

The government can also use contract terms and conditions to mitigate risk. For example, the government can allow variations in delivery schedules to help a contractor who can't deliver the full quantity by a certain date. Likewise, if the contract terms obligate the government to provide existing government data, that will save the contractor time and money in collecting the data. If the government allows variations in delivery quantities, small businesses may be able to compete because the new quantities are within their capacity to deliver.

121. What are the offeror's material costs?

Material costs are the cost of materials used to complete a contract, including raw materials, collateral costs, and material that cannot be used for its intended purpose. Examples of raw materials are parts and subassemblies. Examples of collateral costs are freight and insurance. Examples of material that cannot be used for its intended purpose include materials in overruns or materials that have spoiled and weren't used in manufacturing.

The two types of material costs are direct material costs and indirect material costs. Direct material costs are any material costs that can be identified specifically with a final cost objective. Indirect material costs are any material costs that cannot be identified specifically with a final cost objective.

Collateral costs are expenses associated with getting materials into the offeror's plant, for example, inbound transportation or intransit insurance. Collateral costs may be treated as direct or indirect costs depending on guidelines established by the company.

The government must also identify related material costs in the offeror's proposal and analyze how the offeror accounts for these materials. Related materials represent excess materials the offeror proposes to purchase to ensure that sufficient material is available for production of the item. For example, when a machine on the manufacturing line fails and the product it was working on doesn't pass the quality standard, the product is usually scrapped. Similarly, any raw materials used in overruns or that have spoiled before they are used also get scrapped. Offerors will either propose one number encompassing all forms of related material costs or separate them. These items may still have residual value, however, and the final contract cost should be adjusted to reflect that.

122. How does the government analyze the offeror's material costs?

The government goes through several steps to analyze an offeror's proposed material costs, including evaluating the methodology used to estimate direct material cost, identifying any errors in the direct costs proposed, and ensuring that any cost concerns are well documented.

When the government analyzes an offeror's material costs, it identifies any proposed direct material that does not appear necessary to the contract effort. It also ensures that no direct material cost is classified as an indirect cost. During this analysis, the government pays particular attention to costs that will have the most impact on the bottom line of the contract so that it directs the most analysis to the high-cost items.

The government looks at material costs from two different perspectives, at the summary and the detailed levels. In a summary estimate, material cost is estimated on a total cost basis without the benefit of a detailed cost breakdown of unit and cost per unit. These types of analyses are also called roundtable estimates or engineering estimates.

In a detailed estimate, the government looks at the bill of materials (BOM), which is a list of all the materials (including part numbers and quantities) required to complete the contract. The government uses sampling strategies to determine if the materials are appropriate at either the contract level or the line level. The government is trying to ascertain whether the contractor has included the correct items in the BOM to ensure successful contract performance.

Another type of analysis involves analyzing the unit cost estimates. These estimates can be based on current quotes, historical quotes or purchase prices, or inventory pricing. The government is checking to ensure that the cost per unit seems reasonable based on the requirements.

123. Does the government analyze the proposed offeror's subcontracts at this point?

The government will review all costs submitted by the prime contractor, some of which will be based on prices provided by subcontractors. The government will subject these subcontractor costs to the same scrutiny as any other costs on the proposal. The government will raise any concerns directly with the prime contractor. This approach is based on the privity of contract concept.

Privity of contract means that a direct relationship exists between contracting parties. There is a direct relationship between the prime contractor and the government, which is documented in the prime contract. A direct relationship also exists between the prime contractor and each of its subcontractors, and those relationships are documented in the individual subcontracts. However, there is no privity of contract; in other words, no contractual relationship exists between the government and any of the subcontractors to the prime contractor. So while the government is interested in the prime/subcontractors relationship, the government must not violate privity of contract and must therefore deal directly only with the prime contractor.

124. How does the government analyze direct labor costs?

The government spends a great deal of time analyzing an offeror's direct labor costs because labor costs tend to be one of the most expensive components of the contract. Analyzing labor is a multi-step process.

- The government determines the direct labor classifications that the offeror is proposing to do the work. These labor classifications should be based on the offeror's position classification system, which serves as a guide for personnel selection and assignment.

- The government analyzes how the offeror has proposed its direct and indirect labor costs. An offeror's labor cost represents the amount and types of labor required to complete a contract. Labor costs are broken down into directs and indirects. A direct labor cost is any labor cost that can be identified specifically with a final cost objective, for example a particular contract. An indirect labor cost is any labor cost that cannot be identified specifically with a final cost objective. The way the contractor captures costs will drive whether the cost is direct or indirect. For example, the costs of an engineer's time could be classified as either a direct or indirect labor cost, depending on how the offeror captures costs. The government ensures that the contractor has captured direct and indirect costs appropriately.

- The government identifies and evaluates the methodology the offeror used to estimate direct labor costs. The government must feel comfortable that the offeror's estimating methodology will produce consistent results.

- The government identifies any proposed labor costs that do not appear reasonable or that merit special attention.

- The government analyzes the round-table estimate developed by a team of government experts to determine if it is appropriate. The government is trying to ensure that the benchmark it will use to validate the offeror's prices is reasonable. The government then analyzes the offeror's proposal with the estimates it made on the cost to complete the same or similar work in the past. The idea is that the government could develop an estimate of future contract cost based on historical experience.

- The government analyzes the offeror's estimates against the labor standards, if labor standards are available for the positions the government is seeking, to make sure they consistent. There are two types of labor standards: engineered and non-engineered. Engineered standards are developed using recognized principles of industrial engineering and work measurement. Non-engineered standards are developed using the best information available without performing the detailed analysis required to develop an engineered standard. For example, historical data might be used to determine a non-engineered standard. Labor standards do not exist for every job classification. The government will also assess whether the particular industry it is reviewing relies on labor standards as its commercial practice.

- The government will analyze the labor-rate estimates proposed by the offeror. This analysis is a multi-step process. First the government conducts a preliminary review of the rates and reviews the results. Then it determines whether an audit that has been done or requests that an administrative contracting officer (ACO) conduct a total compensation analysis. The contracting officer responsible for the program will honor the ACO's recommendations and agreements. The factors considered in labor rate comparisons are government labor rate requirements, skill mix of labor effort, time period of labor effort, and company-unique labor factors.

• The government determines whether any government-imposed labor rate requirements apply. The Department of Labor (DOL) has developed labor rates to be used on certain types of government contracts to ensure that employees are compensated fairly. For example, for a services contract, the Service Contract Act (SCA) may apply. The government must ascertain that the rates and benefits meet the minimum requirements. If the offeror's proposed rate exceeds the DOL rate, the government then has to analyze whether the difference is reasonable and whether the proposed rate increases conflict with the Fair Labor Standards Act and SCA clauses. Finally the government must ensure that the rates and benefits meet the minimum requirements established by any governing collective bargaining agreement.

Other labor regulations that impose rates the government may consider are the Davis Bacon Act and the Walsh Healey Act. The Davis Bacon Act applies to laborers or mechanics at any government site on a contract in excess of $2,000 for construction, alteration, or repair of public buildings or works. The Walsh Healey Act applies to contracts or subcontracts in excess of $10,000 for the manufacturing or furnishing of products that will be performed in the United States.

125. What else does the government look at with regard to labor rates?

The government considers several other aspects of labor rates: skill mix, weighted-average labor rates, and company-unique factors. It is important for the government to determine that the offeror has proposed the correct skill mix for the labor effort to ensure that it understands the work required. For example, the government checks that the proposed skill mix is reasonable for the work required and compares the offeror's proposal to labor mixes that were used in performing similar historical contracts.

The government also checks whether the offeror used a weighted-average labor rate. If the offeror did use a weighted-average labor rate, the government wants to ensure that it used the rate correctly and that the rate conforms to the offeror's accounting and estimating practices.

Finally, the government looks at company-unique factors in reviewing labor rates. These include uncompensated overtime and whether the method used to allow uncompensated overtime in the proposal affects labor rates and quality. The government also determines whether differences in other elements of compensation affect the labor-rate comparisons. Finally, the government uses this analysis to determine if the tradeoffs between labor rates and other compensation elements result in a compensation package that appears to be reasonable overall.

After reviewing all these aspects of labor rates, the government is ready to develop its pre-negotiation position.

126. How does the government analyze other direct costs?

During cost analysis, the government contracting officer determines which other direct costs (ODCs) should be analyzed. Examples of ODCs include special tooling; computer services; consulting services; travel; federal excise tax costs; preservation, packaging, and packing costs; production costs; and royalties. For each of these ODCs, the government needs to determine allocability, treatment, and whether they should be characterized as indirect costs. The government reviews the offeror's commercial and government work to determine if the costs are allocated appropriately.

To determine cost treatment, the government must determine if the ODC is purchased solely for the government contract (and therefore should be bought by the government and used by the government after the contract is ended) or if the cost should be shared with the offeror. Finally, the government needs to determine if the ODCs should be characterized as direct costs (contributing directly to the end product) or as indirect costs (that should be considered as part of the overhead rate structure).

127. How does the government analyze indirect costs?

Indirect costs are costs that cannot practically be assigned directly to the production of a particular product. The government carefully reviews these rates because they could help determine the winner of the proposal effort. What is included in these indirect rates varies from company to company, but they typically include overhead costs associated with manufacturing, material, engineering, field service, and the site.

To determine whether an offeror's indirect costs are appropriate, the government first analyzes the offeror's cost estimating systems. This is typically done when the contractor decides to pursue government business by bidding on a particular contract. Once that review is complete, the government considers the rates proposed for the specific contract.

In analyzing indirect costs, the government first reviews the pools and bases for rate development and identifies any inconsistencies and weaknesses. The government then reviews how the offeror developed the rates and examines the proposed rates. It checks to ensure that the rates were applied appropriately. Finally the government ensures that there are no additional indirect costs that were not included in the rates.

128. Are general and administrative (G&A) expenses included in indirect costs?

Yes, G&A expenses are part of a company's indirect costs. G&A includes items such as salary and other costs of executive staff at the corporate office; salary and other costs of staff services such as legal, accounting, public relations, and finance; and selling and marketing expenses.

129. How does a company identify pools and bases for rate development?

For its indirect costs to be approved by the government, the contractor must identify its indirect cost pools and bases. An indirect cost pool is a logical grouping of indirect costs with a similar relationship to the cost objectives. For example, a manufacturing overhead pool would include all the manufacturing indirect costs. An indirect cost allocation basis can include such items as direct labor hours, direct labor dollars, number of units produced, and number of machine hours.

A company generally begins by estimating sales volume for the period. Next the company estimates the indirect cost allocation bases for the period. Then it estimates the indirect cost pools for the period. Finally it estimates indirect cost rates for the period.

130. Is the government looking for anything in particular when it analyzes rates?

The government tries to identify any rate inconsistencies over the allocation cycle. It is important to have accurate indirect cost rate estimates because the actual rates will not be known until the end of the accounting period and by then the contract may be completed. When the government has concerns about inconsistencies, it ensures that these concerns are well-documented in the event of a future contract issue.

The process the government typically uses is to develop a plan for the analysis and to identify any unallowable costs. Next the government analyzes the indirect cost allocation base estimate by converting the indirect cost allocation base and the indirect cost paid to constant year dollars. It then analyzes the base pool relationship and develops and documents its pricing position.

131. How does the government analyze a contractor's forward-pricing rates?

Forward-pricing rates are the rates proposed by the contractor as part of the proposal for its estimates of rates during the duration of the contract. When contracts go on for multiple years, the contractor needs to make assumptions about what its labor rates will be in the future. The government in turn needs to understand what assumptions the contractor is making in developing these rates for the out years. Often, the government has already audited the contractor's forward-pricing rates and has developed audit-recommended rates. The auditor or ACO will then provide formal forward-pricing rate recommendations to any government buying activities within which the contractor is trying to secure business. Achieving agreement on the forward-pricing rates is usually a time-consuming process between the government and the potential contractor.

132. How does the government analyze a contractor's facilities capital cost of money?

Facilities capital cost of money (FCCOM) is the imputed cost related to the cost of contractor capital committed to facilities. The purpose of FCCOM is to compensate the contractor for the capital required for investment opportunities and the return on investment of that capital. To attract investment, the return on investment must be greater than the capital required. The cost of capital is a real cost that must be considered in investment decisions.

To calculate the FCCOM, the company determines the appropriate cost of money rate and accumulates its net book value of the business unit facilities capital. Next it allocates the facilities capital net book value to indirect cost pools. Then it sums the facilities capital net book value to indirect cost pools. At this point it can calculate the FCCOM for each pool, identify the appropriate allocation base for each FCCOM pool, and calculate the FCCOM factors.

133. How does the government analyze a contractor's proposed profit or fee?

Profit or fee is the dollar amount over and above allowable costs that is paid to the contractor for contract performance. Actual profit or fee may vary based on contract performance efficiency, incurrence of unallowable costs, or contract type. In addition, each federal agency has its own guidelines for establishing profit or fee.

The government uses profit or fee to motivate contractors. Profit or fee must be applied consistently to stimulate efficient contract performance and maintain a viable industrial base to meet the government's needs. In addition, profit or fee must be used to attract the best capabilities of qualified large and small business concerns to government contracts. The statutory limits are 15 percent on research and development contracts and 10 percent on all other contracts.

To motivate contractors with profit or fee, the government considers contractor risk; cost risk; federal socioeconomic programs; capital investments; cost control and other past accomplishments; independent development; and any other relevant factors. The government does not allow a contractor to include FCCOM in the profit calculation. Once the profit/fee rate is determined for the contract, the same rate is used on modifications if the work being done is the same as that in the original contract and if the modification has a relatively small dollar value compared to the total contract.

In addition, the government relies on the DoD weighted guidelines to determine the appropriate profit or fee on a contract. The DoD weighted guidelines have technical risk, technology incentive, management/cost control, and contract type risk components. Each of these components is rated on a scale to determine its degree of importance in calculating profit or fee.

CHAPTER 9
The Government's Price Evaluation

Price analysis is the process whereby the government examines and evaluates an offeror's proposed price to determine if it is fair and reasonable without evaluating the separate cost elements. The government conducts several activities in an effort to ready itself for price negotiations with an offeror. Following this preliminary work, the government evaluates an offeror's proposal from a price perspective.

In conducting the price evaluation, the government keeps in mind that certain changes can result in lower overall prices. For example, provided they are acceptable to the government, changes in terms and conditions, delivery dates, and delivery locations may ultimately help the government secure a better deal while keeping a contractor's proposed price intact.

134. Why is the government required to conduct market research prior to issuing the solicitation?

The government conducts market research before issuing a solicitation because it needs to collect and analyze information about the capabilities available in the marketplace. The government then uses this information in developing purchase requests for acquisitions both below and above the simplified acquisition threshold. To collect market research, the government relies on sources such as knowledgeable individuals (in and outside the government), databases, source lists, and catalogs.

Through this market research, the government determines the sources, best practices, and availability of commercial items. The government is also trying to determine whether commercial items or non-developmental items will meet its requirements.

135. What is the relationship between market research and contract pricing?

As a general rule, if the government increases contractor performance costs by having the contractor do a great deal of work, the contract price will increase. Likewise, if the government lowers contractor performance costs, the contract price will be reduced. Accordingly, the government needs to determine which parts of the work it will continue to do itself and which parts it will require the contractor to do. In addition, if the government increases the contractor's risk, the contract price will increase. Thus, the government tries to identify the components of risk for a particular contract and mitigate as many of the potential risks as it can so that the offerors' prices will not be inflated to account for increased risk.

If the government limits competition, it will typically get higher contract prices. If it facilitates competition, contract prices will typically be reduced.

136. How does the government prepare estimates?

The government agency with the need must formally submit its requirement to the contracting office. To do this, the agency develops an independent government estimate using the data collected as part of its market research. The government can use automated systems to prepare purchase request estimates that are based on algorithms previously loaded into the system, such as the last contract price, as a starting point. While this approach is quick and easy since most of the work has already been done, it has limitations. For example, these automated systems do not take market conditions into account. The government can also use a manual approach to develop the estimates. Estimators may use different methods, so the validity and reliability of these estimates are assessed in light of the assumptions used. Asking questions about the assumptions and the market realities is a helpful way for the government to achieve better estimates and more realistic contract costs.

Most government estimators know their product and how often they need to update their information. The items they consider are last price paid, general price changes, current commercial market price, quantity discounts, and availability of substitutes. Government estimators tend to use both quantitative and qualitative judgments. The government looks at individual estimators to determine if their past estimates have been close to the contract prices determined to be fair and reasonable. If the answer is yes, the government tends to have greater reliance on the estimate. Just as the government wants to ensure that contractors are giving it realistic estimates, the government also reviews its own estimating capability to ensure that it is getting consistent and accurate results.

The government can use historical data to prepare its cost estimate but it must document its sources. When no historical data exist, the government can use product analysis; however, with this approach the estimator must consider the labor and materials required to produce the item. In the estimating process, this is any data that are out of date, misleading, or irrelevant to the estimating process. This means that the government wants to ensure that labor or material rates are current, reflect the actual service or item being produced, are accurate and complete, and include only those items that are directly related to the service or product being procured. In addition, the government estimator must retain independence by looking at websites or catalogs and must not contact specific vendors to get quotes to avoid the appearance of bias.

137. What does market research entail?

The government uses a variety of sources to complete its market research. These include:

- *Independent government estimate*—as described above

- *Historical prices*—from contract files, computerized acquisition data files, or manual item records

- *Published prices*—from trade journals, catalogs, Federal Supply Schedules, product brochures, etc.

- *Data from buyers and other experts*—other government buyers, contract administrators, technical experts, or auditors

- *Data from prospective offerors*—current or past contractors

- *Data from other sources*—for example, state and local employees, professional associations, or telephone surveys

- *Pricing history*—showing the pricing trends for the item

- *Current competitive conditions*—how many companies are available to do the work

- *Current overall level of demand*—whether new technology is on the horizon

- *Supply and demand trends*—whether any raw materials are impacting the overall supply to meet the demand

- *Market forces*—whether the country is in a recession or is experiencing inflation

- *Pricing strategies*—whether there is a way to bundle offerings

- *Product characteristics*—unique attributes of the products from various companies

- *Delivery/performance terms*—unique attributes of delivery from various companies

- *Ownership costs*—unique ways of owning the product

- *Terms and conditions*—unique terms or conditions that may impact the buy decision

- *Problems*—anything the government should be aware of with regard to particular vendors or products.

138. What does the government do if it thinks it will not get enough competition?

The government will look at its RFP to determine if changes in either the business approach or the terms and conditions would make the procurement more attractive to bidders. For example, the government might consider improving the RFP by:

- Consolidating requirements with another procurement. Since larger quantities tend to attract more competition, the government may look at adding its future needs, provided that it has adequate storage for the extra items until they are needed. The government may also consider combining this requirement with another procurement. Finally, it may try to use an existing ID/IQ contract to meet its needs.

• Using language that promotes full and open competition and avoiding the use of restrictive clauses unless absolutely necessary. For example, the government should state the function, performance, or essential characteristics necessary to maximize competition and not specify a brand name. Further, it should encourage companies to bid their commercial items if commercial items are acceptable to the government.

• Reviewing the required documents. When the government issues a contract, an order of precedence is stated to resolve any conflicts that arise from ambiguities between documents. The government will review this order to determine whether any conflicts may preclude companies from bidding. The normal order of precedence is:

– Documents mandated for use by law

– Performance-oriented documents

– Detailed design-oriented documents

– Standards and specifications.

• Ensuring that companies know where to obtain any requirements documents, such as federal or military specifications.

• Considering allowing contractors to use other than new material. While the government needs to consider requirements of law or regulation, safety of persons or property, and contract performance requirements first, where appropriate, the government may allow contractors to provide refurbished or government surplus items.

- Reviewing the delivery or performance schedules. Specifying strict performance schedules in the RFP could prevent small companies from participating and thereby restrict competition. In addition, strict performance schedules could result in higher prices.

- Considering liquidated damages. At the time of contract award, the government and contractor agree to a financial penalty on the contractor if the products or services provided under the contract do not work as stated. Since it is difficult to determine the exact amount of downtime and expense the government experiences, an amount like $500 per day is used to incentivize contractors to provide quality products or to fix problems expeditiously. However, these liquidated damages can be deal breakers for companies, thereby limiting competition.

- Improving the business terms and conditions by reviewing the contract type and risk analysis. In a fixed price contract, the contractor is required to deliver the product specified and a limitation is imposed on the amount of money the government must pay. In a cost reimbursement contract, the contractor is required to deliver a "best effort" to provide the specified product or service; all allowable costs are reimbursed, regardless of delivery, up to the contract amount. In a commercial item contract, the government must use a fixed price or fixed price with economic price adjustment contract.

- Reviewing the applicability of socioeconomic requirements. The government's attempt to attract small and small and disadvantaged businesses to the marketplace can have the effect of narrowing the range of potential bidders.

- By other means. This includes matching the payment and finance terms to market conditions, furnishing government property, and considering cost/technical tradeoffs.

139. How does the government publicize the acquisition?

The government usually publicizes acquisitions through www.fedbizopps.gov, a website focused on federal business opportunities. The government may also post notices in the contracting office, in trade association publications, through mass media, or through paid advertisements.

140. What strategies does the government use for making an award?

The government has many different strategies when it comes to making an award. In each case, it must determine which choice is the most advantageous in light of government requirements, level of competition, and general market conditions. These award strategies include:

- Aggregate award of all line items to one contractor—single award to one responsible contractor

- Multiple awards for different line items—award based on lowest aggregate cost to the government

- Family or group buys—award for families of line items based on lowest aggregate cost to the government

- Progressive awards—used when the offeror provides the lowest aggregate cost but does not offer the full quantity; the government awards the first batch to that offeror, then the next batch to the next lowest offeror

- Multiple awards for the same line item—multiple awards for the same indefinite requirement when offerors provide comparable products or services

- Split awards—awards for a single line item split among multiple vendors; typically specified in the RFP

- Partial set-aside award—a portion of the solicitation requirement is set aside for small business; any small business can submit an offer for the set-aside part or the whole requirement.

141. How does the government evaluate a contractor's prices?

The government conducts its price evaluation using a four-step procedure: (1) determine the solicitation provisions; (2) determine the total price offered; (3) evaluate various award combinations; and (4) make the award decision based on price-related factors. Analyzing a contractor's price is only part of the evaluation. In addition to analyzing the top-level price, the government also reviews the individual cost elements (see Chapter 8).

142. What are the inputs into a price evaluation based on solicitation provisions?

The government looks at solicitation provisions such as compliance with the Buy American Act, government-furnished property and production, transportation costs, longer term business relationships, energy factors, lease arrangements, and SDB price adjustments.

143. What are the Buy American Act criteria?

The government reviews its independent cost estimate (performed as part of the pre-solicitation process) and the current FAR requirements (for a civilian agency procurement) or the current DFAR requirements (for a DoD agency procurement).

The FAR criteria include descriptions for:

- Components—articles, materials, and supplies incorporated directly into the end products

- Domestic end product—an unmanufactured end product mined or produced in the United States or if the costs of its components are greater than 50 percent mined in the United States

- Domestic offer—an offered price for a domestic end product

- End product—articles, materials, and supplies to be acquired for public use under a contract

- Foreign end product—an end product other than a domestic end product

- Foreign offer—an offered price for a foreign end product.

The Buy American clause requires the contractor to deliver only domestic end products except those for use outside the United States. In addition, if the government determines that the products are not mined, produced, or manufactured in the United States in sufficient and reasonably available commercial quantities of a satisfactory quality, then non-U.S. products may be used. If the agency determines that domestic preference would be inconsistent with the public interest or that the cost would be unreasonable, foreign products may be substituted.

The DFAR focuses on defense equipment. It defines a domestic concern as a concern incorporated in the United States or an unincorporated concern having its principal business in the United States. A foreign concern is any concern that does not meet this requirement. A non-designated country end product is from a country outside the United States or qualifying country. In terms of national defense, a non-qualifying country, end product, or offer made from outside the United States or outside a qualifying country is ineligible for use in U.S. government DoD work. Only offers, components, and products from the United States or a qualifying country are eligible for use in DoD work.

144. How does the government use government-furnished production and research property factors in its solicitation provisions?

The government must eliminate any potential competitive advantage to any contractor possessing government-furnished production and research property. This situation occurs when an incumbent contractor has been doing work for the government. When there is a re-compete for the work, a new contractor would be at a distinct disadvantage because the incumbent has access to the existing government production and research property that other bidders do not. The government must consider any costs or savings to the government related to providing such property, regardless of any competitive advantage that may result to the non-incumbent companies. The government does this by adjusting the offers of contractors proposing to use government-furnished production and research property or by charging the contractor rent for using these items.

145. How does the government handle transportation costs?

The government's goal is to make acquisitions that are most advantageous and to ensure that supplies arrive in good order, in good condition, on time, and at the required location. The government uses the term FOB—free on board—to help determine responsibility and basis for payment of freight charges and the point at which the title for goods passes to the buyer. FOB Origin means that the government is required to pick up the deliverables at the contractor's warehouse, and FOB Destination means that the contractor must ship the items to the government.

146. Can the government have long-term business relationships with contractors?

Yes, the government can have multiyear contracting and options to acquire supplies and services. In a solicitation for a multiyear contract, the government states that the base contract will extend over two or more years. Multiyear contracting is a special contracting method used to acquire known requirements in quantities and total cost not exceeding planned requirements for up to five years. By using options, the government elects to purchase additional supplies or services called for in the contract or elects to extend the term of the contract. Both of these contracting methods may be used in sealed bidding or negotiation.

147. Does the government consider energy conservation and energy efficiency factors in making award decisions?

Yes, recognizing that the cost of energy is an important cost of operating many items and systems, the government considers energy efficiency in the procurement of goods and services. The government obtains data from independent research, manufacturer specifications, contractors' proposals, and past history. The data include energy conservation data, energy efficiency data, estimated costs, and other relevant factors. The government can apply best value contracting methods to the solicitation requirements as incentive for companies to use more energy-efficient solutions. For example, the extra cost of the energy usage could be applied to the price of the company's proposal offering the more energy-intensive solution. In addition, the government can apply liquidated damages to a contractor if its product fails to produce the energy savings claimed in the proposal.

148. Does the government consider leasing instead of outright purchases in its procurement decisions?

Yes, the government sometimes considers leasing arrangements and will say so in the original RFP. It is important to note that if the government does not specifically ask for leases and they are offered, the proposal may be deemed outside the competitive range because an alternative proposal has been submitted. For example, if the government requests a computer system, the contractor may submit two proposals—one to sell the computer system to the government and an alternative proposal to lease the computer system to the government. However, these two proposals will both be evaluated only if the government allowed alternative proposals to be submitted. When making the lease versus purchase decision, the government considers the estimated length of time for use; financial and operating advantages; cumulative rental payments; contract purchase price; transportation and installation costs; maintenance and other service costs; potential obsolescence; trade-in value; and availability of purchase options.

149. Does the government provide an evaluation adjustment to small, disadvantaged businesses?

The government can provide a Small Disadvantaged Business (SDB) Price Evaluation Adjustment, which is a price-related factor that may be applied in contract award decisions where an SDB is competing with one or more concerns that are not SDBs. The government may also provide federal contracting assistance for qualified small business concerns located in historically underutilized business zones (HUBZones). This is done in an effort to increase employment opportunities, investment, and economic development in those areas by means of a HUBZone Price Evaluation Preference. Joint ventures that include an SDB or a HUBZone may also qualify for the adjustment. All federal agencies now participate in this program.

150. How does the government conduct price analysis with regard to the total price offered?

Price analysis is the process of examining and evaluating a proposed price to determine if it is fair and reasonable without evaluating the separate cost elements and proposed profits. It involves a comparison of two sets of prices, for example, between two contractors' proposals or between a contractor's proposed cost and the government's should-pay cost. The government's should-pay cost is the price the government should reasonably expect to pay for the deliverable based on information concerning competitive offers. The government obtains the should-pay cost during the market research phase of the procurement.

151. With so many companies offering so many different products, how does the government compare products and prices?

When the government compares prices between two or more companies, the products do not have to be alike but they must have some characteristics in common. The government's goal is to make as much of an "apples to apples" comparison as possible by focusing on the similarities and accounting for the differences between the products.

Sometimes, the government uses information gathered in market research to make multiple comparisons in determining price reasonableness and increasing confidence in its pricing decision.

To compare prices, the government selects prices for comparison; identifies the factors that affect comparability; determines the potential impact of these factors on prices selected for comparison; adjusts prices selected for comparison; and compares adjusted prices to the offer in line for award. As a potential basis for this price analysis, the government uses other proposed prices received in response to the solicitation; commercial prices; previously proposed prices; parametric estimates; and independent government estimates.

Other proposed prices are those prices that have been submitted by companies competing independently for contract award. The prices must be part of offers that meet government requirements. The award must be made to the offeror whose proposal represents the best value to the government.

Commercial prices are prices the government obtains from published price lists, published market prices, and similar indexes. In using commercial prices, the government must take into account any discounts or rebates that are offered. The government also must consider differences related to the contracting situation.

Previously proposed prices and contract prices are historical prices the government has paid for previous products or services. The validity of the historical price depends on whether that price is fair and reasonable and whether the comparison is valid.

Parametric and "rough yardstick" estimates are based on parameters established by the government or industry to determine future prices. These estimates are considered valid if they are widely used and produce reasonable results.

Independent government estimates fall into three categories:

- Independent government estimates that accompany purchase requests

- Value analysis estimates, which are the results of a specialized analysis of the function of a product and its related price; these estimates involve taking the item apart to determine how it is made and why it costs what it does

- Visual analysis estimates, which are the results of a visual inspection of an item, or drawing of an item, to estimate its probable value.

152. Which factors affect the government's ability to compare prices?

The government looks at several factors that affect price comparability, including market conditions, quantity or size, geographic location, purchasing power of the dollar, extent of competition, technology, and government-unique requirements.

For each comparison, the government must determine which factors affect the comparison and then determine how those factors affect the comparison. Based on that decision, the government then determines if the comparison, even with its limitations, contributes to the price analysis. Finally, the government must determine if specific changes in the contracting situation will affect the contract price. For example, would the sources, quantities, production/delivery rates, start-up costs, and terms of purchase impact the outcome of the comparison? The government documents the price-related differences (taking into account comparability) and factors out price-related differences. Once the government does this, it can compare the adjusted prices to estimate the range of reasonable prices and then use the price that appears most reasonable as the should-pay price. If the should-pay price differs significantly from the apparent successful offer, the government must determine why there is such a disparity.

153. How does the government analyze the differences?

Price analysis compares the offered price with the available estimates of a reasonable price, which are the government's should-pay price estimates. The offered price should fall within the range of should-pay. If the proposed price is outside the range, the government must determine if the price of the apparent successful offer is reasonable despite the identified differences; if the price of the apparent successful offer is unreasonable; or if the differences result from problems with the solicitation or other mistakes.

154. What vendor-related differences does the government look for?

The government understands that each company has its own personality and way of running its business so the government does not expect every company to be exactly the same. However, the government does check to see if there are circumstances that result primarily from the action or inaction of an individual company. In other words, a contractor who cannot perform is never a good deal at any price.

The government also seeks to ensure that all the vendors understand its requirements. For example, a contractor may have a misunderstanding if the solicitation contains unusual requirements. Varying interpretations may occur when performance requirements are used. Either of these situations could have an effect on contract pricing and could account for the wide variety in prices.

Companies can also vary in their prices based on the technology they use. Technology can be reviewed from several different perspectives. If the product technology is within a company's existing capabilities, the company will not need to conduct expensive R&D, thereby resulting in a lower price. If the government requires a unique production technology that is currently available, the company will not need to invest in a new plant and equipment. Special technology requirements are likely to result in a higher price. Finally, differences in production requirements may cause prices to increase.

Next the government looks at a contractor's operating efficiency and determines whether there are any mistakes in the proposal. Efficiency measures include input, labor, materials, and equipment. Mistakes could range from a simple mathematical error to a mistake arising from the complexity of the procurement.

The government also looks at differences beyond comparing two contractors' prices. It considers the market as a whole to identify possible sources of the differences between offers. Examples of market research include:

- Changes in the level of competition that may affect pricing strategies; for example, if there are many competitors, the prices will be driven down

- Limited competition and collusion, which the government might suspect if it does not get adequate price competition (i.e., two or more sources)

- Differing economic conditions, which could provide one company a competitive advantage based on its location.

The government also reviews its own contract requirements to determine if they include any term or condition that would prohibit companies from bidding. A contract should define who, what, where, when, and how for any task performed under the contract. If any of these requirements are unclear, they are said to be defective. If the government changes requirements, there will probably be an impact on contractor price.

155. Does the government go through the same analysis on a sealed bid?

Typically, the government is looking for very specific items when it inspects sealed bids. It is trying to determine if there are mistakes in bids, unbalanced bids, or any issue that warrants cancellation of the bid.

When the government inspects sealed bids for mistakes, it is looking for unexpectedly low bids or clerical errors, or any other indications of errors. If the government suspects a mistake, it advises the bidder of the potential error. The bidder may then allege the mistake and request permission to correct it; allege the mistake and request permission to withdraw the bid; or verify the original bid.

An unbalanced bid is when the government detects that, despite an acceptable total price, the price of one or more contract line items is significantly over- or understated as indicated by application of cost or pricing analysis techniques. While this may seem like a good deal for that particular line item, it is the government's obligation to reject bids that involve unacceptable risks. The risk is normally the greatest when start-up work, mobilization, or first articles are separate line items. Similarly, if the base quantities and option quantities are separate line items, the government may suspect an unbalanced bid situation.

The government may also determine that there is a need to cancel the invitation for bid (IFB). The government may cancel the bid for price-related reasons if:

1) The IFB did not provide consideration for all factors of cost

2) The bids received indicate that the government's needs can be satisfied by a less expensive article

3) All bids are at unreasonable prices

4) Bids were not independently arrived at in open competition

5) A cost comparison shows that performance by the government is more economical.

156. What price-related decisions are involved in a negotiated procurement?

The government must determine the need for cost information. The contracting officer can ask for additional information to make an evaluation decision but must give contractors extra time to prepare it.

The government also must determine if it will have discussions with the offerors. Unless it is stated in the original RFP that the government intends to award without discussions, it is assumed that the government will conduct discussions with the offerors. These discussions can take the form of clarifications or full negotiations. The government can also have a limited exchange with an offeror by having clarifications without discussions.

157. What does the term "cost and pricing data" mean?

The government states that cost and pricing data are all facts that, as of the date of price agreement, prudent buyers and sellers would reasonably expect to significantly affect price negotiations. When a contractor is required to submit a certification of current cost and pricing data, it must certify the data as accurate, complete, and current. This includes vendor quotes, nonrecurring costs, make-or-buy decisions, estimated resources to attain business goals, and information management decisions. The Truth in Negotiations Act drives whether cost or pricing data must be submitted.

158. When can the contractor get a cost or pricing data exception?

The contractor can get an exception to submitting cost and pricing data if:

- Two or more offerors are submitting independent proposals, neither is offering unreasonable prices, and one is expected to win based on being the best value

- The price is set by law or regulation

- The items being procured are commercial

- The head of the agency contracting activity has waived the requirement.

Even if certified cost and pricing data are not required, the government still needs information from offerors to prove the reasonableness of their cost or price. This information could be catalog prices, market prices, annual sales volume, etc.

159. How does the government determine the competitive range?

Sometimes it is not efficient for either the government or the offeror to continue with the solicitation process because the government has determined that there is no opportunity for the offeror to win based on the other proposals submitted. In this situation, the government goes through a competitive range determination, ranking the proposals and determining which are eligible for award. Those that are not eligible are removed from the solicitation process.

The process the government uses is:

1) Evaluate all proposals

2) Identify evaluation score groupings

3) Identify the most highly rated proposals

4) Determine whether to limit the competitive range

5) Notify unsuccessful offerors.

160. Does the government communicate with the offerors after it receives the proposals but before it makes an award decision?

Yes, in a competitive negotiation, the government can determine that there is a need for pre-negotiation exchanges. The government may have clarifications with the intent to award without discussions, known as the clarification and deficiency process. Or the government may have open communications with contractors before it establishes the competitive range. Finally, the government may have exchanges after establishing the competitive range but before negotiations. In a noncompetitive negotiation, this process is called fact-finding.

The government uses this communication process to address any adverse past performance that must be explored; understand any ambiguities in the proposal; cure any proposal deficiencies; materially alter the technical or cost elements of the proposal; or revise the proposal in any way it deems necessary.

The government uses all the information gleaned throughout the communications process to establish a pre-negotiation price position. The pre-negotiation objectives are based on field pricing assistance, audit reports, technical analyses, fact-finding results, independent government estimates, and price histories.

161. How does the government evaluate risk?

The government analyzes the risk on contractors' proposals to determine which solution will be the most cost-efficient over the term of the contract. There is a range of risk. For example, the acquisition of standard commercial items may involve little pricing risk while a state-of-the-art acquisition will have a higher level of pricing risk.

When the government negotiates with the contractor, it is trying to mitigate as much risk as possible. The government comes up with three different price positions based on the risk associated with the contract. The minimum price position is the starting point in negotiations and represents the lowest price that can be supported by reasoned analysis. The objective price position represents the most reasonable price. The maximum price position represents the highest amount that the government can reasonably accept.

The government must consider potential tradeoffs between price and other terms during negotiations. In non-competitive discussions, all elements of the contract are subject to change during the negotiation process. In competitive discussions, the government cannot change minimum contract requirements unless all offerors remaining in the competitive range have the opportunity to revise their proposals based on the change.

162. Does the government keep a record of its pricing decisions?

Yes, the government documents all of its pricing actions as the final activity in the contract pricing process. These actions include events, actions, and decisions. The government does this so it will have a record in case there are any contract disputes, as well as for future reference if the contracting officer is replaced by someone else. The documentation includes enough detail to explain what the contracting officer did and why to someone not related to the negotiations.

The government has a process for documenting all types of procurements. In a sealed bid, the government records all bids, the reasons for rejection of bids, how ties were broken, and the basis for determining that the award price was reasonable. In micro-purchases and other simplified acquisitions, the government documents all quotes, the analysis used to determine price reasonableness, and, if there was only one source, why there was an absence of competition.

In a negotiated procurement, the government develops a pre-negotiation memorandum. It documents the purpose of the negotiation (for example, new contract, final pricing), description of the acquisition, reasons why the offeror did not provide cost or pricing data, and a summary of the most significant facts and events.

CHAPTER 10
After Proposal Submission

When a company prepares a proposal, it should realize that the government could accept it as is and it will become a contractually binding document. In that case, nothing in this chapter needs to occur before contract award. However, sometimes the customer has questions about the proposal or would like to modify the solution. When the customer has questions, it will issue clarification reports (CRs) or deficiency reports (DRs). Sometimes the customer wants to see the solution demonstrated or wants to negotiate certain portions of the contract. Other times the customer believes that the proposal prices are too high and wants the companies to submit best and final offers (BAFOs), which are also known as final proposal revisions (FPRs).

The types of tasks that could be required before contract award include:

- Customer questions

- Customer amendments

- Live test demonstrations

- Competitive targets

- Discussions with government customers

- BAFO

- Contract award.

163. How does a contractor answer customer questions or respond to proposal amendments?

After the customer receives the company's proposal, it begins the evaluation process. The first step of this process is to compare the proposal with the RFP requirements and the source selection plan to determine if the solution proposed by the company is compliant. If the customer's evaluator decides, based on his or her initial reading, that the solution is compliant, then a score is assigned to that section and the evaluation process is finished. If the evaluator cannot decide whether the customer's solution is compliant, further action is usually taken. In such instances, the first step is for the customer's evaluator to issue a question to the company.

Government customers refer to this process as the clarification report (CR) and deficiency report (DR) process. The government uses a CR when the solution requires clarification; it uses a DR when it deems the proposed solution to be noncompliant. When a company receives a CR or a DR, it goes through a formal response process, including solution review and perhaps modification, writing the response, updating the proposal, and reviewing the responses before it submits them to the government customer in writing. In some instances, the government will allow a company to provide oral responses to the government's questions, but more typically the government requests written responses so they can become part of the contract file.

Another method of responding to a proposal is for the customer to issue an amendment. A government customer can issue an amendment when it wants to change part or all of the RFP. The customer may have reason to modify, remove, or add requirements to the solicitation document or RFP, such as technology advances, company questions, new regulations, changes in the cost model, or the inability of all companies to meet a certain requirement. The customer communicates these changes only to companies that are within the competitive range.

The overall process for a company to respond to questions and amendments is basically the same and includes the following steps.

Receive CRs, DRs, or Amendments from Customer

The customer can issue CRs or DRs to evaluate each contractor's response to the requirements at any time after the proposals have been submitted. The customer may issue CRs and DRs many times throughout the procurement cycle, and they usually are specifically developed for and issued to the company from which the customer received an inadequate proposal. Therefore, not every company will receive CRs and DRs.

The customer may issue RFP amendments any time during the procurement process after it has released the RFP. Similarly, the customer may issue an amendment at any point in the procurement process to inform contractors of a change in RFP requirements. Commercial customers may choose to issue the amendment either verbally or in a written format. Government customers typically release all amendment information in written form, sent to the companies within the competitive range, posted on the agency's web page, or noted on fedbizopps.gov

Acknowledge Receipt

For government programs, the company must inform the program's contracting officer (CO) that it received the documents using the procedures prescribed by the RFP. The typical method of acknowledging receipt of questions is a phone call, email, or fax to the CO stating that the company received the documents. To acknowledge receipt of amendments, the company must send back a signed Standard Form 33 to the CO before, at, or after proposal submission.

Review the Question, the RFP Requirement, and the Proposal to Determine the Issue, or Review the Amendment to Determine Effect

The customer usually issues questions to a company by email but may also send them in paper format or on a disk.

Some customers will inform a contractor orally of a problem in its proposal and require the company to respond to the question in a proposal update.

The customer's question report should contain the following information:

- Contractor's name or identifier

- CR/DR tracking number

- RFP section number corresponding to the requirement of the response in question

- Contractor's proposal section number corresponding to the response in question

- Description of the specific issue with the response

- Description of what the contractor needs to do to fix the problem area.

Questions may be issued on any section of the proposal or procurement activity, including the technical, management, contracts, or price volumes; the live test demonstration; or the site visits. When a company's proposal team receives questions, the team must review the relevant RFP requirement, proposal section, and issue being raised to determine if it affects the solution as proposed. In some cases, the issue may be resolved with a brief explanation; for example, the customer may have become confused because the company used two different names for the same product throughout the proposal. The customer's response would be to explain the inconsistency in a memorandum. Other times, the company must change its solution to accommodate the customer's issue.

When the customer issues an amendment to a company within the competitive range, it typically puts the amendment on the agency's web page, fedbizopps.gov, or through a "push" email (for which the contractor signed up with the agency).

A customer attaches a Standard Form 33, which serves as a transmittal cover sheet, to an amendment and includes RFP update pages that have sidebars to denote any changes. A company must incorporate the updated pages into the original RFP and determine the effect of the changes to its proposed solution. In some cases, the company's response is not required, such as when the new requirement is already met by the company's existing solution and the company's proposal already states that the requirement can be met. If the proposal does not already state that the requirement can be met, or if new products must be offered to meet the additional requirements, the company must issue a proposal update.

Notify Subcontractors of Issues within Their Areas

The proposal team must review any CR, DR, or amendment that affects a solution provided by a subcontractor with that subcontractor to ensure that the solution proposed is compliant. In the case of a customer question, the subcontractor should write the first draft of the response because it is familiar with the solution and then have the proposal team review it. In the case of an amendment, the subcontractor should help the proposal team update the proposal to reflect accurate information. If a CR, DR, or amendment renders the subcontractor's solution noncompliant, the proposal team must find a new subcontractor with a product that meets the requirements.

Determine If Additional Items Are Required

Sometimes additional products are required to address the issue stated in the question or to meet the modified requirements of an amendment. If this is the case, the company must find another product on the market that can meet the customer's requirements and that complies with the rest of the solution. Once the company has identified this product, the proposal team must gather all the necessary data about the product to update the proposal and assess the cost effect of the new product. Some of the proposal sections that the team may need to update for a new product include technical data, pricing information, representations and certifications, management information, and documentation.

Assess Cost Effect

The proposal team must assess the cost of the new product in terms of its overall contribution to the bottom-line price. It does not make sense, for example, to add a superior technical feature if the associated cost takes the team out of the competitive range. However, if the new product is expensive and necessary, the team should cut costs in other areas to remain competitive.

Understand How the Customer Wants to See Changes

The RFP proposal instructions section may explain how the customer expects to see changes made. Sometimes the customer provides additional submission information in the cover letter with its questions or amendment. For CRs and DRs, the government agency usually expects a written response to the issue raised and proposal update pages. For amendments, the customer usually expects proposal update pages or a certification stating that no changes are required.

The proposal team must provide the revision number, revision date, and highlighted revisions on each proposal page that is updated. The customer may want each revision on a different color of paper. Sometimes the customer wants the company to mark which revision was generated by each question. The customer may limit the number of pages used for proposal revisions. The customer does this so that companies do not submit a lot of pages after the customer has already conducted most of the proposal evaluations. If the customer limits page counts, the total number of pages that each volume may contain will be outlined in the RFP. The customer may also stipulate that only changes driven by a question or an amendment will be accepted and evaluated. This is to prevent companies from proposing a brand new solution.

Write Response

Once the proposal team reviews all the relevant documents and decides which solution changes are required, the team can formulate a response. When responding to customer questions, the company is usually required to provide a written response to each question. If the company does not understand the issue being raised in the question, it should seek clarification from the customer either verbally or in writing.

Determine Effect of Changes and Update the Proposal

Changes made to one section of the proposal typically affect the entire proposal. For example, when adding a new product to the solution, the following sections may require changes:

- *Technical volume*—All charts, text, and graphics that contain a description of the revised product

- *Management volume*—All charts, text, and graphics that contain a description of the support being provided for the revised product

- *Contracts volume*—Percentage of business for the company providing the revised product and small business status

- *Live test demonstration volume*—All test plans for the revised product, if required

- *Price volume*—All exhibits that provide unit and life-cycle pricing for the revised product

- *Documentation*—All user and system documentation, if required for submission

- *Executive summary*—Description of all solution components.

Any of these changes typically mean that the company must obtain additional information from its subcontractors to be eligible for award. A subcontract relationship could fall apart at this stage because more negotiations and reassurances will be needed, and the subcontractor may not be able to provide them. For example, if the customer believes that part of the solution provided by the subcontractor will not work, the company must either gain assurance from the subcontractor that the product will be modified to meet the customer's solution or the company will have to replace the subcontractor's product with another product.

Review Changes

Once the proposal team has answered all the questions and made the proposal updates, the team conducts a review of all the revisions to ensure that:

- No contradictions exist between sections

- Changes have been made in all the appropriate proposal sections

- Changes made as a result of the questions do not contradict previously written sections

- All team members are aware of each revision and its effect

- All references to the old information have been removed.

This review is critical because if changes are not made properly, more questions from the customer can result.

Produce Proposal Changes

Once the proposal team responds to all the questions and updates the proposal, it can begin the production process.

The production process entails editing the changes, making the changes to the proposal, formatting the proposal changes according to the customer proposal instructions, producing the requisite number of copies, and conducting a quality check of the final document. The customer typically wants each question, response, and corresponding page packaged together so that the evaluators can review the effect of a change on the entire proposal. The company usually has to provide the same number of proposal updates as it did original proposals.

Submit Revised Proposal and Question Responses

The company must submit the revised proposal and responses to the customer by the designated date and time. The customer evaluators will review the changes and, if necessary, issue additional questions, which starts the process all over again.

164. How does a company prepare for a demonstration?

The customer may require the company to present a demonstration as part of the evaluation process. Demonstrations give the customer an opportunity to verify and validate the company's solution against the RFP requirements and to ensure that the company's solution will work as proposed. In addition, demonstrations give the customer the opportunity to ascertain the level of risk associated with the proposed solution. The company is expected to design and produce a technical demonstration that complies with the customer's demonstration requirements and to present the proposal team in the best manner possible.

Demonstrations provide an excellent opportunity for company and subcontractor to work together and share solution information. The company may need to obtain product and technical support, marketing brochures, demonstrators, presenters, and subject matter experts from the subcontractor organization to make the demonstration a success.

The overall process for preparing for a demonstration includes the following steps.

Determine the Requirements for the Demonstration

Demonstrations vary in type, duration, and format depending on the customer and the solicitation requirements. Demonstrations can also vary as to when they occur—either before contract award, which will be the focus of this chapter, or after contract award. After contract award demonstrations are used when the program is large and has many components that require frequent updating. In such cases, the customer may require the company to present a demonstration each time the company adds a new component to make sure it works.

All of the subcontractor's products may not be needed for a demonstration. The company must decide, based on the customer's requirements, which, if any, of the subcontractor's product line is necessary for the demonstration.

Determine the Demonstration Length

Demonstrations vary in length from several hours to a month or more for large programs. The length of a demonstration can provide a significant competitive advantage for some companies. For example, a customer uses a lottery to determine the order in which companies will demonstrate. The demonstration is expected to last a couple of weeks and many companies are involved. Because of the duration of the demonstrations, some companies may have extra weeks or even months to prepare for their demonstrations. Such instances can provide a significant competitive advantage to companies, particularly when procurement events, such as proposal submission, question response, and demonstrations, are occurring concurrently.

Review RFP Requirements for Demonstration

When the customer requires a demonstration, the customer usually provides demonstration requirements in the original RFP or through an amendment to all offerors. The customer may require each company to submit a demonstration plan as part of its proposal submission depicting what the team plans to demonstrate (if the customer allows the company to decide) or how the team intends to comply with the customer's demonstration requirements.

Develop a Plan for Conducting the Demonstration

Regardless of whether the customer requires a demonstration plan, the company's proposal team should develop a plan for managing the demonstration to ensure that it occurs flawlessly. The team has much riding on a successful demonstration, and the customer does not allow for makeup demonstrations in the event that the team's first attempt fails. The demonstration plan should contain the steps listed in this section with specific dates established for each step.

Determine Solution Components to Be Demonstrated

A major part of the demonstration plan is determining what components to demonstrate. The proposal team will want to highlight its company's strengths and demonstrate capabilities that are superior to the competition's, but what is actually shown will be driven by the customer's demonstration requirements. If the customer conducts operational capability tests, the team must demonstrate the solution components that correspond to the components required by the tests. If the customer allows for a contractor-driven demonstration, the team has much more flexibility in choosing what to demonstrate.

Assign Responsibility for Each Component of the Solution

The team should assign one person to each component of the solution to ensure that the component is ready on the day of demonstration. A knowledgeable person from either the company or subcontractor may be selected for a solution component. Some companies prefer to have each component covered by two people: one to handle the presentation (to talk during the test, describing all activities and answering evaluator questions) and one to handle the demonstration (to show how the product is intended to work). These two people must work closely to present a well-orchestrated demonstration.

Determine Degree of Readiness of Each Component

Determining the degree to which each component is ready for demonstration will require input from both the company and its subcontractors. To determine readiness, the demonstration team should develop test plans for each functionality that will be demonstrated and establish criteria to determine how well the product will meet each requirement. If actual tests are required by the customer, the team can:

- Define all requirements related to a specific test

- Develop a standard format for test plans

- Develop plans for testing how a particular product meets each requirement

- Conduct a management team review of the test plans to ensure adequacy.

If actual tests are *not* defined by the customer, the team can:

- Develop a plan for how to demonstrate as many requirements of the RFP as possible given the time constraints

- Select the solution components that will show the team in the best possible manner and develop a demonstration plan for those components

- Complete and review test plans.

The company's solution will always have areas that are not as strong as others. The best way for the demonstration team to handle this problem is to carefully analyze its solution's strengths and weaknesses, as well as those of the competition. This analysis will allow the demonstration team to emphasize the competitor's weaknesses and downplay its own. The team can also try to fix as many of its own solution's weaknesses as possible to decrease the problem's effect on the solution. For this approach, the proposal team will need assistance from its engineering department for products developed internally and from teaming partners and subcontractors for products developed externally.

Submit Any Demonstration-Related Questions to the Customer

During demonstration preparation, the company should call the customer if it has questions. It is much better to get any open issues resolved before the demonstration than to present the demonstration in a manner that the customer did not anticipate. Typically, a CO will require the company to submit the question in writing. The CO then answers the question in a formal amendment that is sent to all companies.

Determine the Role of Subcontractors in the Demonstration

If products or services are provided by subcontractors, the demonstration team should consider asking representatives from those companies to participate in the demonstration. The roles of the representatives can vary depending on the demonstration requirements. For example, members from the teaming partner or subcontractor company could be identified as the responsible person for a solution component because they know the product best. Other roles that representatives can fulfill include demonstration support, presentation support, integration support, background documentation support, helpline support, emergency support, and facilities and equipment support.

Locate Demonstration Space

The customer has the option of requiring that the demonstration occur at a customer or company facility. If the demonstration is to occur at the company's facility, the proposal team must locate enough space to handle the demonstration requirements. Typically, a minimum of three rooms is needed for the demonstration: one in which to conduct the demonstration, another for the support personnel required to conduct the demonstration, and the third for the customer evaluation team to conduct sidebars.

The demonstration room must be large enough to handle the customer evaluation team, contractor support personnel, demonstrators, presenters, and necessary equipment. The customer often limits the number of company personnel allowed in the demonstration room at any one time. Support personnel, therefore, need an area in which to wait before conducting their piece of the demonstration or in the event of an emergency. The customer evaluation team usually requests a private area in which it can retreat each day before, during, and after the demonstration to compile notes, compare evaluation scores, and assign risk assessments. Also, if the customer requires or if the company chooses to demonstrate manufacturing facilities, the demonstration team may need to organize a tour of the facilities.

Alternatively, the government may decide that the contractor has to provide a sample for it to evaluate. This is particularly relevant in the construction arena; for example, the government may ask an electrical engineering firm to wire a room so that it can assess performance prior to award.

Provide Amenities

Besides demonstration space, the proposal team will need to provide other amenities for the customer during the visit. Furniture, projection systems, maps of the area, telephones, secretarial support, computers, and food and beverages may all help the demonstration run more smoothly.

Develop Demonstration Documentation and Presentations

To present a polished demonstration, the team should develop a carefully defined agenda and use standard presentation and documentation formats. The agenda should follow the demonstration requirements listed in the RFP or, if the company can develop the agenda, it should match the evaluation criteria established in the RFP. An agenda will help the proposal team stay focused on what the customer wants to see, rather than on what the company wants to demonstrate, which may be of little interest to the evaluators and, therefore, doesn't keep the evaluators' interest.

Following is a sample demonstration agenda that a company could use:

- Welcome and introductions

- Keynote address

- Technology presentations

- Solution overview

- Individual tests, presentations, or demonstrations

- Manufacturing facilities tour

- Scheduled breaks/meals

- Status at the end of each day

- Schedule for the next day's events.

The agenda should also include time for the company to answer any customer questions either at specified points throughout the day or during a presentation. Sometimes the RFP states that the company has the opportunity to retest if the team fails a test the first time. If the customer allows retesting, it is usually permitted under strict conditions. For example, the customer may stipulate that testing will occur for eight hours each day. If the company completes all the tests scheduled for the day under the eight-hour requirement, the customer may allow retesting for any failed test during the remaining time, but the retesting may not exceed the eight-hour time schedule.

The proposal team should also highlight any concerns the customer expressed during the demonstration. If the customer expressed any major concerns, the company may wish to present its position as an agenda item.

Once the team has prepared the agenda, it can establish standard formats for its presentations and documentation. Presentations include all formal addresses given to the evaluation team throughout the demonstration. Documentation includes any handouts, samples, and test reports that are provided to the evaluators as part of the evaluation process or as background information. The team should develop standard formats early on and provide them to the presenters and demonstrators. Standard formats minimize the amount of rework associated with taking existing presentation and documentation and reformatting it into the new standard demonstration format.

Once the formats have been established, the team and/or presenters can prepare scripts for each test or presentation. The extent of script writing depends on the presenters and demonstrators used. If the presenters and demonstrators have been working on the proposal and are familiar with the RFP requirements, little, if any, script writing may be necessary. If the team uses professional demonstration personnel, however, it may be prudent to write a script that tailors what is said about the product to target the specific customer evaluators.

Make Contingency Plans

If the company fails the demonstration, the company's chances of winning the procurement are minimal. Therefore, the company should have contingency plans in place in case a component fails before or during the demonstration. The contingency plans can include having backup components available on site, having the technical experts at the demonstration in case there is a problem, or assigning backup personnel to conduct the presentation. All these contingencies need to be worked out with the subcontractor early in the process.

Determine Accommodations for the Customer

Usually, the customer will request a list of hotels in the immediate area of the company facility if the demonstration is scheduled over multiple days. Some companies put together visitor's guides outlining the restaurants and amenities in the area.

Ensure That Demonstration Personnel Are Prepared

Demonstration personnel need to be prepared for the pressured environment of a demonstration. Written scripts, rehearsals (including videotaping, if necessary), and external reviews are all approaches to help demonstration personnel prepare for the actual demonstration. It is also important that all demonstrators and presenters understand the evaluation criteria so that they can emphasize those characteristics of the solution that illustrate the team's ability to meet the evaluation criteria.

Test the Solution and Finalize the Demonstration

The proposal team will need to continually test the solution to ensure that it works as intended. Sometimes the team finds that changes are needed to make the solution functional. Any changes to the solution must be carefully documented in proposal updates. As discussed, the team must decide when to stop making changes and begin working on finalizing the solution for presentation. Once the team has finalized the solution, it will want to conduct a requirement compliance check to ensure that all RFP requirements have been addressed.

Complete Production of Demonstration Materials

The last preparation step is to produce the final version of all demonstration materials.

NOTE: Some companies like to give the government evaluators items that have the company logo emblazoned on them. These gifts can be notebooks, pens, etc. However, the contractor must be aware that government personnel cannot accept gifts in excess of $20 from contractors and that many government officials choose not to accept any gifts at all. While gifts may be considered a nice gesture and perfectly acceptable in a commercial environment, they should be carefully considered in the federal environment because of the perception that the government is accepting gifts in return for a favorable award decision.

Conduct Demonstration

The team is now ready to conduct the demonstration. Any tests that the team fails should be conducted again, if the customer allows. The customer and company must agree on what tests were completed. The customer may share with the company which tests it passed and which it failed.

Answer Demonstration-Related Questions and Update the Proposal

The company will need to update the proposal if any of the following situations occur:

- Solution changes were made in preparing for, or as a result of, the demonstration

- The customer issues questions based on the demonstration

- The customer asks questions at the demonstration, which the company wishes to clarify in the proposal.

Answering demonstration-related questions ensures that the solution the company demonstrated is the exact solution that it proposed.

165. How does a company finalize its competitive target?

Because of the highly competitive nature of customer procurements, many companies develop competitive targets. A competitive target is the price a company believes that its competitors will bid to win the procurement. Armed with a competitive target, a company then tries to get its own price below what it believes the competitors will bid to win the procurement. Developing a competitive target is both an objective and a subjective activity. It is based on actual numbers (where they exist) and on assumptions (when real data are not available).

The competitive target is typically done early in the procurement (usually as part of the bid decision process) and then revalidated throughout the process. The following steps describe how a company develops a competitive target.

Select People to Work on the Competitive Target

The right people must work on the competitive target. Ideally, a company should select individuals who understand the technical solution being proposed and who have a broad understanding of the competitor's product offerings to work on the target. In addition, it is helpful if the people selected can conduct thorough research, because the competitive target team will need to uncover what companies the competitors are likely to team with, what their strategies for winning will be, and what price they are likely to bid.

Although the technical team members probably possess these characteristics, it is best *not* to have them identify the competitive target. This is because the more the technical team discovers about the competitor's solutions, the more likely it might be not to develop a different solution of its own.

Once the competitive target team has uncovered the competitors' solutions, the team might want to review its discoveries with the technical team. In this way, the technical team might be able to apply strategies that the competitive target team identified as part of its research.

Sometimes it is easier for a company to hire an outside market research company to conduct the research and provide a competitive target for a particular program. A market research company can provide good data, if the proposal team selects a market research firm that specializes in the solution germane to the program. If the firm selected has a database full of information it has gleaned over the last several years in an industry, it makes sense for the proposal team to tap into these resources to develop its competitive target. Of course, the team should decide which alternative—developing the target internally or externally—will yield the best information at the most reasonable cost.

Subcontractors are a tremendous source of information for developing the competitive target. They can help the company acting as prime contractor identify realistic estimates for what the competitors may bid for individual components on the program. The company can take the information gleaned about the individual components and estimate what other companies will bid.

Identify Major Solution Components

The company conducts several steps to develop a competitive target. First, it identifies the major solution components required to meet the requirements of the RFP. The company already did this when it developed its own solution, so that information can be provided by the technical team. For example, if the procurement was for information technology, the team might identify printers, workstations, and modems as the hardware components of the solution.

Select Competitors to Use for the Competitive Analysis

Next, the competitive target team reaches consensus on the one or two teams on which it would like to develop competitive targets. The company cannot conduct targets for all the competitors because it probably does not have the time or resources to develop a target for each program competitor. Therefore, the company should select the competitors that are strong contenders for winning the procurement. Once it has selected one or two companies, it develops models on the selected competitors.

Determine How the Competition Will Bid

The competitive target team needs to determine which pieces of the solution the competitor company will provide itself and which components it will likely contract out. To do this, the company needs to understand the competitor's product lines and how the products are configured. Next, the team determines which companies the competitor will work with for the solution components that will likely be contracted out. Understanding the competitor's strategic alliances, the companies it has teamed with in the past, and the companies it is conducting marketing activities with are all ways to determine this information.

Estimate Prices for Each Component

Finally, the team attempts to ascertain the pricing that the competitor will use for each component. Commercial price lists, General Services Administration (GSA) schedules, and data obtained through the Freedom of Information Act (FOIA) process are all ways to gather these data. The pricing information is the hardest to obtain. Often, the team will have to make some assumptions about what the competition will bid. Ideally, after the team conducts several competitive target analyses, it has data that it can use to pursue future programs.

Finally, the competitive target team estimates the loads that the competitor will use on the products and services it offers. *Loads* are percentage rates that include general and administrative (G&A) costs, overhead costs, and a fee. Once all the component prices and rates have been established or estimated, the team adds them together to equal the competitive target for the program.

Validate the Competitive-Analysis Target

Developing a competitive target is an evolutionary process. Once the team has captured all the initial data, it reviews the data with internal and external people to try to validate as much of it as possible. As more information becomes available about the competitor's solutions, the team adds that information to the competitor model to develop the competitive target. By now, the company's technical and business teams have developed and priced the solution offering. The competitive target team then shares the information it obtained with the technical and business teams. If the competitor is using strategies that would prove useful to the proposal team, the proposal team may implement them. In addition, the technical and business teams review each solution component to determine if the current product offering is cost-competitive.

At this point, an education process occurs. The technical team may try to convince the competitive target team that the price it has established is unreasonably low. The technical team will cite solution components that could not be offered for the price that the competitive target team established. The competitive target team also tries to justify why the numbers it has developed are the price to beat. There is typically give and take on both sides, and then the information is presented to upper management.

Upper management uses the information provided by the competitive target team and the business and technical teams to determine the price the company should offer for its products and services. The company wants to offer its solution at a price that covers its costs and makes a profit. The strategy and gaming occur because the company wants to come in at a price low enough to win the award but high enough to earn as much profit as possible.

Conduct Follow-Up Activities After Contract Award

The company should review the competitive target after contract award to determine the lessons learned from the analysis. At this point in the process, the winning competitor's unit prices may be available through the FOIA process or through catalogues distributed to the customer. The company should use these data to update its competitive target files for future procurements. If the company is the winner, it should still analyze the losing company's total price with the competitive target established. Though detailed product pricing will not be available on the losing company's solutions, analyzing the competitor's total price with the competitive target will indicate how proficiently the company establishes competitive targets.

166. How does a company prepare for and conduct negotiations?

Discussions and negotiations are designed to clear up any misunderstandings between the customer and the company before contract award. The customer expects the company to strive to resolve any open issues during the discussions phase. To do this, the company must solve open issues and develop alternatives for solution components, if necessary.

Several points in our review of the procurement's negotiations phase deserve emphasis. First, government customers typically refer to the negotiations between the government and potential prime contractor as *discussions*. Discussions basically begin during the questions stage and can last up until the BAFO. The commercial customer typically refers to a set period of time when the customer and potential prime contractor negotiate the contract.

Second, the government customer may choose not to conduct discussions. If this is the case, the company should ensure that the customer is aware of any open issues that the company believes need resolution at the time of proposal submission. The next round of discussions and negotiations usually occurs before the BAFO, so that the company can make any necessary proposal updates before the customer makes a contract award. However, some customers have, on occasion, conducted discussions with the apparent winners after BAFOs were submitted. In this scenario, the contractors are usually required to update their proposals to reflect the final negotiated contract between the customers as a result of the discussions.

The last point to understand about the customer's requirements for discussions is that the customer is not obligated to conduct discussions with every company. Typically, the customer will conduct discussions only with companies still within the competitive range, either in the interest of time for a commercial customer or to avoid potential protests after contract award for government customers. However, a customer may choose to not to have discussions with all parties, for example, when the customer conducts discussions with only the apparent winner.

The overall process for preparing for discussions includes the following steps.

Receive a Call to Discussions

If the customer wishes the company to participate in discussions, the customer will send a letter, or call the company, and provide the date, time, and location for the discussions. In addition, the customer will send a copy of the discussion agenda items to the company to assist it in its preparations.

Prepare Any Company Issues for Discussion

Once the company knows it is invited to discussions, it must prepare its items for discussion. Throughout the procurement process, the company should identify any issues that require discussion with the customer. Items for discussion could stem from confusion about a particular requirement or the company's desire to have certain requirements relaxed. For example, the proposal has a clause that requires the company to assume a great deal of risk. Because of it, the company must inflate its price to mitigate its exposure. The customer likes the company's solution, but cannot work with the company because its price is too high. In this case, the customer and company may be able to develop a mutually beneficial solution to the problem, perhaps by developing a risk-sharing scheme. The company may bring up issues during initial RFP evaluation, proposal development, demonstration, questions, marketing efforts, BAFO preparations, or any conversations with the customer personnel.

Review and Prepare Responses to Any Items for Negotiation

Sometimes a customer will issue one more round of questions to a company to resolve any remaining outstanding items—sometimes referred to as items for negotiation, or IFNs. IFNs are handled in the same way that questions are handled (i.e., the company reviews the issue raised by the customer, assesses its impact, develops a solution, and documents that solution in a response to the customer and in a proposal update).

Prepare Negotiation Strategy

Now the company is ready to compile all the information it developed for its negotiation strategy. The management team reviews its list of items previously developed and decides which issues to discuss. The team then conducts research to determine the position the company wishes to take on a particular issue. These findings will then be presented to the customer. The company hopes to convince customer personnel to proceed as the company wishes.

For key issues, the company may want to prepare several different solution scenarios in case the customer does not approve of the first option. Most important, the company should identify the most important issues so it can discuss them first. The company should do this in case the customer sets a time restriction. It is also important to include subcontractors in the negotiation strategy preparation, particularly if they have issues that need to be addressed as part of the discussions.

Determine the Members of the Negotiation Team

Next, the company decides who should participate in the discussions. Typically, a company will select its contract representative as the spokesperson for the team. Other people the company may select to be on the negotiation team include the program manager, salesperson, and any other person who is an expert in the areas being discussed. The customer may restrict the number of people the company may have at the discussions. If this is the case, the company may bring as many people as necessary to the discussions and swap people in and out of the meeting as various topics are presented. The company may or may not ask the subcontractor to participate in the negotiations.

Participate in Discussions

The discussions are held at the designated date, place, and time. The customer typically discusses its open items first. For commercial negotiations, the customer may choose to have any number of people present. For government negotiations, the CO will conduct the discussions for the government and technical personnel are in the room only for the time during which technical discussions are held. When the business or contractual issues are raised, the customer has its technical evaluation team leave the room. This is because the customer wants its technical evaluators to select the best solution based on technical merit without regard to price or contractual issues. The contractor is not obligated to follow suit. Discussions will continue until they are complete or until the customer states that time is up.

Government customer personnel stay as neutral as possible during the discussions so as to avoid giving one company a real or perceived advantage over another. The customer may not answer all questions raised during the discussions but will provide answers to the company's questions after the discussions are concluded. The customer may choose to continue discussions when the answers are obtained. These techniques are used to maintain the integrity of the procurement by keeping all companies on equal footing.

167. How does a contractor work with the customer to develop a negotiation summary?

At the conclusion of discussions with the government, either the customer or the company will develop a negotiation summary. If the company develops the summary, then the customer has the opportunity to review it before it is finalized. If the customer develops the summary, then the company reviews the summary before it is finalized.

Information about the discussions is disseminated in two ways. First, the information about relevant sections discussed may be provided to the teaming partners for their review. Second, the information from discussions is disseminated through a negotiation summary. The purpose of a negotiation summary is to provide an audit trail of the discussions in case any issue arises in the future. The summary contains the following information:

- Author

- Date

- Subject, including contract number

- Discussion's begin and end date

- List of personnel from both sides.

Also included is a list of issues categorized in the following manner: contractual, cost-related, technical, or miscellaneous. Each of the issues contains the related clause, a brief description of the issue, highlights of the discussion, and a summary of the final text or how the contract will be modified.

Information helpful for discussions and negotiations includes:

- Items raised by the proposal team throughout the procurement cycle

- Issues the customer has raised

- Data obtained during the CR/DR process

- Discussion agenda items issued by the customer

- Demonstration comments made by the customer

- Information on why the customer has concerns about an issue

- Data on alternative solutions to the issues

- Data to justify why the task must be completed in the manner proposed if the company does not wish to change its solution

- Information to rate alternatives; for example, what is the best, worst, and most likely resolution to the open issue

- Information that helps the company understand the bottom-line effect of an issue

- Information to prioritize the issues.

168. How does a company prepare a best and final offer?

A best and final offer (BAFO) is typically the last formal information exchange before contract award. The customer asks for BAFOs only from companies still within the competitive range. Bear in mind that the customer could have made a second competitive range determination after the discussions phase to further limit the competition. The reason the customer conducts a BAFO is to secure the best value. Most times, this means that the customer expects the company to lower its prices for the goods and services it is offering.

The customer is under no obligation to conduct a BAFO. Sometimes it awards a contract based on a first and final offer. For governmental contracts, the current Federal Acquisition Regulation (FAR) states that if the customer puts a clause in the RFP stating that the contract may be awarded without a BAFO, the customer may, but it is under no obligation to, conduct a BAFO. (Commercial companies do not have to adhere to any such regulations.) If the customer does not include this clause, the customer must conduct a BAFO. Likewise, the customer may conduct more than one BAFO if it deems this necessary. If multiple BAFOs are required, all companies within the competitive range may submit a revised BAFO.

The customer expects the company to update the proposal, if applicable, to provide best value pricing and to resubmit the cost proposal. When a company receives a call for BAFOs, the customer typically gives the company a very short period of time to prepare its response. For this reason, most companies prepare their BAFOs long before the actual call is received so they have enough time to complete their response. Likewise, many companies will prepare BAFO plans to anticipate all the steps required to complete a timely, compliant response.

The overall process for BAFO preparation begins before the company receives a letter requesting its BAFO. For a large program, the proposal team may begin its preparations one to two months before it believes the BAFO is due. These preparations will occur as the team prepares for discussions and completing the CR/DR phase. The steps include the following.

Prime Contractor Develops a BAFO Plan

Once again, a plan is used to develop a strategy for accomplishing a procurement task. The customer typically gives a company several days to two weeks to submit its BAFO. The proposal team typically develops a BAFO plan before a BAFO is even requested because of this tight timeframe and all the tasks that the company must complete before its submission. The plan details the specific strategies, methods, and approaches that the proposal team will use on outside companies to lower their prices. In addition, the team looks internally at ways it can reduce its operating costs once the contract is awarded. Part of this BAFO plan includes determining the risks that the company is exposing itself to and the techniques that it will use to mitigate those risks during contract performance. Many of the following steps are milestones for the BAFO plan.

Prepare Subcontractors

For the prime contractor to submit a lower, responsive BAFO submission, it must secure lower prices and, perhaps, better terms and conditions from its subcontractors. Obtaining a subcontractor's approval on innovative pricing approaches takes time. Ideally, the prime contractor wants to give the subcontractor as much time as possible to secure the lowest prices it can. If the company gets the subcontractor involved too late in the process, the subcontractor may not be willing or able to lower its prices.

Alternatively, the company can use the prices the subcontractor already quoted and try to negotiate lower prices after award. This strategy, though, could cause the team to not be included in the customer's competitive range because the prices are too high. Similarly, the company could assume it can get lower prices after award and discount the prices to the customer based on that assumption, but this approach is risky because the contractor has no guarantee that the subcontractor will lower its price.

Complete Validation of Competition Analysis Target

During this preparation phase, the team continues to validate the competition analysis target. As more information becomes available, the price the company believes it needs to beat may become more realistic. The company will not know the actual price until the contract is announced. The company's estimate drives additional cost-cutting strategies for the BAFO team.

Validate Technical, Management, and Business Solutions

Before the proposal team begins extensive work on the BAFO, the team should ensure that it has the current technical, management, and business solutions. This step, coupled with reviewing labor estimates and validating subcontractors' proposals, is part of an iterative process. As requirements are further refined, labor estimates and product mix may vary and subcontractors' proposals may need to be updated.

Review Labor Estimates

Labor is typically one of the most expensive items on a contract. Even having just one extra person on the contract for the life of the contract can add hundreds of thousands of dollars to the firmed fixed price proposal. Likewise, if the proposal team underestimates the labor requirements, the company could end up losing money during contract performance because additional personnel resources are required. Therefore, the proposal team needs to understand the exact number of personnel needed to run the contract and ensure that the appropriate labor costs are included in the price proposal. In a cost reimbursable contract, the contractor is concerned about exact labor estimates because, although the government will pay for all costs, the contractor's profit margin will be impacted if it underestimates the level of resources needed.

Validate Subcontractors' Proposals

Another step in the BAFO preparation process is to validate each subcontractor's proposal. This is important because the subcontractor may have proposed more than what is required to meet a particular technical requirement. In addition, the technical team needs to ensure that the products offered will actually meet all the customer's requirements. The team needs to conduct several reviews:

- Review the subcontractors' technical proposals against the team's cost proposal to ensure that what is proposed has an associated price

- Review the subcontractors' lists of products against the actual RFP requirements to ensure that all requirements have been addressed

- Ensure that accurate subcontractor costs have been used to develop the price proposal

- Determine ways that subcontractors might be able to reduce their prices.

Negotiate with Subcontractors

Once the team understands the subcontractors' proposals, the next step is to negotiate any outstanding issues between the company and the subcontractors. The company wants to help the subcontractors develop pricing strategies that can allow the company to be more competitive.

Request BAFO Pricing from Subcontractors

At the conclusion of discussions, the company typically asks for the subcontractor's BAFO submission. The BAFO submission reflects the products and prices that are incorporated into the subcontract between the company and the subcontractor. The team inserts the subcontractor's prices into the cost model and uses them as the basis for its price proposal to the customer.

Develop and Document Pricing Strategies

Ideally, once all of the suppliers' prices are put into the cost model, the company will have a proposal that comes in under its competitive target. Seldom, however, is this the case. Usually, the company has to take some additional risk for the overall deal to come in under the competitive target. Management must understand and be willing to commit the resources necessary to manage the contract given the risks that have been taken to win the contract. Management must understand this as it conducts a management review of the pricing strategies and final BAFO price.

Price Reduction Strategies

Brian T. Fisher, in his article, "Winning on FAFOs: A Proposal Manager's Tailoring Techniques" (*Contract Manage-*

ment, May 1997), suggests two different types of price-reduction strategies: cost-based and process-based. For cost-based strategies, he suggests that the company:

- Reevaluate the direct labor structure

- Propose a low or negative rate escalation

- Reclassify indirect laborers into the direct cost pool

- Use a value-added general and administrative rate

- Reduce the proposed fee or profit.

For process-based strategies, he suggests the company:

- Create a new business unit

- Base the proposal on aggressive performance data

- Use review teams

- Reduce indirect rates

- Outsource

- Replace existing employees with job shoppers

- Eliminate mid-level supervisors or managers.

Components required to document pricing strategies include:

- Statement of the area to which the pricing strategy is being applied (e.g., hardware)

- Actual strategy being applied (e.g., reducing product prices in the out-years)

- Anticipated costs saved (e.g., $20 reduction per item in years two and three of a three-year contract multiplied by 100 items per year yields a $6,000 contract savings)

- Rationale for taking the risk (e.g., the price of hardware typically declines over time as newer technology is introduced into the marketplace)

- Risk mitigation strategy, or how the company intends to make up the money it could potentially lose (e.g., if the contract contains a technology refreshment clause, the company may decide it will offer a new product in its place in the out-years).

Receive Notification from the Customer if It Makes a Competitive Range Determination

As discussed earlier, the customer may make a competitive range determination at any point in the procurement cycle. If, after discussions, the customer does not believe that a company can possibly change its proposal enough to warrant award, the customer may make its first or second competitive range determination and eliminate nonresponsive contractors from the competition.

Complete a Profile for How the Contract Will Do Over Its Life and a Business Case

A company typically develops a contract profile to determine how profitable a contract will be during performance. This information is used to ensure that the company will not lose money on the proposal submitted. During contract performance, the company uses the profile for budgeting purposes and to establish how well an account is managing its costs.

To establish the contract profile, the team must determine a likely business case for the program. A *business case* is the team's best estimate of how many products and services will be purchased during the life of the contract. A team makes these assumptions based on actual RFP language, customer meetings, customer buying patterns, assessment of the customer's need, and potential budget available. Subcontractors will request this information from the company so that the subcontractor can use the data internally to obtain the necessary approval for quantity discounts and better terms and conditions.

Receive a Call for BAFO from the Customer

Once the customer requests BAFOs from contractors still within the competitive range, it may allow a few days or a few weeks for BAFO submission. The customer may also include any final instructions to the companies in preparing their proposals. (Notice how much work should be completed *before* receiving the BAFO call.)

Prepare BAFOs

The company makes several final checks to validate its readiness for BAFO submission. First, it ensures that the cost model is in the proper format to meet BAFO requirements. Frequently, the customer will ask for additional data to be provided at BAFO, such as GSA price lists or commercial price lists. The company may then be asked to give a discount percentage off those price lists in the price proposal. The company will want to quality-check its costs. To do this, the company reviews what products have been proposed in the technical volume against the price quote submitted by the subcontractor and ensures that it is the same cost listed in the cost model. The company also validates its overhead, G&A, and profit rates and ensures that they are applied appropriately.

Produce and Deliver the BAFO

Once the team has prepared its BAFO, the team prints it, reproduces it, packs it, and ships it to the customer by the due date. On government contracts, from this point until contract award, the company should not contact the customer. Any conversations between the company and the customer during this period may be questioned and become grounds for protest if a competitor should learn of them. Because protests are not an option for companies bidding on commercial contracts, contact with the customer after BAFO submission is not a problem on commercial contracts.

Prepare Audit Package

As the team finalizes its BAFO for a government program, the team should focus its attention on finalizing its files for the contractor purchasing system review (CPSR). Any contract purchase made during the audit period is subject to review. The team must ensure that the company's files are current as soon as the contract is announced.

The following information is needed for the BAFO:

- The final solution so that the BAFO team prices the correct components.

- An idea of the acceptable price to the customer so that the team does not bid a price that is too high for the customer's budget.

- Information on the competition to determine what price the team should bid in order to price the program as competitively as possible.

- Trend analysis data, so the team has an idea of the trends within a particular industry. The team can then decide the amount of risk it wants to take to win the program. It can do this by analyzing some widely accepted beliefs about what the future will hold so that it can price its products accordingly.

- Current rates disclosed to DCAA for overhead and G&A. These are necessary to bid the program properly so that the company can later pass an audit for government contracts.

- Quotes from companies that include the final discounts offered by the companies for their BAFO submission. These will allow the company to develop its BAFO submission to the customer.

- Strategies on more efficient ways to conduct business that can help drive down the contract price (e.g., merging several program requirements to obtain discounts through economies of scale).

169. What are the key components of start-up planning?

Although customers usually do not require a company to conduct account start-up planning, contractors should conduct such planning because it is crucial to the success of the contract. Often, the customer requires the company to start work immediately after contract award. A contractor, more often than not, claims in its proposal that it has established processes and procedures to manage the program. The customer, therefore, expects the contractor to be able to immediately begin providing the necessary contract deliverables and to begin performing the work as stated in the proposal.

For the contractor to be able to begin working on the contract immediately, up-front planning is critical. This planning must take place before the contract is awarded so that the company can begin work immediately after award notification. The contractor must meet its requirements from the start to establish a solid relationship with the customer. If it does not plan for the contract, chances for initial customer satisfaction are limited.

The main objectives for the contract start-up planning process include:

- Prepare for deliverables

- Identify personnel

- Establish processes

- Understand data requirements

- Establish working relationships with subcontractors

- Establish marketing channels.

Prepare for Deliverables

In the RFP, the customer states the deliverables it expects to see during contract performance. There are usually two types of deliverables: written reports and products. Written reports may be required one time only, periodically, or on some predefined schedule. The customer could require a few deliverables or hundreds. When the proposal team developed its management plan, the team considered what data was required for each deliverable, how often that deliverable needed to be produced, how many people were required to produce the deliverable, and how many people it would take to produce and review the final report.

Now the proposal team must determine precisely how these deliverables will be produced. It will need to answer questions such as the following:

- Will it need to develop a database to store all the data?

- Who will populate the database? Who has ultimate responsibility for each deliverable?

- What software package will be used to develop the deliverables? (The customer may require an electronic copy of the document, so it may tell the team which software package to use.)

- How will the quality control and management review processes work?

- How will the proposal team orchestrate delivery to the government?

- Will a draft be produced for the customer to review before it receives the final document? (Again, sometimes the RFP stipulates that this will occur.)

The other type of deliverable on a contract is the product that must be provided. A customer requires product deliveries to be made within 30 days after the contractor receives a delivery order. If, at contract award, the customer hands the contractor several delivery orders, the contractor is obligated to provide the ordered goods and services within 30 days of contract award. For the contractor to make these deliveries, the contractor must review delivery orders, create purchase orders for suppliers, manufacture and ship products, and pay invoices. The contractor must establish company contact points, ordering procedures, subcontracts, delivery terms, and shipping procedures so that orders can be processed in a timely fashion. In addition, if the products must be manufactured or assembled at the prime contractor's site, extra time must be built into the schedule for these tasks.

To maintain control of all these processes, the contractor will have to track the data pertaining to each order. If the contractor fails to meet the customer's required delivery schedule, it could be terminated for contract default.

Identify Personnel

Finding well-trained, efficient personnel presents a major challenge to the new program team. Contract success depends on each person doing his or her job effectively and efficiently. Top-notch people may be scarce in a company, and even if they are accessible, they are typically so good that they cannot be extracted from the project on which they are currently working. However, it would not be prudent to have all the company's stellar performers work on one contract to the detriment of the others. The program team must prepare alternatives for when it cannot get all the best people to work on the contract. For example, it could look for less-experienced people within the organization or try to hire people from outside the company.

Coordinating with a subcontractor to get the specific expertise from its organization when and where the program team needs it is also a challenge the team will need to address. The subcontract should have clearly defined roles and responsibilities so that the subcontractor is prepared to meet the customer's objectives.

Establish Processes

The team needs to develop processes so that the team performs tasks consistently to obtain consistent results. Processes are also important to reduce the training time needed for people new to the contract. The proposal team developed high-level processes when it developed its management proposal. Now the program team must decide the details of how each process on the contract will work.

The individual processes needed for a contract are numerous and are geared specifically to the requirements. The types of processes needed on most contracts are as follows:

- Contract and program training

- System training

- Product development

- Purchasing

- Invoicing

- Office administration

- Financial reporting

- Management reporting

- Customer reporting

- Company correspondence

- Customer correspondence

- Prime-contract administration

- Subcontract administration

- Customer delivery order

- Career development

- Employee appraisals

- Employee salary administration

- Quality assurance

- Proposal development

- Contract modifications

- Time cards

- Travel-expense tracking

- Written-deliverable production.

The company may have already developed some processes, so the program team will just need to implement them on the contract. Not all the processes will apply to a specific contract; for example, a labor-type contract would not require any of the processes for design and engineering.

The contractor or the proposal team should document processes so that they are not perpetually recreated. Processes will be refined over time as people become more sophisticated about the job requirements. As these processes are refined, the contractor may be able to save itself and the customer money through greater efficiency.

Understand Data Requirements

Once the team understands the deliverables it needs to turn in to the customer and the processes required to manage those deliverables, it can assess what data elements are required to support those activities. The program team should break down each deliverable into its data elements. Then the team should analyze each data element in terms of how it should be obtained. By starting off with the customer deliverables, the contractor can maintain focus on what the contract actually requires. The team may expand the data requirements after the process-definition phase if the team realizes that additional data are required to manage all the components of the contract.

Associated with the data required are the tools necessary to capture the data. Whether the team uses an internally developed database, spreadsheet, program management tool, or a combination of all three, data must be managed on the contract. Data must be accurate, easily accessible, and as integrated as possible. For example, if the database tracks all the steps in filling a customer order, ideally, the team would like the database to track all the contract financials as well. That way customer order data from the database do not have to be re-keyed into the financial spreadsheets before they can be used to develop a management report.

The team should store as much contract data as possible in one central repository that has the ability to generate programmed and ad hoc requests. This approach minimizes report generation because all reports are generated from the same data, it minimizes user training because users need to be trained on only one system, and it minimizes data correction because data need to be corrected in only one system.

Keep in mind that as the government moves toward implementation of an earned value management system (EVMS), the contractor will be required to collect different data than what it normally collects. In EVMS, the government wants to ensure that if the contractor has used 50 percent of the funds, 50 percent of the value has been attained and 50 percent of the work has been completed. For the contractor to demonstrate these percentages, its EVMS system must be closely linked to its cost estimating system, project management and control system, and budgeting system.

Establish Working Relationships with Subcontractors

The team must determine who in each subcontractor organization is responsible for helping the contractor meet the program objectives. Throughout the proposal process, the subcontractor has worked on the team based on the contents of a nondisclosure agreement and a team agreement. By the end of the BAFO stage, the prime contractor and subcontractor companies should have agreed on price and price-affecting terms and conditions. During this phase, the prime contractor and subcontractor negotiate all the rest of the terms and conditions for the subcontract.

Additionally, the prime contractor must understand how to accomplish program objectives through the subcontractor organization. Ideally, the prime contractor should know who in the subcontractor organization is responsible for:

- Subcontract issues

- Business issues

- Technical issues

- Marketing issues

- Purchasing and delivery issues

- Overall program direction.

The prime contractor and the subcontractor must work together as a team if the program is to be successful. The subcontract is the tool that is in place to ensure that both parties live up to their obligations to one another. By establishing these points of contact for each subcontractor, program team members can go to the right person within each of the organizations to get the program objectives completed.

Establish Marketing Channels

With the government's emphasis on indefinite delivery and indefinite quantity-type contracts, all the contractor actually wins when it is awarded the procurement is the right to sell its products and services. It is up to the program team to market its wares to the customer community if it expects the contract to be profitable. Marketing the contractor's products can be simple—relying primarily on word-of-mouth marketing—or complex—offering incentives to salespeople from subcontractor companies to push the products. Either way, the team's marketing efforts must be evaluated by comparing the money it costs to implement them versus the potential revenue streams they may generate.

Marketing efforts the team can use include:

- Trade show booths

- Trade magazine advertising

- Providing guest speakers at conferences

- Catalogues

- Brochures

- Internet advertising

- Product demonstrations

- Customer visits

- User meetings.

170. How does a company conduct start-up planning?

To conduct contract start-up planning, the company and the program team conduct the following process.

Ensure Corporate Support for the Planning Effort

Planning efforts take time and money and are not typically reimbursable by the customer. Therefore, the company must decide if the plan is worth doing and determine the number of resources it is willing to devote to its development. Once the team has secured a corporate commitment to spend the funds necessary to develop the plan, the team is ready to select its planning team members.

Select Planning Team Members

The program team members for a start-up plan should consist of individuals who will be responsible for bringing the plan to its fruition. Ideally, the team will have a representative from each functional area; however, that approach may be too costly for the company to implement. A more cost-effective approach is to have three to five individuals who are responsible for key functional areas and who understand the contract as a whole so that they can develop a plan that is workable and makes good business sense. The individuals selected should have the ability to envision all aspects of the contract and should be able to logically think through the processes required to run a government contract.

Develop the Components of the Plan

The company can use whatever planning approach it deems necessary to develop a workable, usable plan.

Communicate the Plan

Once the plan is developed, the company must communicate it to the team that will implement it. The contract start-up plan may be shared with internal team members, management, and outside companies. It may even be shared with the customer after the company is awarded the contract. As new team members are brought on board, the plan serves as a useful overview of the tasks that need to be accomplished for contract start-up success.

Implement the Plan

The people assigned to implement the plan work on the projects defined and stay within the stated budget. If the customer delays the award, the company can work on refining the start-up plan or actually begin the start-up plan. Usually, the planning steps take longer to implement than anticipated. This is a natural outcome, particularly if the people who are working on the plan have never estimated resources or started up a contract. The team cannot predict how smoothly its plan will run. However, planning improves over time, and soon the team will reap the rewards of its labor.

Develop and Use Feedback Mechanisms to Update the Plan

Periodically, the team should review the status of the plan. The team does this by developing feedback mechanisms and by assessing its performance against those mechanisms. In the case of assessing a start-up plan, the team can check whether objectives are being met, if projects are being completed on time, if the stated resources are actually required for the project, and if the project is staying within budget. If the team answers any of these questions negatively, the team needs to reassess that particular area to determine what is causing the problem. Possible reasons include lack of knowledge by the planning team of the true resources required, members who are less experienced than anticipated, or nonresponsive companies. Feedback mechanisms allow the planning team to make changes in the plan so that the team can accomplish its intended purpose.

Receive Notice of Contract Award

When the customer makes an award to the procurement winner, the customer usually notifies the winner by calling the contract administrator of the winning company. The customer informs losing companies by phone call or by letter. In rare instances, the customer does not notify the losers individually. In the case of federal programs, the customer publishes the award in one of the procurement periodicals, such as *Government Computer News* or *Federal Computer Week,* or in a major national newspaper, such as *The Washington Post.* A commercial company may just stop all communication with a company and it's not until the company calls the customer that it learns that the customer made an award.

The customer may award the contract to multiple offerors. Some customers are using the multiple award contract vehicle much more frequently in their procurements. In fact, in government contracts, the Federal Acquisition Streamlining Act (FASA) has mandated that all advisory and assistance procurements over $10 million be awarded to multiple contractors. In these procurements, the customer stipulates in the original RFP that the award may be made to multiple contractors. In addition, the FAR encourages the customer to use multiple awards or indefinite quantity contracts. Once the awards are made under these indefinite delivery/ indefinite quantity (ID/IQ) task order procurements, each of the winning contractors must compete for work to be done under the contract.

The overall process that the company follows for notification of contract award is as follows:

Wait

Waiting for the contract award is one of the toughest tasks about the procurement. People will ask the team members daily, "Have we heard yet?" or "Do you think we won it?" If a company is not doing well financially, upper management may put increasing pressure on the team by stating how this procurement is a "must win." Rumors among contractors spread quickly, and the team may spend a lot of anxious moments second-guessing itself as to whether the strategy it used was the best one. If the customer runs into problems with the award, the announcement may be delayed, so the company continues to wonder if it won. The only advice for this situation is for the team members to do whatever they can to keep their own spirits up until the award is announced.

Learn of Contract Award

The company will eventually learn if it won when the customer makes the contract award. Typically, the customer publishes a schedule detailing when the award will be made. If the company has not been notified of an award by that scheduled date, the company may call the CO to determine when the award decision will be announced. The company will usually receive a letter or a phone call from the CO stating whether the contract has been awarded.

Determine If the Company Has Won or Lost the Contract

The next steps in the process depend on whether the company won or lost the procurement. We will discuss the steps for the winning company first.

Winning Company

Execute Prime Contract between the Customer and the Contractor

The first step for the winning contractor is to execute the prime contract with the customer. Execution occurs after contract discussions have been completed. Discussions may have begun before BAFO submission, in which case all that is left to do is for both parties to sign the contract. Discussions may also have been conducted after BAFO submission and after an apparent winner was selected. Again, the only task left to do in this situation is for both the customer and the winning contractor to sign the prime contract. However, the customer may wait to conduct discussions until after announcing the winner. If this is the case, the customer and the contractor complete their discussions, and pending satisfactory resolution of all outstanding issues, sign the contract.

Notify Relevant Parties of the Award

The most fun the contractor may have on a proposal effort is when it announces to the world that the team has won the procurement. The company should notify the following groups, at a minimum: upper management, proposal team members, teaming partners, subcontractors, newspapers, internal publication channels, and internal support groups. The purpose of this notification is to provide as much preparation time as possible to the groups that will support the contract. Each of these teams will need to begin preparations for providing resources to meet the first contract deliverable.

Implement Account Start-Up Plan

Once the award has been announced, the winning contractor team begins implementing the account start-up plan. Each of the steps discussed in the account start-up planning section must be completed to meet the initial contractual requirements.

Execute Subcontracts

Companies take different positions regarding when to negotiate subcontracts. Most prime companies prefer that the subcontract negotiations occur before they submit BAFO pricing, so they have firm subcontractor pricing and understand the degree of risk to which their companies are being exposed. Subcontractors, on the other hand, prefer to wait until after contract award to negotiate the subcontracts with the prime contractors. Subcontractors believe they have more leverage after the contract has been made because the prime contractors have included the subcontractors' products and services in the proposals and, therefore, must provide the stated products and services. Subcontractors believe they can determine whatever price they want because the business is virtually guaranteed, at least for contract start-up.

Plan Win Party

At last it is time to celebrate. A win party is a way to publicly recognize the people responsible for the contract win. It allows team members to pat themselves on the back and reminisce about the long hours, the challenges, the heroes, and the seeming impossibilities that were overcome. It is good closure for people. Although a party would make for a good proposal-to-contract transition, the proposal team members likely will never work together again. Individuals go off to other efforts, and new people are brought in to work on the contract. The win party gives the recipients the feeling that the company really appreciates the effort that goes into winning new business. This appreciation is what builds employee loyalty to the company and gives them a reason to work on the next proposal effort when asked.

Win parties can be either a small affair with just the team members attending a luncheon or a dinner, or it can be a gala event with a theme, entertainment, and door prizes. Inviting spouses or significant others is a way of thanking them for the time that the proposal team members spent away from home. It also helps the spouses or significant others understand what their partners do at work. The size of the win party should be commensurate with the significance of the deal to the company, the amount of time the members worked, and the size of the deal. Dollars spent on the win party should be evaluated against the potential revenue that the contract will bring to the company.

Public recognition of the team effort should be the order of the day. Public recognition of individual members is good provided no one is left out. Gratitude speeches by top corporate people also emphasize what the team has accomplished. In addition, there should be special, private recognition of outstanding contributors in the form of a special gift or bonus. Additional vacation days can be awarded to make up for all the additional work time required during the proposal effort.

Arrange Kickoff Meeting with Customer
Soon after contract award, the customer will usually schedule a kickoff meeting with the winning contractor. If the customer does not do so, the contractor should take the lead in getting this meeting established. Both parties need to understand how the contract will operate on a daily basis.

The discussion items for the kickoff meeting include:

- Introduce management team members from both parties

- Determine appropriate ways to communicate with each other (e.g., phone, fax, electronically)

- Review the organization chart

- Discuss the first deliverables

- Conduct tour of contractor and customer facilities, if needed

- Instruct how to obtain badges for each site, if needed

- Discuss the specifics of how the contract will operate

- Obtain all customer-furnished equipment

- Submit any contract deliverables that are due at contract award

- Review work breakdown structure, if required

- Determine access methods for systems that both parties need to use.

On government contracts, the contractor may be required to provide a redacted copy of its proposal to the customer to use for FOIA purposes. FOIA allows any individual or business entity to request information from the customer, and for a modest fee, the customer will provide it. There are certain stipulations outlined in the FAR; for example, the information cannot be of a proprietary nature to give one company an unfair advantage over another. This is the reason that the customer allows the winning contractor to take a copy of its proposal and redact, or mark out, those items within the proposal that the contractor believes are of a proprietary nature. If the customer agrees, the redacted copy will used for any FOIA requests.

Ensure That Procedures Are Established with All Subcontractors

As part of the contract start-up plan, the prime contractor discovered the points of contact within the subcontractor organization. Now it is time to work with those points of contact to determine how the purchasing and invoicing procedures will be implemented. For example:

- Will a forecasting process be used?

- Will a draft order process be used?

- Who should receive purchase orders?

- How will orders be received?

- Where will products be shipped?

- What is the method of shipment?

- When will products be accepted?

- When may invoicing occur?

- How will payment occur?

These discussions should occur initially with the subcontractor that is providing a large number of the products on the contract or that is providing products required for the first deliverable. Discussions can be held with the remaining subcontractors soon thereafter.

Transition All Proposal Files Over to the Account

After the award has been announced, all proposal files become the contract files. This includes all company correspondence, customer correspondence, final RFP, and final proposal. All data for the contractor purchasing system review (CPSR) file, including solicitation; evaluation criteria; memorandum of negotiations; justification for why one company was selected over another, suspended, or debarred from listing; selection of a small or small and disadvantaged business; and price analysis must be retained by the team for the next review.

Losing Company

Notify the People Who Worked on the Program

The worst news that a proposal team can get is to find out that the program it worked so hard on for the last several months, or even years, was awarded to another company. It is a tough time—emotions run high, pride is crushed, and there are a lot of unanswered questions. Some commercial customers will explain why a company lost the program. The government customer gives formal debriefing to the losing contractor. It is important that the company take the information gained through this process and apply it to a lessons-learned exercise so that the company's next program can be a winner.

Schedule Debriefing

In a government program, the company may request and be granted a debriefing to more fully understand the source selection process. This information may assist the company in upcoming procurements.

Close Out Proposal Effort

As soon as the customer announces the award, the company should close out its proposal effort. Steps in that process include:

- Closing out cost centers

- Returning equipment to subcontractors

- Filing a copy of the proposal

- Finding other projects for the proposal team members

- Conducting a lessons-learned exercise

- Deciding what portions of the proposal might be re-used on other proposal efforts.

CHAPTER 11
Exchanges with Offerors

The government is not required to sit down and negotiate with companies pursuing contracts. In fact, the government doesn't even have to talk to the companies in a negotiated procurement. In some cases, there is *no* talk or negotiation. The government simply awards a contract on the basis of initial offers. This means that the deal is made solely on the basis of the paperwork submitted by the companies. It's like sealed bidding without the public opening!

When the government awards "on the basis of initials," there's little if any conversation or exchange between the government and the offerors. The only kind of exchanges that can occur is "clarifications."

Although awards "on the basis of initials" are possible, what occurs more often is that the government wants to discuss the offers with the companies submitting them. After all, talking with the companies typically leads to a lower cost offer.

When discussions are held, there are a lot of ways the government can negotiate with offerors. The government does not have to have face-to-face discussions during a negotiated procurement. It can negotiate on paper, in person, or by oral presentations. But it can negotiate only with those in the competitive range.

171. What is the competitive range?

The competitive range is the short list of the companies with whom the government will hold discussions. This "range" of companies consists of those whose initial proposals seem to be competitive enough to make it worth the government's time and effort to pursue.

For example, in a professional golf competition, there's a first cut of the competitors. Anyone who makes the first cut gets to keep going. If you don't make the cut, you're out. That's what the competitive range is. It's the first cut that determines who gets to keep going. The competitive range is a wonderful work saver for the government.

"Full and open competition" is the law in procurement. But over time, this law has come to be seen by Congress as good news for contractors, but bad news for the workload of contracting officers (COs). If the CO had to have discussions with everyone who could possibly submit a proposal, the CO's job would be nearly impossible. A good part of the CO's efforts and time would be wasted because some of the proposals don't have a chance of winning the contract.

172. How does the government decide who is in the competitive range?

The competitive range is determined when the CO decides which proposals are the most highly rated. Prior to 1997, the competitive range could be huge. The standard was "when in doubt, leave them in." The emphasis was on keeping as many companies as possible in the competition, which placed COs under pressure to include as many proposals in the competitive range as possible.

In 1997, a CO got the right to use, as a guide, the saying "when in doubt, throw them out." If the CO is in doubt about whether a proposal should remain under active consideration by the government, the CO is supposed to leave it out of the competitive range. This new approach allows the CO to decide which proposals are the highest rated and then select those for the competitive range.

However, there's no guidance in the FAR regarding how many proposals should be in the competitive range. It depends on the circumstances. All the FAR says is that the "highest rated proposals" are to be in the competitive range, making it a judgment call for the CO, who must ask, "How can I get the best deal for the government?"and include that many in the competitive range.

173. What is the one great advantage of the competitive range?

The one great advantage of the competitive range is that it cuts down on the amount of work the government has to do. The competitive range *limits the number of companies the government must have discussions with*. From a contractor's point of view, it forces the government to deal only with the best offers. If a company's offer is in, it has a good chance of winning; if its offer is not, the company doesn't have to waste any more time and money on pursuing the contract.

174. Is there only one competitive range determination?

There may be more than one competitive range determination, but that depends on a number of factors. First, a CO must decide which proposals are the most highly rated. As discussions are held with companies, the government might decide that a company's proposal is no longer one of the highly rated proposals. If so, the government can throw it out of the competitive range—effectively altering the competitive range determination. FAR 15.306(d)(4) says that a highly rated offer can be eliminated from the competitive range if after discussions have been held, that company's proposal is no longer one of the most highly rated. Significantly, the FAR says the company can be eliminated "whether or not all material aspects of the proposal have been discussed, or whether or not the offeror has been afforded an opportunity to submit a proposal revision." This seems to say that if something a company says or does knocks down its score, the company can be eliminated from the competitive range regardless of the unanswered (and unasked) questions that the government may have had about the proposal.

The FAR is silent on whether a CO can set a second competitive range that further reduces the number of competitors in the competitive range. However, information given out at the time of the FAR 15 rewrite states, "Additional competitive range determinations are possible based on the result of discussions with offerors."

Thus, two or more competitive range determinations are possible.

175. What are "clarifications," "discussions," and "communications," and what are the distinctions among them?

These words are "terms of art," that is, they mean something special to government contractors and COs.

These terms let everybody in the procurement process know how much they can say to each other during a specific stage in the process. These terms also help ensure that all companies have the same chance to sell their solutions to the government. Clarifications, discussions, and communications are basically just categories describing how much conversation there can be between the government and the companies pursuing contracts.

How much a company can talk to the government depends on how much information the government really needs at a particular point in the contracting process. If the government doesn't need much information and it's on a minor point, the government only has to ask one company to get the information. But if the information from one company really impacts that company's offer, such as giving the company a chance to change its price, the government in fairness should give the same opportunity to all the other companies pursuing the contract.

Thus, there are three categories of conversations:

- *Clarifications* prior to awarding on the basis of initial offers

- *Discussions* with those in the competitive range

- *Communications* prior to establishing the competitive range.

Clarifications

According to FAR 15.306(a)(1), *clarifications* occur only if the government wants to award on the basis of initial offers. Prior to the FAR Part 15 rewrite in 1997, clarifications could occur at any point in the process to handle minor issues, such as typos. With the 1997 change, clarifications occur if the government will award on the basis of initial offers. So *when* clarifications can occur changed in 1997.

What clarifications deal with also changed. In 1997, clarifications took on another role when past performance became more important in the procurement process. Now, clarifications can also deal with past performance issues.

Under the old rules, the government might not be able to discuss past performance with only one company. Clarifications, in the post-1997 system, therefore, got a new job: now there can be clarifications when the government wants to award on the basis of initial offers but there is uncertainty about past performance. For example, the government needs more past performance information on one company or the government is going to use adverse past performance information on which the company has never had an opportunity to comment.

FAR 15.306(2) deals with this issue. It says that companies "*may* be given the opportunity to clarify certain aspects of their proposals (e.g., the relevance of the company's past performance information and adverse past performance information to which the company has not previously had an opportunity to respond)." The new job of clarifications, therefore, is to help the government and the company work with the past performance information if the government wants to award on the basis of initial offers.

Discussions

The government has *discussions* for major aspects of offers in the competitive range. To be fair, if the government has discussions with one company, it must also have discussions with the other companies pursuing the contract.

The classic distinction between clarifications and discussions is that if an agency needs a point clarified, it need not involve other offerors. But if it has discussions with one offeror in the competitive range, it must have discussions with all in the competitive range. The heart of the distinction between clarifications and discussions, what GAO refers to as "the acid test" for whether discussions occurred, is whether the agency gave an offeror an opportunity to revise or modify its proposal. In addition to GAO's acid test, the courts have several other helpful points to consider in distinguishing a clarification from a discussion.

When a protester argued that a competitor providing any additional information had to be a discussion, the court pointed to precedent that concluded that "any meaningful clarification would require the provision of information." And if an offeror's response to an agency question "provides information essential to evaluation criteria, increases the past performance score or tips the scales toward the offeror providing the clarification, it still may be only a clarification." The U.S. Court of Appeals for the Federal Circuit has held that courts should "give deference to an agency's permissible interpretation of its own regulations." Thus, if an agency considered its question to an offeror to be a clarification, courts should respect that conclusion as long as the conclusion was permissible and reasonable.

An Improper Clarification

In one case, during the oral exchange between an offeror and the agency, the agency said the offeror had not submitted a pricing spreadsheet with its oral presentation materials. The offeror later sent one by email but had changed its prices. GAO said, "Providing an offeror an opportunity to make a material change in its proposal constitutes discussions. Moreover, it is clear from the record that ITE's revised pricing was tendered after the point in time it was supposed to be submitted and that this resulted in the agency improperly engaging in discussions with only one offeror after the deadline for submitting proposals." *Global Analytic Information Technology Services Inc.*, B-298840.2, February 6, 2007.

A Proper Clarification

In one case, the Air Force used several "evaluation notices" or ENs to get additional information from offerors. All ENs were labeled "FAR 15.306(a) Clarifications." The court agreed: "This court resolves very close questions about an

EN in favor of the government, if the EN was intended as a clarification, was labeled as such, did not clearly violate the limitations on clarifications expressed in FAR 15.306(a), and do not clearly stray into the forbidden zone of discussions described in FAR 15.306(d)." Applying this test, the court did not find any of the ENs to be discussions. One good example: The winner's proposal had stated that "for now" it had selected a specific subcontractor. In response to a "clarification," the offeror's response "simply confirmed this choice, clarifying a minor aspect of its work plan. This is a classic example of a clarification." *Dyncorp International LLC v. The United States,* No. 07-84C, May 24, 2007.

Communications

Once the competitive range became narrower, the government had to ensure that it had good information before deciding which companies would be in the competitive range. To make the process as easy as possible, it should be one-sided and not a free-for-all involving all companies. *Communications* occur before the competitive range is established. To help the government decide who is within the competitive range, the government can get involved in communications.

What can the government do with communications? The regulations have a "shall" and a "may."

The government *shall* have communications with companies whose past performance information is the determining factor on whether they are included in the competitive range. These communications *shall* deal with adverse past performance information to which the company has not had the opportunity to respond.

There are other conditions when the government *may* have communications with companies. Again, the government would only have communications with those on the edge of being included in the competitive range. Communications *may* be held with those whose inclusion or exclusion is uncertain and *may* be conducted "to enhance government understanding of proposals; allow reasonable interpretation of the proposal; or facilitate the government's evaluation process." FAR 15.306(b)(2). Communications cannot, however, be used to cure deficiencies or omissions or make changes in the proposals themselves.

Thus, in *clarifications*, the government gets only minor corrections or past performance information prior to the award on the basis of initial offers. In *communications*, the government gets a little more information, but only on its competitive range decision. In *discussions*, the government gets a lot of information from all the companies in the competitive range.

176. What happens if an offer doesn't get to the government by the deadline? What do the new late submission rules allow?

Things have gotten much simpler. The late submission rules have been streamlined by the November 1999 FAR changes. (See FAR 52.214-7 for sealed bids and FAR 52.215-1 for negotiated procurements.) Thrown out are hyper-technical rules for next day mail, hand-delivered bids, etc.

The new rules simplify the whole process. Now the government simply has to consider, according to FAR 15.208, whether there is "acceptable evidence to establish that the offer was received at the government installation designated for receipt of proposals and was under the government's control prior to the time set for receipt of proposals." This new rule has greatly simplified the decision on whether to accept the late offer.

Government receiving agents should take special precautions to make sure that the processes for receiving bids and offers are secure. One special precaution might be to keep the date-time stamp machine behind the counter, rather than on the counter, where it would be easily accessible to bidders and contractors who could stamp in their materials whenever they please. Another precaution would be to ensure that your systems work (for example, that the fax machine has paper and is turned on).

A contractor should take special pains to allow enough time for government processes to work. For example, don't expect to be able to fax in a modification to your price proposal several seconds prior to bid opening. There may not be enough time for the government to get the modification to the bid opening room. The test is whether government handling was the paramount cause of the late submission.

177. What happens if both the government and the bidder cause a bid to be late?

The trickiest late bid problems are those where both sides—the government and the company—do something that contributes to an offer or bid being late. But notice: only where the government is the "paramount" cause of the bid or offer being late is the government responsible. For example, if the government gave companies bad directions for submitting their offers, the bid will still be considered late because the offeror following the bad directions showed up at the government building only three minutes before offers were due. To be improper, the government action must be, in the words of GAO, "affirmative action that makes it impossible for the company to deliver the proposal on time. Even in cases where the late receipt may have been caused, in part, by erroneous government action, such as bad directions, a late proposal should not be considered if the company significantly contributed to the late receipt by not acting reasonably in fulfilling its responsibility to deliver a hand-carried proposal to the proper place by the proper time." (*Integrated Support Systems Inc.*, B-283137.2, September 10, 1999.)

CHAPTER 12
Final Proposal Revisions

Final proposal revisions (FPRs) result from the government having "meaningful discussions" with all in the competitive range. After the discussions are over, the government asks all companies still in the competitive range to submit an FPR. However, there is no requirement that a company has to change anything in its proposal. The company can stand pat, make no changes, and simply go with the original offer.

The interesting thing about discussions in government contracting is that they are not what you or I would consider discussions. For example, in procurement, discussions are considered to have been held even if all the government does is request an FPR from a company. In procurement law, discussions have been held because the company got a chance to submit an FPR. Discussions have been held even though there is no actual conversation between the government and the company after the submission of the initial offer.

If the government does decide to exchange information prior to requesting an FPR, its discussions can take many forms. In some cases, the government will have discussions solely in writing. In other cases, the government will use face-to-face discussions. And sometimes a combination of both.

A lot can go on in these negotiations. FAR 15.306(d) says that these negotiations may include bargaining. To the government, bargaining means "persuasion, alteration of assumption, scan positions, give and take. . . ." The positions of both sides, but especially the government, should be flexible during the discussion phase.

Not only is there a broad range of styles in discussions, but discussions can cover a broad range of contract items. The FAR says that these discussions "may apply to price, schedule, technical requirements, type of contract, or other terms of a proposed contract." Notice how many aspects of a contract can be open for discussion—the discussions can go way beyond topics usually negotiated between parties, such as price.

178. What happened to BAFOs?

When these discussions are over, the government calls for FPRs. Up until 1997, the government called for BAFOs. The trouble with the phrase *best and final offer* was the suggestion in the language that the government did not receive a best offer until it was to be the final offer. Now, there is the more accurate phrase, *final proposal revisions*.

179. What are "meaningful discussions"?

The whole purpose of the competitive range is to give the government and companies a chance to exchange information so that companies know exactly what the government wants and the government can learn exactly what a company can provide.

To make it worthwhile for both sides to exchange information, those in the competitive range are entitled to "meaningful discussions" with the government. "Meaningful" involves what parts of the proposal have to be discussed and how obvious or direct the government has to be in explaining what the problems with a proposal are.

There is a constant struggle going on here. Companies want the government to alert to them to every possible shortcoming in their proposals, so that they can maximize their score when submitting a final proposal revision to the government.

That's nice, but that's not the law. The government has no obligation to steer companies into every area that could be improved and that could increase the score awarded a proposal. All the government has to do is alert companies to ways that they could enhance their proposals so that they have a fair chance to win the contract. In legalese, the CO must discuss "significant weaknesses, deficiencies, and other aspects of its proposal" (such as cost, price, technical approach, past performance, and terms and conditions) that could, in the CO's opinion, be altered or explained to enhance materially the proposal's potential for award." FAR 15.306 (d)(3).

So the first problem with meaningful discussions is that the government can pick and choose what part of the proposal it will discuss with a company.

The second problem is how obviously the government has to point out problems in the areas it has decided to discuss with the companies. Does the government have to tell companies precisely what is wrong with their proposals and precisely how to fix it? Not exactly. While a company obviously wants to be told precisely what the government wants, a CO needs to be careful not to disclose to one company any proprietary information or solutions proposed by another company.

It seems like smart business for the buyer to tell the seller exactly what the buyer wants. But that may not be legal in government procurement. Legally, all the government has to do is to steer the companies into the areas that need to be addressed.

Of course, the government can point out to offerors all the areas that need improvement and precisely what within those areas has to be addressed. And why not? If an offeror knows exactly what the government wants, the likelihood of the government getting what it wants—at a good price—is much greater.

Let's make an important distinction. All we have been talking about in this questions so far is what the government *has* to do during meaningful discussions. We've been talking only about the bare minimum the government has to do. A CO does have the discretion to be more precise, and the sellers want that to happen. But the CO must always be careful that proprietary information is not disclosed.

180. How can the government accept a good offer that comes in late?

All offers submitted to the government have to arrive before the deadline. That's one of the basic principles of government contracting. Every solicitation requires that all the initial proposals be submitted before a specific date and time. And all FPRs must also be submitted before a specific date and time, which is the same for everyone.

However, the government has developed a number of rules for deciding whether it can consider a proposal that comes in after the established deadline. Even though the offer is late, it can still be considered by the government if it meets one of the exceptions listed in FAR 15.208.

One exception for late offers that is not mentioned in the FAR allows the CO to, in effect, declare a late proposal to be early—for a new deadline which the CO is establishing only after all the other proposals have been submitted and after the late proposal itself has come in.

Several GAO decisions have sanctioned this peculiar way that the government makes a late proposal early. GAO allows the government to do this because it increases the number of proposals in the competition. If a CO can consider a late offer, the competition increases.

And to GAO, this late-becoming-early device is good. But to the companies that followed the rules and got their proposals in on time, this late-becoming-early device is bad. It likely will provoke a protest in the future.

While this process is clearly legal, it will also clearly not seem fair to the companies that submitted their offers by the original deadline. They will feel it is unfair to give a benefit to a company that didn't care enough about the solicitation to submit its proposal by the original deadline.

181. What are unbalanced bids and what is the best way to determine whether one exists?

An unbalanced bid is one in which some of the items in a multi-item procurement are significantly overstated or understated. An unbalanced bid is bad because fair pricing of items requires that prices for several items in a bid be reasonably related to the actual value of the items. The government should pay what the item is truly worth, no more and no less. For example, if a company has overpriced an item, such as the cost of mobilizing to a site, the company gets more money out of the government sooner than it should. This leaves other items underpriced. If the government terminates the contract, there is less money in the contract than needed and the government will have paid more than the delivered work is worth—a bad deal for the government.

What especially presents problems are bids that are *materially* unbalanced. FAR 52.214-19 defines it this way:

> . . . a bid is materially unbalanced when it is based on prices significantly less than cost for some work and prices which are significantly overstated in relation to

cost for other work, and if there is a reasonable doubt that the bid will result in the lowest overall cost to the Government even though it may be the low evaluated bid, or if it is so unbalanced as to be tantamount to allowing an advance payment.

It is important to be careful about the "advance payment" language in the FAR provision dealing with sealed bids. Is it still something a CO should look out for? Not according to GAO. GAO has said that "under the recently revised unbalanced pricing provision in FAR 15.404-1(g), neither the term 'advance payment' nor the concept is any longer used in discussing unbalanced pricing. It is not clear why the term has been retained in FAR 52.214-10 and 52.214-19." GAO is saying that the concept of an unbalanced bid has been updated for negotiated procurements in the FAR, but not in the sealed bid regulations of the FAR.

But even though time may have changed the focus and eliminated the advance payment concern, the test remains very similar: making sure that the government does not run an unacceptable risk of nonperformance from a bid.

For example, in one case, the winning company bid a price for mobilization/demobilization that was twice the government estimate and more than three times a competitor's bid. But GAO did not consider this to be a materially unbalanced bid because the government intended to order all the bid quantities so that the "unbalanced" bidder's price remained low throughout the course of the contract. In another example, the winning company bid a price way out of whack with the government estimate and a losing company claimed an unbalanced bid. But the CO said it wasn't an unbalanced bid because other companies had even more unbalanced prices for some items.

CHAPTER 13
Past Performance

Past performance is the new kid on the procurement block. Since 1997, it has been a mandatory evaluation factor for negotiated procurements over $100,000. The FAR allows exceptions, such as when it doesn't make sense because the item is brand new. In the past, negotiated procurements did not have to consider past performance as a specific evaluation factor. Nor was past performance as such considered in sealed bidding.

But past performance has always played some role in the award of a government contract. For both types of procurements, past performance was considered one element of the responsibility determination made by the CO for the apparent winning proposal. So a CO could refuse to award a contract to a bad performer by finding it nonresponsible. But that was theoretical.

As a practical matter, a low price from any contractor, good or bad, is hard to resist. A CO would be hard-pressed to refuse to award a contract to a less-than-perfect contractor offering a low price by finding the low-priced contractor nonresponsible for its previous poor past performance. And what if the contractor had bad performance on only one contract? Plus, finding a contractor nonresponsible might well provoke a protest. What the government really wants to do is pick the best-performing companies in the solicitation process, not eliminate ones that have a record of defaults—and making past performance an evaluation factor lets the government do this.

182. If a company filed claims, can the government hold that against the company and consider claims filing as part of (adverse) past performance?

A typical element of contract performance is the filing of claims by the contractor under the disputes clause. However, previous claims by a company should not affect a past performance rating. The fact that a contractor filed claims cannot be used against it in considering past performance because in filing claims a contractor is simply exercising its legitimate rights under the contract.

Companies still are concerned about the government using against a contractor in evaluating past performance the fact that the contractor filed claims against the government in previous contracts. GAO in the past has discouraged this. The rationale GAO uses is that the government cannot penalize a contractor for exercising legitimate rights the contractor has under the contract. An open question, however, is whether an agency can hold against a company the filing of frivolous claims.

GAO does find it appropriate, in evaluating past performance, to consider a contractor's "combative" attitude. A combative attitude could interfere with contract administration and make it more difficult for both sides to get the job done on time and within budget.

GAO takes the position that, absent some evidence of abuse of the contract disputes process, contracting agencies should not lower a company's past performance evaluation based solely on its having filed claims; firms should not be prejudiced in competing for other contracts because of their reasonable pursuit of such remedies.

What is reasonable? One indicator of *reasonable* is the percentage of claims filed and won by the contractor. In one case, a company was reasonable in filing its claims because it had won all the claims filed and even the number filed—9 over 15 years—was not an unreasonable number. In this same case, there also was no evidence that the claims had an adverse impact on contract performance. For example, there was no evidence suggesting that the contractor had failed to perform the contract changes effectively, delayed contract performance, or failed to respond to or cooperate with the agency in performing the contract changes.

183. What are the rules on how an agency should evaluate a vendor's past performance in the solicitation process?

An agency's past performance evaluation can make the difference between a vendor winning or losing a contract. Therefore, how an agency evaluates past performance is important. Here are some rules:

1. *An agency must follow whatever rules it set out in the solicitation.* The solicitation can also establish who is responsible for getting completed questionnaires from references to the offeror or the agency. In one case, the government did not put that burden on the offerors and GAO found the agency's evaluation of past performance inadequate. But if the agency puts that burden on the offeror and the offeror's references do not contact the agency, the losing offeror cannot complain. *Family Entertainment Services, Inc.*, B-298047.3, September 20, 2006.

2. *If the solicitation does not prohibit an agency from using information it receives, the agency may properly use that information.* In another case, the agency's solicitation required offerors to identify contracts they had completed within the previous three years. A protester complained that an agency considered its past performance from a contract that was older than three years.

GAO found that to be irrelevant. The solicitation said the government could consider information concerning the offeror's past performance since it was not contained in the proposal. In addition, nothing in the proposal prohibited what the agency had done: "There is nothing in sections L or M, or elsewhere in the solicitation, that precluded the agency from evaluating relevant past performance information, whether or not it was listed in the proposal or concerned a contract completed within the past three years." *BST Systems, Inc.*, B-298761, December 1, 2006.

3. *An agency must treat all offerors equally.* GAO has criticized agencies for not treating all offerors equally. In one case, it said: "Although the contract specialist attempted to contact each of IMC's references by telephone, and was able to forward the agency's past performance questionnaire by e-mail to the Fort Campbell, West Point, and Fort Knox references, these references were instructed that they were to return the completed questionnaires in 1 to 2 days. The record provides no explanation as to why the contract specialist imposed these deadlines on IMC's references, nor does the record provide that the contract specialist made any attempt to contact any of IMC's references after June 1." An agency may impose such strict response deadlines but there must be a stated reason for doing so and it must be a good reason. *Family Entertainment Services, Inc.*, B-298047.3, September 20, 2006.

184. What if the evaluation information on past performance is wrong? Must the government give the offeror a chance to correct it?

Recent changes have let the government make past performance a critical evaluation factor. The more critical the factor, the more accurate the information should be. This importance of past performance information puts a premium on its accuracy. But sometimes the information that the CO uses to determine past performance is simply wrong. For example, a reference might tell the CO that the contractor was late and behind schedule on the reference's contract. But that wasn't true. Or maybe the references made an innocent mistake and based their past performance reference on the wrong company.

Can the contractor get GAO to correct that erroneous information? This is a real problem from a contractor's perspective. GAO will not independently review past performance information a CO uses to award a contract. All GAO looks for is whether the CO's decision was reasonable and consistent with the stated evaluation criteria and applicable statutes and regulations. GAO believes that determining the relative merit of a company's past performance information is primarily a matter within the contracting agency's discretion so it takes a generally hands-off approach.

This limited review highlights a related problem: the limited review of the references by the CO. A CO does not have to look beyond what is in front of him or her.

Having described what a CO has to do at a minimum, what more can the CO do? For one thing, a CO can try to verify the information given about the company's previous experience.

For its part, a company has to be more aggressive in this area. There is no law that says a contractor cannot give its references notification that a reference check will be made by another agency. A wise contractor will also give its references a copy of whatever information the agency has put into the solicitation regarding the references, such as a copy of any questionnaires or evaluation criteria that will be used in the past performance evaluation.

185. When can an agency properly refuse an offeror a chance to rebut adverse past performance information?

It all depends on where in the process the agency is: wanting to award on the basis of initial proposals without discussions, trying to decide on the competitive range, or having discussions with those in the competitive range.

If an agency will be using adverse past performance information against a company, the company wants to know about it and be given a chance to rebut it. And while this seems like simple fairness, the FAR does not demand that an agency always give the company an opportunity to rebut adverse past performance information.

The FAR has a "shall" and a "may." The *shall* is for adverse past performance information keeping a company from the competitive range. FAR 15.306 (b)(1)(i) requires an agency to tell a company about the adverse past performance information that a company hasn't had a chance to rebut if that information is keeping the company from the competitive range. The government must give the company a chance to rebut that information.

But that's not the rule when the agency wants to award on the basis of initial proposals. The FAR also has a *may*. FAR 15.306(a)(2) deals with award without discussions. It says that when an award will be made without conducting discussions, "offerors may be given the opportunity to clarify certain aspects of proposals (e.g., the relevance of an offeror's past performance information and adverse past performance information to which the company has not previously had an opportunity to respond) or to resolve minor or clerical errors." An agency has discretion to ask for rebuttal information.

When does a CO not need to ask for rebuttal? Simplistic as it sounds, the CO does not have to give a rebuttal opportunity if the agency has no clear reason to question the adverse past performance information or if the government uses a valid database containing information that the company has previously had the chance to rebut.

For example, in one case, the government had already given the company a chance to rebut the adverse past performance information when the information was going into the agency's past performance database. Refusing to give the company another chance in that case was fair.

What does a valid database look like? Here's an example of one that's valid.

The Corps of Engineers keeps a database on construction projects called the Construction Contractor Appraisal Support System (CCASS). In this process, a Corps contractor is evaluated by the contracting agency within 60 days of substantial completion. This evaluation is then reviewed by someone else, who must be familiar with the contractor's performance on the project and must be one level above the evaluator. A contractor must get a copy of the evaluation. If the evaluation is "unsatisfactory," the contractor gets a chance to address the report and respond to it, and the contractor's comments should be included in and addressed by the government in the final evaluation. A contractor that gets a final unsatisfactory report gets a chance to appeal that evaluation to someone above the CO. Similar opportunities to comment on interim performance evaluations are also available, although no appeal is allowed. Because companies have been given a chance to rebut information in the CCASS, another chance to rebut during the solicitation stage is not necessary.

Here's an example of a database that's not valid.

The Department of Education has about two million accounts, worth about $9 billion, of debts students owe the government. It hired companies to track down the former students and resolve the accounts by garnishment, litigation, or other administrative resolutions. In evaluating past performance on one procurement, the agency used its Competitive Performance and Continuous Surveillance (CPCS) evaluation process to assess how each company was doing. The CPCS evaluates a contractor's work every four months. Based on that evaluation, a contractor might get more work if it was performing well or less work if it was not. As described by GAO, "Under the CPCS methodology, the contractor ranked the highest under a particular performance indicator receives the maximum number of points available for that indicator, and the remaining contractors receive points in proportion to their standing relative to the leading contractor. Each contractor's overall CPCS score for each four-month period is the sum of its scores for all of the performance indicators for that period."

GAO criticized this system: "The CPCS methodology set forth in the current contracts envisioned not a cumulative evaluation over the life of the contract, but a series of discrete periodic evaluations of performance." GAO wanted "an examination of each of the CPCS periodic scores, and the underlying data [as] a component of the past performance evaluation." In addition, the CPCS system could be manipulated by the contractors. They could reduce the size of their workload by returning unresolved cases to the government for reassignment to other contractors during the same evaluation period. Thus, contractors could manipulate the size of their inventory to move up in the rankings.

186. Does an agency have to verify the past performance information submitted by references?

An agency does not have to verify the past performance information submitted by a company's references. When an agency evaluates past performance, it need not contact the references if the solicitation does not obligate the government to do so; nor does an agency have to investigate adverse past performance information. Clearly, the company has the obligation to make its case that it has performed well in the past—it cannot rely on the government to make its case for it.

The only exception would be if the contracting officer has a reason to question the validity of the past performance information. What would give a contracting officer "reason to question" the information? Here's one example. Many questionnaires have room for narrative comments and then a summary evaluation. If there are obvious inconsistencies between a reference's narrative comments ("average") and the actual ratings the reference gives the offeror ("great"), the contracting officer would have a clear reason to question the information.

187. How is the government supposed to rate someone new to the work?

When considering the qualifications of a new supplier, an agency must be careful to not hold lack of experience against the company in a best value award. Congress demanded that new suppliers' lack of experience be considered a neutral factor in evaluating past performance.

This is a nice idea, but it is proving difficult to work with. One way agencies can successfully do so is to explain why a new supplier lost a procurement and explain why the lack of past performance by that company was not a factor in the agency's decision.

Also, the use of a neutral rating approach to avoid penalizing a company without prior experience does not preclude a determination to award to a higher priced firm with a good past performance record over a lower priced company with a neutral past performance rating. Indeed, such a determination is inherent in the concept of best value. But, there must be documentation showing that the CO performed an analysis comparing the companies concerning best value.

188. In evaluating past performance, can an agency consider only the past performance of the corporate entity and not that of the key personnel?

Even though the FAR states that agencies should evaluate the past performance of key personnel, considering only the past performance of the corporate entity is allowed.

Typically in evaluating past performance, the government wants to know not only how well the company performed in the past, but also how each individual key person performed in the past. FAR 15.305(a)(2)(iii) even goes so far as to say that agencies *should* take into account relevant key personnel past performance information.

Sometimes, however, key personnel past performance is not relevant and need not be considered. For example, in one case, the Navy was concerned with the performance history "of the corporate entity, which the agency believes is indicative of the entity's future performance." Moreover, the

Navy acknowledged that it was contracting with the corporation and not with any key personnel (who might not stay for the duration of the contract).

189. Can a settlement agreement limit what an agency may say about a contractor's bad performance?

A settlement agreement can limit what an agency may say about a contractor's past performance—if it is clearly stated in a settlement agreement.

Because settlement agreements are narrowly construed, any agreement that parties reach about an agency's future recommendations on the contractor's past performance must be expressly stated in the settlement agreement. Not only are settlement agreements binding on the parties; they are very narrowly construed if a dispute over the settlement terms ever arises.

For example, in one case, a settlement agreement included language that stated that the parties "will deal with each other in good faith." Several years later, the company lost a procurement on the basis of its past performance and protested. It lost. More careful language would have yielded the company better results. For example, the agreement should have required the agency to disregard the protester's performance under the terminated contract. Also, the agreement should have said that the parties were considering future contracts when they were drafting the settlement agreement on that contract.

Chapter 14
Debriefings

After the government awards a contract, any of the losing companies can get a debriefing from the government. A debriefing is a meeting between the government and an individual "disappointed" offeror (as a losing company is politely referred to). Both sides discuss the company's proposal so that the company can improve future submissions to the government. The briefings are supposed to be learning experiences for the companies. To the extent that the government can help the companies understand what the government wants and allow the companies to say it better, a debriefing will be beneficial for both the government and the participating companies.

190. What information is usually provided at a debriefing?

Usually there is a subtle battle going on at a debriefing. COs are wary of disclosing proprietary or source selection information because it's against the law. On the opposite end of the spectrum are the companies, which want to know everything they possibly can—not only about their own losing proposal but also about the winner's proposal and the proposals of their competitors. Thus, the two sides are often coming from opposite ends of the information spectrum.

Unfortunately for companies, there is little chance that they can get all the information they think they are entitled to. The cheapest remedy for agency abuse of the solicitation process is GAO. But GAO takes the position that the contents of the debriefing are beyond its jurisdiction. The only other alternative is the courts, a process far too costly to invoke simply to get additional information.

In addition, companies do not want to be put in the awkward business position of suing potential customers to get information. In some instances, the request for information under the Freedom of Information Act may help the company get the government paperwork from the solicitation process. But that's about all.

The government has to give companies more information about the winning company since the winning contract is a public document. The real disagreements that arise at debriefings stem from the company's interest in its competitors' proposals and the government's extreme reluctance to share any information on a company's competitors.

191. What form does a debriefing take?

The debriefing can take any form. It can be an in-person meeting. It can be done by telephone or by videoconference. Or it can be done in writing. FAR 15.505(c) also allows a debriefing "by any other method acceptable to the contracting officer (CO)." So there is flexibility in the debriefing process.

192. When do debriefings occur?

The debriefings can occur at one of two points in the solicitation process. There is a preaward debriefing and a postaward debriefing.

If the company is thrown out of the competition prior to award, it is entitled to a preaward debriefing. *Entitled* is a key term. Companies are only *entitled* to a pre-award debriefing;

they are not *guaranteed* a preaward debriefing. The government has the discretion to decide when a preaward debriefing will be held: preaward or postaward. If the preaward debriefing is put off until after the award is made, the CO must document why the debriefing has been delayed.

Who wants a preaward debriefing? Possibly, companies that are excluded from the competitive range, companies that are initially in the competitive range but are later excluded from the competitive range, companies excluded from the competitive range after a final proposal revision and prior to a second final proposal revision, or simply a company that is in the running all the way to the end of the competition and loses.

193. How does a company get a debriefing?

Timing is critical. To get any kind of debriefing, preaward or postaward, a company excluded from a competition prior to award must request a debriefing within three days after receiving notice that it was excluded from the competition. Any company that misses this three-day deadline is not guaranteed a debriefing. The government, of course, may decide, as a business relations gesture, to provide a debriefing even if the deadline is past.

Contractors should not use the phone. A request for a preaward debriefing requires written notice to the government.

The government can grant either a preaward or postaward debriefing to companies that meet the three-day deadline.

One advantage to a company getting a preaward debriefing after the award has been made is that the government has to provide more information to the company in a postaward debriefing than in a preaward debriefing. Let's look at what information that has to be given out in a preaward debriefing.

Preaward debriefings have to disclose:

1. "the agency's evaluation of significant elements of the offeror's proposal"

2. "a summary of the rationale for eliminating the offeror from the competition"

3. "reasonable responses to relevant questions about whether source selection procedures contained in the solicitation, applicable regulations, and other applicable authorities were followed in the process of eliminating the offeror from the competition."

What has to be disclosed at a preaward debriefing makes better sense if some background is provided. In 1997, the debriefing took on a function other than simply disseminating information—it took on the role of discouraging protests. Over the years, it had become clear that losing companies would file protests to get additional information about their proposals. It was only through the protest process that this additional information could be obtained. But once the protest process provided the information, companies often realized that they would lose not only the protest but the contract as well. And they realized this only after the companies had spent time and effort on the protest and the government had also spent time and effort defending the protest.

Congress realized that if protesters used the protest process to get information, it would be better to give them that information at a debriefing to avoid a "data gathering" protest that the company would ultimately lose anyway.

Congress also wanted to improve the debriefing process while discouraging protests. Accordingly, during the mid '90s, Congress became much more specific about the information the government had to release during a debriefing. The FAR debriefing regulations show the broad range of information that the government has to disclose.

194. Should a lawyer come to a debriefing?

Obviously, whether a company brings a lawyer to the debriefing is a business judgment based on the specific facts and circumstances of the particular situation.

One disadvantage of bringing a lawyer to the debriefing is that it will be perceived as raising the stakes of the debriefing. Having a lawyer at the debriefing might suggest to the government that the company is planning to file a protest. This in turn could make the CO extra cautious about what he or she says at the debriefing. In addition, the government might then want to have its lawyer present at the debriefing.

Along the same lines, taking a tape recorder or a court reporter to the debriefing sends a very specific—and probably the wrong—message to the CO. Whether a particular company believes it is a good business judgment to raise the stakes in this way is a decision that only the company can make.

195. What information does the government have to disclose at a postaward debriefing?

The FAR tells a CO what must and must not be disclosed at a debriefing.

First, let's look at what must be disclosed.

The CO must follow FAR 15.306(d). The very first words in that paragraph are the most critical from the contractor's perspective. That paragraph starts out with "At a minimum, the debriefing information shall include. . . ." Two points must be made about this short but important phrase. First it describes what the government has to disclose because the phrase uses the word shall. There is no discretion about disclosing the listed items at a debriefing. The language is mandatory. The government must give out the information listed in that paragraph, which includes the following:

- Whether the CO broke the law in the procurement process

- The company's rankings

- The company's rating

- Why the company lost (its weaknesses and deficiencies)

- The rationale for award of the contract.

But that's not all the phrase says. It also says that the government shall disclose this information "at a minimum." In other words, what's listed in the paragraph is simply the starting point of the information that has to be given out. But as mentioned, at the debriefing tug-of-war between the CO and the losing vendor, the CO often minimizes the information given out and the losing vendor often tries to maximize the information given out.

So as we talk about the specific information that must be given out, it's important to keep in mind the Congressional intent found in this opening phrase: "at a minimum, the debriefing information shall include. . . ."

196. What information cannot be disclosed at a debriefing?

What cannot be disclosed at a debriefing is also described by the FAR, first in general terms and then in specific terms.

In general, the FAR says that a debriefing "shall not include point by point comparisons of the debriefing offeror's proposal with those of the other offerors." From the company's perspective, the important phrase is "point by point." Clearly, any comparison that makes a detailed analysis of a competitor's proposal in comparison with the winning company's proposal and the proposals of the other losing competitors is improper.

But only point by point comparisons are prohibited. A general comparison is not. And because the general comparison is not prohibited, reading the language of the FAR, which says "at a minimum," companies should be able to get some, although not detailed, comparison information at a debriefing.

197. Does the government really have to admit at a debriefing that it made a mistake?

The self-incriminatory language in FAR 15.506 (d)(6) seems hard to believe. It tells a CO that he or she must include at the debriefing "reasonable responses to relevant questions about whether source selection procedures contained in the solicitation, applicable regulations, and other applicable authorities were followed." The language seems to require a CO to disclose at a debriefing that he or she broke the law— that, for example, in conducting the discussions, he or she did not follow a particular regulation or broke the law dealing with meaningful discussions.

Would anybody in their right mind want to tell a losing company that the company lost because somebody in the government broke the law? As difficult as this language is to believe, and as tough as this language is to apply fairly, this language nevertheless requires the CO to disclose every law violation resulting from a solicitation.

There's very good logic behind this bewildering requirement. The logic is that violations of law often come to light during a protest. Despite this, however, the company does not win a protest automatically on the basis that there was a violation of the law. This clause is designed to require the government to disclose at an early stage of the process, before a protest has been filed, that the law has been broken. The government can follow up the disclosure with information showing that the company still would have lost the procurement, even if the law had been followed to the letter. If the government is going to win a protest down the road even though it broke the law, it makes sense to try to avoid a protest over the law violation by disclosing the violation at the beginning of the process.

198. The government has to tell losing companies their rankings and ratings. What are rankings and ratings? What is the difference?

One of the most helpful pieces of information that companies can pick up in a debriefing is their rating and their ranking.

The *rating* is the point score difference between the losing company and winner. Typically, the government will evaluate the technical and cost proposals on the basis of 100 points. For example, a company will get a score of 90 on the technical proposal and 85 on its cost proposal. What this debriefing requirement demands of the government is that it disclose the score of the winner and the score of the loser.

The rating discloses two very helpful pieces of information: (1) how far behind the winner the losing company actually was and (2) how many points the losing company would have to make up as a result of a protest to win the contract.

The *ranking* is simply the order of finish. In other words, the winner obviously came in first. Where did the debriefed company come in and where did the other companies come in? This is a controversial issue. The FAR language says that the government must disclose "the overall ranking of all offerors."

From the company's perspective, the FAR promises companies that the government "shall" disclose rankings to "offerors." Use of the word "offerors" suggests that the government give the identity of each offeror and its ranking. But the government often uses abbreviations or some other identifier that does not disclose the specific identity of a company. To companies, it seems that the government is not following the letter of the law. For example, if the government says that the winner (obviously) came in first, and the debriefed company came in fourth, the government may say that "Company A" came in second, "Company B" came in third, and "Company C" came in fifth, while not identifying who Company A is. The problem with this approach is that there is no offer sheet with the signature "Company A" on it.

However, the government usually argues that "the government's job is not to provide commercial intelligence to losing companies." So demanding the specific identity of competitors is probably a lost cause for companies. As mentioned, there is no effective way to challenge the government's incorrect interpretation of this provision.

CHAPTER 15
Protests

Not to put it too delicately, a protest is a fight by a loser to get the contract it lost. The protest rules are very precise and must be rigidly observed. In this chapter, we discuss where protests can be filed, the advantages of the various forums, and ways to avoid a costly, time-consuming protest.

199. What are the chances of a company winning a protest?

The chances that a protesting company may win are surprisingly high. And the best results are not found at GAO. In fact, a very small percentage of protests resolved by GAO end up in a favorable decision for a contractor. The best results come from working directly with an agency. To understand why this is true, let's take a look at the overall protest process.

There are three places a protester can go: the agency (the contracting officer or someone higher up in the agency), GAO, or the U.S. Court of Federal Claims.

If the protest will be filed at the Court of Federal Claims, the submission will be very complicated and technical. It will be filed by a lawyer following the rules of the court. Protests to the court are rare, and therefore this chapter will not discuss them in detail.

Most protests are filed at the contracting agency or at GAO.

Agency Protest

A protest to the agency simply involves writing a letter to either the CO or someone higher than the CO as provided in agency regulations. The company gets a response from the person the protest was addressed to—either the CO or someone higher than the CO. The agency's response to the protest ends a protest to the agency.

A protest to the agency is often the first step a company takes. While most companies believe there's no harm in seeing if the agency will reverse its decision, a protest to the agency has many limitations. And, unless the time limits are strictly observed, a protest to the agency could cause a follow-up protest to GAO to be late and therefore not considered.

GAO Protest

Protesting to GAO is more complicated. Obviously, the first step in the protest process is filing the protest. A protest to GAO, like a protest to the agency, can simply be a letter explaining why the losing company thinks it did not get a fair chance to win the solicitation. There need be nothing fancy about the protest letter. It simply has to identify what the company thinks went wrong with the solicitation and ask that the wrong be corrected. The company may also request specific documents.

A protest to GAO is only slightly more complicated than a protest to the agency. It's more complicated only because GAO requires that a number of specific magic words and phrases be included in the protest. To its credit, GAO puts out a booklet, available at its website (www.gao.gov), describing in plain English what a protest to GAO must look like. As a result, it's easy for the average businessperson to file a protest to GAO without a lawyer being involved.

The second step in the GAO protest process is the agency report. This is the agency's answer to the company's protest letter. It often includes documents as well as a statement by the CO and a memorandum of law from the agency's lawyers.

The third step in a GAO protest is protester comments on the agency report. This is a rebuttal by the protester to the agency's position. On occasion it serves another purpose. It can be used to raise new protest issues discovered only from the protester's review of the agency documents in the agency report.

200. What is the best approach for a company to take?

For a company, the best approach may well be to go to GAO and try to convince it that the company is correct. A side benefit is that this process also allows access to the agency's lawyers. During the GAO protest process, a protester might convince the agency's lawyers that the company did not get a fair deal. So the GAO process also provides an opportunity to convince the agency's lawyers that the agency did not treat the company fairly.

201. What are the advantages and disadvantages of filing a protest to the agency?

The big advantage is that it's easy. A protest to the agency is simply a letter complaining about the treatment the company received during the solicitation process. And, because it's easy, it's cheap. Companies don't necessarily need a lawyer to file a protest before the agency.

One of the big disadvantages, however, of filing a protest to the agency is the lack of any discovery. In other words, the losing company has no ability to rummage through the CO's file to see if any (other) mistakes were made by the government during the solicitation process. GAO offers a better discovery alternative.

Another real disadvantage of going to the agency, or more specifically, to the CO, is that the protester is going back to the individual who denied it the contract in the first place. It seems unlikely that the CO, who refused to award the losing company the contract in the first place, is going to have any second thoughts about it later on.

A better approach might be going to the CO's superior—an option the agencies offer. This alternative certainly has less CO "pride of authorship" or involvement in the solicitation.

202. What are the advantages of filing a protest at GAO?

Better data are available through GAO's discovery process. That's the good news. The bad news is that only a lawyer can get much of this information. And the lawyer must not be on the company's staff. The lawyer also must have no employment connection to, or business interest in, the losing company. So the only lawyers who can get this information are lawyers retained by this company.

The discovery process is limited primarily through what is called a "protective order." The order gets its name from the fact that the government must release data to the company but the lawyer is ordered to protect any proprietary or source selection information from disclosure to the client. A lawyer under a protective order must not tell the client any proprietary or source selection information that the lawyer discovers through the process.

As a practical matter, the government prepares two sets of documents. One set of documents is for lawyers under a protective order. This set includes all sorts of raw data, such as the evaluations given the government by references from prior projects (with the names of the references disclosed) and the source selection plan the agency used (describing how a source selection panel evaluated proposals).

The second set of documents will be for the client. This set includes all the documents given the lawyer under the protective order but with any proprietary or source selection information whited out.

Any protest, whether to the agency or to GAO, means a lot of work for the CO. And the work must be completed in a very short time, under the scrutiny of the CO's supervisors and the agency's lawyers.

A protest to GAO, however, is much more detailed and involved. Because protesters to GAO demand documents used in the solicitation process, it's the CO's job to collect the documents, copy the documents, index the documents, and ship them off to the agency lawyer. If the protest involves facts that are contested, the CO may have to testify in any fact-finding session presided over by GAO. Although these sessions are not formal trials, the CO will feel the pressure of the sessions as if it were a trial. In addition, such sessions require the CO to prepare to testify.

GAO sessions are generally informal, although lawyers are often involved on both sides. Each side presents evidence and cross examines the other side's witnesses.

203. What can a contracting officer do to avoid a protest?

A CO can avoid a potential protest by providing the company a fair and exhaustive debriefing. If a company can walk away from a debriefing feeling that it was treated fairly during the solicitation process and simply lost the contract to a better proposal, the chances of the company filing a protest are reduced. On the other hand, to the extent that a company walks away from a debriefing feeling that the government was hiding something, the company may believe that a protest will be able to uncover additional information that could support the company's (usually unfounded) belief that the government was hiding something.

Clearly, a CO cannot disclose proprietary or source selection information to a company at a debriefing. The CO should closely follow the FAR's description of the "minimum" information he or she should disclose; however, this still allows the CO to disclose a wide range of information. Doing so should help a CO minimize the risks of receiving a protest.

204. What are the disadvantages to a company protesting?

Suing customers is not smart business practice. Companies believe that filing protests will get them black-balled by the agency and a protest will mean that they will receive no future contracts from that agency. While that may be true in isolated instances, generally COs try to be fair in evaluating and awarding contracts. So while a company may think it is bad business to file a protest, as a practical matter it may not be. COs want good performers. Successful contractors will receive contracts, whether they file protests or not.

205. Is it smart for a company to argue that the contracting officer showed bad faith?

Arguing bad faith is a sure loser at GAO. GAO defines bad faith out of existence. To GAO, bad faith is the specific and malicious intent to injure the protester. COs may dislike a particular company, but none has a specific and malicious intent to injure it. Over the years, protesters arguing bad faith on the part of the government have consistently lost the argument and the protest.

206. What's the worst thing a contracting officer can do after getting a GAO protest that seems to have merit?

Dawdle, stall, delay. It may cost the government money. Here's why. A protest that has merit can be remedied in several ways. The typical remedy is to put the protester back into the solicitation process and give the protester another chance to win the contract. A protester typically will not receive bid protest costs and attorneys' fees if it gets another chance to win the contract.

Congress, however, anticipated that an agency, either out of negligence or out of malice, could decide to not let a company know the agency was going to let the company back into the solicitation process until the end of the process. The agency could drag out the protest process, intentionally or inadvertently, and cost the protester money with the only remedy being put back into the competitive range.

To discourage agencies from stalling or simply not seriously considering all of the protester's arguments until the very end of the protest process, GAO may provide a successful protester with a double remedy: being put back into solicitation process and providing bid protest costs and attorneys' fees. This double hit was designed to spur agencies to seriously consider protests from the very beginning.

GAO may award attorneys' fees as well as allow a protester back into the solicitation process when an agency unduly delays resolving a "clearly meritorious" protest. This double hit applies only if a protest was clearly meritorious. Often, a government agency will raise a good argument or the legal or factual issues involved are close questions. In these instances, agency delay is really extended consideration of a protest's merits and will not cost the government bid protest costs and attorneys' fees. The government has the right to give due deliberation to protests raising difficult issues.

207. What is an automatic stay?

An automatic stay is an injunction that stops the government from any further work on the contract. It's designed to ensure that if the protester wins, there's something left of the contract to actually win.

Up until 1984, it was possible for a protester to win a protest, but only after the contract had been finished. Obviously, in those cases, there was nothing left for the protester to win. To make sure that there was something left to win, Congress in 1984 instituted an stay. The automatic stay was designed to automatically stop any work on the contract or, even before that, the award of any contract, if a protest was filed before the contract was awarded or within ten days after award of the contract had been made.

While the stay may be automatic, holding up the work is not. Congress made it easy not only for the contractor to invoke the automatic stay, but also for the government to override the automatic stay. Congress provided that an automatic stay could be overridden if the government could establish one of two huge loopholes: (1) continued performance was in the government's best interest, or (2) there were urgent and compelling circumstances for continued performance of the contract.

One of the best examples of when the automatic stay can be easily overridden is at the start of a new fiscal year. If the building security contract is to take effect October 1, but a protest has been filed and the automatic stay has been imposed, the building still needs security. In that instance, it would be easy for the government to establish that "urgent and compelling circumstances" require continued performance of the contract while the protest proceeds.

CHAPTER 16

Inspection, Acceptance, and Warranties

Getting what the government pays for is the purpose of a contract. And the way to know whether the government gets what it pays for is to use the inspection clause. To provide a "plain English" understanding of the inspection clause, this chapter explores the inspection of construction clause (FAR 52.246-12), which tends to be typical of other inspection clauses.

208. In plain English, what does the inspection clause say?

First, the definition of what's covered by the clause is very broad. The government gets the right to inspect not only the final product but also anything along the way and, in fact, even before the work starts. The clause covers the manufacture and fabrication of any of the components that go into the final product:

> (a) Definition. Work includes, but is not limited to, materials, workmanship, and manufacture and fabrication of components.

Notice that the definition does not simply cover what's listed in the clause. The definition simply says that the work "includes" what's specified. According to this definition, a lot more can be covered by the inspection clause.

There is an affirmative obligation on the contractor's part to make sure that the work complies with the contract.

It's not only up to the government to make sure the work complies—the contractor has that obligation too. And the way the contractor ensures that the work complies with the contract is by having an inspection system that verifies that what goes into the project meets the contract's requirements:

> (b) The Contractor shall maintain an adequate inspection system and perform such inspections as will ensure that the work performed under the contract conforms to contract requirements.

A surprise government inspection is clearly allowed. All the work done under the contract can be inspected at any time and place, and the government can use any reasonable test to determine whether the work satisfies the contract requirements. The government is entitled to strict compliance with the specifications:

> [The work] is subject to Government inspection and test at all places and at all reasonable times before acceptance to ensure strict compliance with the terms of the contract.

The government has no duty to inspect the work and alert the contractor to inadequate work. Inspections are for the government's benefit, not the contractor's benefit. When noncompliant work is discovered, the contractor can't complain that the government had the right to inspect work earlier in the process and if the government had done so, the work would have been found to be noncompliant much earlier in the construction process:

> (c) Government inspections and tests are for the sole benefit of the Government and do not—
>
> (1) Relieve the Contractor of responsibility for providing adequate quality control measures;

(2) Relieve the Contractor of responsibility for damage to or loss of the material before acceptance;

Whether a government inspector is on the job or not, and whether the government inspector tells the contractor to do something different from what the contract requires, the inspector's work, or lack thereof, has no bearing on the contractor's ultimate duty to do work that complies with the contract:

(d) The presence or absence of a Government inspector does not relieve the Contractor from any contract requirement, nor is the inspector authorized to change any term or condition of the specification without the Contracting Officer's written authorization.

Inspections and tests are paid for by the contractor. Government contracting assumes that the costs of inspections and tests are included in the contractor's prices. And if the inspection does not go off at the time arranged, the contractor is responsible for any additional costs that the government incurs because the tests are rescheduled:

(e) The Contractor shall promptly furnish, at no increase in contract price, all facilities, labor, and material reasonably needed for performing such safe and convenient inspections and tests as may be required by the Contracting Officer. The Government may charge to the Contractor any additional cost of inspection or test when work is not ready at the time specified by the Contractor for inspection or test, or when prior rejection makes reinspection or retest necessary.

The government must fix what doesn't comply with the contract. The only alternative is that the government could take a price reduction if it wants to accept something less than full compliance with the contract:

(f) The Contractor shall, without charge, replace or correct work found by the Government not to conform to contract requirements, unless in the public interest the Government consents to accept the work with an appropriate adjustment in contract price. . . .

If the contractor doesn't fix it, the contractor pays for the fix made by someone else. Or the government could simply terminate for default the contractor's right to proceed:

> (g) If the Contractor does not promptly replace or correct rejected work, the Government may (1) by contract or otherwise, replace or correct the work and charge the cost to the Contractor or (2) terminate for default the Contractor's right to proceed.

Who pays for interim inspections depends on whether the work after inspection is found to be done correctly. If it's been done correctly, any damage the contractor suffers by a disruptive interim inspection gets paid for by the government. And if the contractor has lost time, it gets additional days added to the contract performance period. But it's the other way around if the interim inspection shows that the work was not done properly. In that case, the contractor pays for the inspection and any necessary rework:

> (h) If, before acceptance of the entire work, the Government decides to examine already completed work by removing it or tearing it out, the Contractor, on request, shall promptly furnish all necessary facilities, labor, and material. If the work is found to be defective or nonconforming in any material respect due to the fault of the Contractor or its subcontractors, the Contractor shall defray the expenses of the examination and of satisfactory reconstruction. However, if the work is found to meet contract requirements, the Contracting Officer shall make an equitable adjustment for the additional services involved in the examination and reconstruction, including, if completion of the work was thereby delayed, an extension of time.

The timing of the government inspection can't be delayed. If a project can be finished in pieces, the government is supposed to inspect and accept individual pieces as soon as possible. Once something has been accepted, that's it. It's final. The only exceptions to this "finality of acceptance" are if there are latent defects, fraud, gross mistakes amounting to fraud, or warranty rights:

> (i) Unless otherwise specified in the contract, the Government shall accept, as promptly as practicable after completion and inspection, all work required by the contract or that portion of the work the Contracting Officer determines can be accepted separately. Acceptance shall be final and conclusive except for latent defects, fraud, gross mistakes amounting to fraud, or the Government's rights under any warranty or guarantee.

Having looked at the clause in detail, let's look at some common questions that arise during the inspection process.

209. The government had a chance to inspect the work, but didn't. Now it's time for the final inspection and the government finds something wrong with the work. Since the government had a chance to inspect the work that was being done but didn't do so, can the government now complain that the work was not done correctly?

The government always has the right to inspect, and reject, the work at any time before acceptance. The inspection clause says that the government inspection is solely for the benefit of the government. It is not for the benefit of the contractor. The government has no duty to inspect the work while it is going on.

There are, however, benefits to the government inspecting as the work proceeds, rather than waiting until after all the work is done. The first benefit is that the government will have a chance early in contract performance to see if the work is being done properly. If it is not, the government has the right to terminate the contract for default. When the government waits until the end to inspect, and then finds the work improper and wants to default the contractor, the government may have lost significant rights.

Second, if there is a delivery date specified in the contract but the government does not inspect until after that date, the contractor has a good argument that the government waived the original contract completion date.

Third, a government inspection as the work proceeds gives the contractor a good idea of what the government will ultimately demand at the end of the contract. Periodic interim inspections indicate the government standards that will be applied at the end of the project. Periodic interim inspections, therefore, can avoid extensive punch list work at the end of the project. These inspections alert contractors to what the government will demand and allow a contractor to meet the government standards as it goes along.

210. What are the differences in the concepts of strict compliance, substantial compliance, and substantial performance?

Strict compliance means that the government always has the right to demand that the contractor fully comply with a specification. It is not the contractor's job to decide that "close enough is good enough for government work." For example, a contractor wanted to use a slightly different shade of an undercoat of paint, having no effect on the top coat. The court ruled that the government had the right to demand whatever color of undercoat it wants to use, even though it had little or no impact on the top coat.

This is strict compliance with a vengeance. But it is justifiable. Any other rule would allow contractors to run the government procurement system. It would also lead to the waste of government money.

Sometimes, however, close enough gives a contractor some rights. In supply contracts, *substantial compliance* gives a contractor a second chance to get it right and avoid a default. If the contractor doesn't get it right the second time, it's in default.

Under substantial compliance, the contractor that delivers, on time, goods that are close, but not quite up to what the government wants, gets a second chance to deliver conforming supplies.

There are other requirements. The company must reasonably believe that the goods comply with the contract. The defects must be minor and easy to correct.

A company that complies with all this gets a reasonable period of time to present supplies that fully comply with the contract. If the company does not do so, the contract can be terminated for default. Again, ultimately, the company is held to strict compliance.

A construction company is also ultimately held to strict compliance. If a construction company wants to get paid 100 percent of the contract price, it must strictly comply with a contract. But the "substantial compliance" exception also applies in construction. This allows a contractor to get paid for the value of what's been installed, even though it doesn't fully comply with the contract. Substantial compliance avoids the injustice of having the construction company build a building, typically on government land, and then be paid absolutely nothing because the company, for example, used plastic pipes instead of copper pipes. The contractor is entitled to get paid the value of what was completed because the pipes, whether plastic or copper, will do the job they are intended to do.

This is especially true where the cure is worse than the disease. For example, if the construction company installs between the bricks of a dam a water stop that will do the job but is not 100 percent what the contract called for, it might well cost millions of dollars to pull out the nonconforming water stop and replace it with a water stop that fully complies with the specifications. The water stop may cost only thousands of dollars to install. It would be wasteful to spend millions to correct what cost thousands—an example of "economic waste." Where correction of the defect in construction would lead to economic waste, the government's remedy is a reduction in the price paid to the contractor. The government does not have the right to require replacement and strict compliance.

What if the issue is not just a price reduction because everything isn't 100 percent per the specification? What if the issue is whether the government can terminate a constuction contract after the building is finished simply for minor deviations from the specification? At this point, two phrases, closely related to each other and to the phrases "strict compliance" and "substantial compliance," come into play. *Substantial performance* or *substantial completion* is used in construction contracting when the possibility of a default is being considered. Substantial performance or substantial completion prevents the government from terminating a construction contract for default when the deviations from the specification are minor.

211. The government approved something with defects it knew about. Now the government rejects it. Can it do that?

As usual, it all depends. It depends on whether it seems fair to hold the government to its original acceptance of the product. This is called *estoppel*. Estoppel means that the government can't do something after the company has justifiably relied on what the government did. To prove estoppel, however, requires a very specific set of circumstances. The action must involve someone with *actual authority* to waive the requirements, like the CO. The person with authority must have *actual or imputed knowledge* that the product does not conform to the specifications. And even though the work did not conform to the contract specifications, the government accepted the work to get the contractor *to continue to work*. And the contractor, *relying* on this, actually did continue to work and would be harmed if not paid for the work. Under these circumstances, who wouldn't think it fair to pay the contractor?

212. The government used it. It bought it, right?

Not necessarily, especially if it's a construction project. In a construction project, there's a special clause: "use and possession prior to completion." That clause clearly states that "the government's possession or use shall not be deemed an acceptance of any work under the contract."

And another sentence, one from the "permits and responsibilities" clause (FAR 52.236-7), says that the contractor "shall also be responsible for all materials delivered and work performed until completion and acceptance of the entire work, except for any completed unit of work, which may have been accepted under the contract." As a result of all this, the government is liable only if its use or possession causes damage. If the damage is caused by a third party or by acts of nature, the contractor is still responsible until acceptance. Use by the government therefore doesn't mean that the government accepts it. All it means is that the government will pay for any damage it causes.

213. If work that has been accepted breaks, the government can call in the warranty. Under a warranty, who has to prove what? Does the contractor have to prove that it did it right or does the government have to prove that the contractor did it wrong?

The government has to prove that the contractor did it wrong and that the defect existed at the time it was accepted. This can be tough to do. This is based on the idea that warranties are to be strictly construed against the government. For the government to win on a warranty issue, it must show that the contractor was given timely notice of the defect, the affected work was the contractor's responsibility, and the government did not cause or contribute to the failure.

This last point can be difficult, so there has been a little relaxation of what the government has to prove. All the government now has to prove is that the contractor was "the most likely or probable clause of the failure." The government doesn't have to prove that the contractor unequivocally caused the defect.

214. Is the contractor off the hook when the warranty period ends?

The contractor isn't necessarily off the hook when the warranty expires. The contract clauses typically say that any remedies under the warranty clause are in addition to those given under the inspection clause. And the inspection clause excludes from "the finality of acceptance" any defects that are latent or that result from fraud or gross mistakes amounting to fraud. As a result, the contractor stays on the hook for latent defects, fraud, and gross mistakes amounting to fraud. The theory behind this is that the government has to use reasonable but not extreme diligence in its inspection process.

It's valuable to examine more closely each of the exceptions. *Latent defects* are defects that are not obvious and cannot be found through a reasonable inspection. They are hidden defects. Opposed to latent defects are patent defects. *Patent defects* are those that are obvious or known. The government has an obligation to identify patent defects that exist at the time of acceptance, but that's all. Latent defects are still a contractor's responsibility. Of course, if something would be a latent defect but the government knows about it when the government accepts it, the defect becomes a patent defect.

Fraud is a knowing misrepresentation or hiding of something with the intent to mislead the government. The inspection clause, however, is rarely used in fraud situations because the government has much bigger guns: the False Claims Act and the False Statements Act. The False Claims Act gives the government civil and criminal remedies, and the False Statements Act gives the government criminal remedies.

Gross mistake amounting to fraud is all of the above without the intent to deceive. It's a major mistake that no responsible contractor could justify. For example, a contractor decided to submit to the government bolts that were not heat-treated (the industry routinely uses heat-treated bolts). This would be a gross mistake amounting to fraud.

CHAPTER 17
Closeouts

The closeout of a contract is a critical point in the contracting process. From a legal standpoint, once final payment has been made and the contract has been closed out, no additional claims can be made under the contract. From an administrative standpoint, the contract is over.

215. How soon after the contract is over should the contracting officer close out a contract?

A CO generally closes out a contract six months after completion. The specific time periods are addressed in the FAR. The FAR also deals with when each specific time period begins—something called "physical completion."

Time Periods

The time periods for fixed-price contracts and simplified acquisitions are addressed in FAR 4.804-1. Except for contracts that are being litigated or terminated, the general rules are: Files for contracts using *simplified acquisition procedures* should be considered closed when the contracting officer receives evidence of receipt of property and final payment, unless otherwise specified by agency regulations. Files for *firm-fixed-price contracts, other than those using simplified acquisition procedures*, should be closed within six months after the date on which the CO receives evidence of physical completion.

The FAR also gives detailed descriptions of when a contract is physically completed:

...a contract is considered to be physically completed when

(1) (i) The contractor has completed the required deliveries and the Government has inspected and accepted the supplies;

(ii) The contractor has performed all services and the Government has accepted these services; and

(iii) All option provisions, if any, have expired; or

(2) The Government has given the contractor a notice of complete contract termination.

The end product of a contract closeout is a contract completion statement with basic information such as the contract administration office name and address, contracting office name and address, name and signature of the CO, contract number, last modification number, contractor name and address, and voucher number and date, if final payment has been made. Another important part of the contract completion statement is a statement that all required contract administration actions have been fully and satisfactorily accomplished.

The last step in the process is putting the statement in the contract file.

216. How long must the files be kept?

For most construction contracts, it's six years and three months after final payment. It's the same for all other types of contracts over the simplified acquisition threshold (currently $100,000). Below that threshold, it's three years after final payment.

217. Is there some way the government can take money from a contractor to pay a debt the contractor owes?

The government can take money away from a contractor to pay debts owed by the contractor. There are numerous ways contractors can owe the government money: damages or excess costs related to defaults in performance; breach of contract obligations concerning progress payments, advance payments, or government-furnished property or material; government expense of correcting defects; overpayments related to errors in quantity or billing; or deficiencies in quality.These debts are referred to as "contract debts." Specific FAR provisions deal with contract debts.

Why use the phrase "contract debts"? Because it's important to distinguish contract debts from other debts someone might owe the government. For example, someone might owe the government for an educational loan or for tax liens. The FAR provisions discussed here don't deal with these types of noncontract debts. They deal only with debts the contractor as a contractor owes the government.

The point person for contract debts is the CO. For most kinds of contract debts, the CO has the primary responsibility for determining the amounts of, and then collecting, contract debt.

The CO must quickly go after contract debts. The FAR urges the CO to collect contract debts quickly because delay hurts: funds unavailable for the work for which they were initially provided, increased difficulty in collecting the debt, and actual monetary loss to the government.

In determining the amount of any contract debt, the CO "shall fairly consider both the Government's claim and any contract claims by the contractor against the Government. This determination does not constitute a settlement of such claims, nor is it a contracting officer's final determination under the Contract Disputes Act of 1978." FAR 32.606(b).

If the contractor does not sign a deferment agreement or go into bankruptcy, the contractor must pay the debt in a lump sum cash payment on demand or as a credit against existing unpaid bills due the contractor.

While a CO should try to negotiate contract debts bilaterally, a CO can unilaterally determine that a debt is owed if a contractor is delinquent in any of the following: furnishing pertinent information, negotiating expeditiously, entering into an agreement on a fair and reasonable price revision, signing an interim memorandum evidencing a negotiated pricing agreement involving a refund, or executing an appropriate contract modification reflecting the result of negotiations.

These unilateral debt determinations must be done with the disputes clause as a government claim. The decision must include a demand for payment. Significantly, no demand for payment can be issued prior to a CO's final decision.

The demand itself must notify the contractor that any amounts not paid within 30 days from the date of the demand will bear interest from the date of the demand, or from any earlier date specified in the contract. The interest rate is the rate the government itself pays on contractor claims.

Also, the demand must tell the contractor that the contractor can submit a proposal for deferment of collection if immediate payment is not practicable or if the amount is disputed.

The FAR allows the CO to show some mercy. It allows the CO to consider whether deferring the debt collection is advisable to avoid possible disputes over collection.

Deferments pending disposition of an appeal may also be granted to small business concerns and financially weak contractors, with a reasonable balance of the need for government security against loss and undue hardship on the contractor. Installment payments, the mainstay of the modern economy, are allowed.

Claims under the disputes clause won't suspend or delay collection. Until the action is decided, deferments will only be granted if, within 30 days after the filing of such action, the contractor gives the CO a bond, or other collateral, in the amount of the claim.

Smaller debts give the CO more options. For debts under $100,000, excluding interest, if further collection is not practicable or would cost more than the amount of recovery, the agency may compromise the debt or terminate or suspend further collection action.

218. When a contractor signs a release for a modification, does that prevent the contractor from getting additional costs at the end of the contract?

It depends on the wording of the release. If the modification's release did not exclude impact costs, the doors to the U.S. Treasury remain open. A release that excludes impact costs allows a contractor to recover at the end of contract performance additional costs unknown at the time a modification was agreed to.

When the parties to a contract sign a modification for changed work, they usually also sign a release or accord and satisfaction. Typically, a release says that the money and/ or time provided with the modification is all the contractor will get for the modification. This procedure is designed to eliminate any future fights over additional costs or time for the modification. But, if a contractor inserts into a release specific language that allows recovery in the future for "impact" costs associated with the change, the accord and satisfaction that went with the modification will not have settled everything.

For example, a contractor put the following language in releases that went along with a modification: "modification covers all direct and indirect costs, but the contractor expressly reserves the right to seek additional time and compensation at a later date for impact or suspension work." When the contract was over, the contractor filed a claim for impact costs for a subcontractor. A board concluded that costs that the contractor could know and quantify at the time the modification was signed were included in the modification's release. Significant was the fact that the modifications were signed well after the work was completed, leaving the contractor in a good position to know what the actual costs of the change were. Unknown costs, however, would still be allowed at the end of the contract.

219. Is a release with a broad exceptions clause really effective for keeping the contractor's options open for future claims?

The so-called "blunderbuss exception" in releases actually closes the U.S. Treasury door on a too-clever contractor. If a contractor wants to keep possible claims alive and still sign a release, the exceptions the contractor states must be specific.

This is based on the following theory. After the contract is finished, the contractor must sign a release that says that the contractor has no claims against the government. Releases put an end to the contract. If a contractor is not sure whether it wants to file any claims in the future, it will identify in the release any claims that are to be excepted from the release.

In the past, some contractors have used blunderbuss exceptions. This kind of exception claims to release the government from any future claims except any future claims that may arise in the future. In other words, it is really not an exception because the exception is so broad as to be meaningless.

A tricky issue is "how specific must an exception be?" It should be very specific or a contractor might be better off not signing a release until it knows the nature and value of any possible claim.

For example, a contractor signed a government-drafted release reading as follows: "NOW THEREFORE, in consideration of the above premises and payment by the United States to the contractor of the amount now due under the contract, to wit, the sum of Six Thousand Thirteen Dollars and Sixty-eight cents ($6,013.68), the contractor hereby remises, releases, and forever discharges the United States, its officers, agents and employees, of and from all manner of debts, dues, liabilities, obligations, accounts, claims and demands whatsoever, in law and equity, under or by virtue of the said contract except:" At this point, the contractor wrote in the following attempted exception: "We reserve the right to submit a claim on the above-referenced contract. And to submit for any taxes due." Later, the contractor wanted to file claims against the government.

The CO refused to allow the claim and so did a board of contract appeals. A clause in the contract said that an exception in a release had "to be specifically excepted and in stated amounts." The contractor did not do that:

> Exceptions to releases are strictly construed against the Contractor, because the purpose of a release is to put an end to the matter in controversy. The exception noted by Appellant in its release, even if it had specifically referred to its prior letters, is likewise a blunderbuss exception, which does nothing to inform the Government about the source, scope or substance of [the contractor's] contentions. Vague, broad exceptions...are insufficient as a matter of law to constitute 'claims' sufficient to be excluded from the required release....To allow Appellant's exception to govern would not only permit it to resurrect a submission that did not constitute a claim either prior to the release, or in the release itself, but which would enable it to assert no more than a naked intention to file an indeterminate future claim in an undetermined amount as a precursor to subsequent development of arguable and previously unknown claims. (*Eagle Asphalt & Oil*, IBCA 4173-1999, December 28, 2000.)

220. Will the FAR release language for modifications work to prevent claims at the end of the contract?

Perhaps not, because the FAR language has some ambiguous words in it that can cost the government more money at the end of the contract. The current FAR modification release language at FAR 43.204(c) encourages vague language. It purports to be a release from additional equitable adjustments "attributable to such facts or circumstances giving rise to" the proposal for adjustment or modification. What exactly does that mean? What does the release deal with?

Vague government-drafted language in modification releases does not protect the government from additional claims. For example, a modification gave more money and different tasks to a contractor under an option. The release stated that the release covered any claims "arising out of Modification P00013. This document contains the complete agreement of the parties. There are no other collateral agreements, either written or oral." A board of contract appeals held that the release covered only the work to occur during the next option year, not the increased costs for the work the year before, even though it might appear that the modification did affect the previous year. Important to the Board was the fact that "the terms of the modification do not plainly bar the present claim.... "

221. When is it too late to file claims?

A contractor cannot file claims after receiving final payment. But final payment is not as simple as it seems. The government needs a final payment date to ensure that claims are filed while the contract is still alive and to protect the government against stale claims. But sometimes, deciding when final payment has occurred is difficult. Courts and boards look to the totality of facts and circumstances of a particular case. If the payment in question is labeled "final" and if such payment comes at a sequence in time and events consistent with finality, then it would seem that final payment has been made.

The problem with final payment is that often several payments are made on a contract and the contract ends up being terminated. Should the last payment the government made be considered the final payment? Probably not, because the last payment was made not with the intent that it be the last one. It simply turned out to be the last one.

To see if final payment has been made, courts and boards look for indicators such as any notation or indication of finality on the invoice or last check, execution of a modification after issuance of the "last" check, still-pending equitable adjustments, failure to request a release, and the government's in-house treatment of the contract as being open.

As one court stated, "final payment should not be found as a matter of surprise. Rather, it is the payment which can reasonably and logically be considered the 'final payment' under the contract that marks [the] cut-off point for the contractor." (*Historical Services, Inc.*, DOTCAB Nos. 72-8, 72-8a, and 72-2BCA¶9592 at 44,839.)

CHAPTER 18
Contract Interpretation

If a construction drawing includes a note "Est. 2000 ft." next to a pile of dirt that has to be removed, does "Est." mean established or estimated? What difference does it make? The difference becomes important when it turns out that the pile of dirt is 2200 feet tall. If the drawing tried to convey the idea that the height of the pile of dirt was *established* at 2000 feet, a contractor would be entitled to the costs incurred in removing an unexpected additional 200 feet of dirt. On the other hand, if the drawing tried to convey the idea that the height of the pile of dirt was simply *estimated* at 2000 feet, the contractor's argument for getting paid to remove the additional 200 feet is much weaker.

What we have here is a problem of contract interpretation. The contract has an ambiguity. The abbreviation *Est.* can mean two different things. And each of the two meanings could be reasonable in the context it is in. A pile of dirt can be either established or estimated at 2000 feet.

When the parties entered into the contract involving the pile of dirt, it's unlikely that anybody noticed the problem with *Est.* The drawing was probably one of many, if not hundreds, of drawings that the government prepared and all the bidders probably ignored in their rush to prepare a bid for the project.

Contracts have ambiguities all the time. When a specification of the building maintenance contract tells a company to clean as well as "stock" the restrooms, what does *stock* the restrooms mean? With what? We can guess that paper products would be required. But of what quality? Do the paper towels in the dispensers have to be one-ply or two-ply? What about the quality of the toilet tissue?

222. What are some of the rules for contract interpretation?

There have to be some guidelines to help contracting parties resolve these contract interpretation issues. And there are. Over the years, rules have been developed and applied to help resolve contract interpretation problems.

At the heart of all these rules of contract interpretation is the concept, or the problem, of ambiguity. Many of the contract interpretation problems that arise are caused by ambiguities.

What is an ambiguity? Curiously, the word *ambiguity* itself is ambiguous. It can mean three different things. It can mean that words are vague, such as the phrase "stock the restroom." It can also mean words that have two or more different meanings, even though spelled the same way, such as the abbreviation, *Est.* Or it can mean words that have contradictory meanings.

The primary rule of contract interpretation is that "the contract interprets itself." What this means is that, ideally, any problem with what one part of the contract means should be resolved by looking at the other parts of the contract.

But this primary rule does not work with an ambiguity. Looking elsewhere in the contract for its meaning doesn't help because the word has several different but equally reasonable meanings. So the parties can't look to the contract for help. In legal terms, they must go "outside the contract" to find assistance. Or maybe instead of going outside the contract, the parties should simply rely on mechanical rules, such as that the contract is interpreted against the party who drafted the language.

223. What is the parol evidence rule?

The parol evidence rule allows the parties to go outside the contract to find an interpretation of the contract that makes sense. Other interpretation aids become available under the parol evidence rule. For example, you can look at what the parties did, what they said during negotiations leading to the contract, and what the ambiguous words would mean in that particular business.

Looking at what ambiguous words mean in a particular business is called trade practice. For example, a contract required a building to be built and as it was built, light bulbs were to be installed. The contract also said that "new lamps" had to be installed immediately prior to completion of a construction project. To lay people, this means that any lamp previously installed during construction had to be replaced. But that is not what it means to the lighting industry. *New lamps* in the lighting trade means only that defective, burned out, or broken lamps had to be replaced. Installing all new lamps is called *relamping*. To lay people, the word *new* is not ambiguous. To the lighting industry, it is. How does a contracting officer interpret this language?

Two questions have to be answered. Before you can use trade practice, you have to have an ambiguity. Is the phrase *new lamp* ambiguous to you? No. New means new. So, to us nonexperts, there is no ambiguity and so there is no need to resort to trade practice. But *new lamps* in the lighting industry raises problems because there are several meanings of the phrase. So, first, in deciding whether there is an ambiguity, you must look at the context of the word.

Contract interpretation law allows the use of trade practice to establish the context of the parties. In the industry, replacing all the lamps is not putting in *new lamps*—it is relamping. So because the government wanted all new lamps, the term *new lamps* became ambiguous in context.

That allows us to go to step two: What does this ambiguous phrase mean? If the context discloses an ambiguity, contract interpretation law allows trade practice to be used to resolve it. New lamps is replacing burned out ones; relamping is replacing all the lightbulbs, whether they're burned out or not. A court held that a government *new lamp* requirement meant that only burned-out bulbs had to be replaced.

224. The contract says one thing, which is different from the way it's being carried out. Does this change affect the interpretation and meaning of the words of the contract?

The way a contract is actually carried out (in legalese, the course of conduct) can affect the interpretation of the contract. A course of conduct involving the same contract, the same contracting agency, and essentially the same contract provisions can give meaning to, supplement, or qualify an agreement between two parties. So it is critical that the parties watch carefully the way the words of the contract get carried out. Conduct can add, subtract, or otherwise change a signed contract. Actions speak louder than words.

To prove that conduct has changed the actual words of a contract, a contractor has to prove that it justifiably relied on a prior course of dealing with the same contracting agency, the same contractor, and essentially the same contract provisions. For example, the Department of Defense had an indefinite quantity contract for vehicle parts with a company. The contract called for two types of service: delivery of the parts to a warehouse (a cheaper method) and delivery to the user (a more expensive way). Over the years, the contract was mainly a warehouse-delivery contract. Suddenly, it became mainly a user-delivery contract. A board found that the course of conduct over the earlier part of the contract established a warehouse contract so that when it became a different kind, the company was entitled to an equitable adjustment as a constructive change to the contract.

225. What is the difference between a design specification and a performance specification? Why does it matter?

Money. This is an ongoing battle in procurement circles: whether a specification is a design specification or a performance specification. The consequences are significant: The government is responsible for any errors in a design specification, while it is much more difficult to hold the government responsible under a performance specification.

"If you follow these government plans, the project will work or we'll pay." That's the warranty the government gives to contractors when the government provides a design specification. With a performance specification, there is no warranty because the government essentially is paying the contractor to figure out how to do something.

The warranty that comes with a design specification is a valuable warranty, since any problems a contractor encounters caused by the specification get paid for by the government. Obviously and unfortunately, the government does not put in big bold letters the word *design* or *performance* on the first page of a specification. When the government and a contractor get into a dispute, the contractor often argues that the problem is caused by the specification, which the contractor labels a design specification. Predictably enough, the government responds that the specification is a performance specification.

Are there any clear indicators of a performance specification? Yes—discretion. If a contractor has discretion in how the work gets done, it's a performance specification. All a performance specification sets forth is an objective or standard to be achieved. The winning company has to use its ingenuity to achieve that objective or standard of performance, selecting the means and assuming responsibility for it.

For example, in a construction contract, the contractor sued the government for damage caused by "over blasting." The contractor said the government had to pay because the specification was a design specification since it set forth all the required elements of the blast plan and set out in detail all aspects related to the blasting, such as the amount of concrete to be removed; the height, width, and depth of removal; and the length, size, and depth of embedment of all anchor and reinforcing steel. A court disagreed, finding it a performance specification. The specification gave the contractor the discretion to specify the diameter, depth, and spacing of the drilled holes; the size and location of charges; the blasting sequence; and the personnel who would be working with the explosives. The contractor had complete discretion in the development of a blasting plan. The government didn't require any specific blasting procedure or the contractor to use certain explosives or equipment. The contractor therefore determined how the blasting would be executed and what explosives and materials would be employed. The specification, accordingly, was a performance specification for which there was no warranty—so the contractor was responsible for the damage.

On the other hand, a design specification is a road map. It lays out in pretty precise detail the materials to be employed and how the work is to be performed.

For example, a government contract required the construction company to remove and control water from the construction site. The government was responsible for getting all necessary permits. The government submitted drawings indicating that a 24-inch pipe would be used to dewater the construction site. On the basis of these drawings, the government was issued a permit. The contractor followed the drawings and laid a 24-inch-diameter pipe to dewater the site. The construction site, however, flooded and suffered significant damage. The contractor tried to get the damage paid for by the government. The contractor argued that the 24-inch pipe was required by the government but the pipe was too small for the site and that damage resulted. The government argued that the contractor could have used any size pipe it wanted because the drawings were only conceptual and part of a performance specification.

A court concluded that the contractor was following a design specification. If drawings show the location, width, and depth of certain elements, the drawings "approach design specifications." The court based its conclusion on the facts that "the drawings are precisely detailed; that the permit was obtained, in part, based on the basis of the drawings; and that the plaintiff was required to perform the contract in accordance with the permit."

226. How does the principle of words being construed against the drafter work?

This is the principle of "contra proferentum." It means that words are construed "contra," or against, the party that proffered or offered it. The theory behind this principle is that it is fair to construe language against the party who did not draft it correctly or clearly the first time. Typically, this rule hurts the government because, in government contracts, the government typically drafts the language.

But, it is not automatic. If a contractor takes an unreasonable interpretation of the contract provision, the language will not be construed against the government. It is only when a contractor makes a reasonable interpretation of language drafted by the government that the principle of contra proferentum applies.

227. What's the harm in a contractor making an aggressive or at-the-fringe argument? It might win.

The harm in a contractor making an "aggressive" argument is fraud. A frivolous interpretation can lead to a false claim.

Parties are allowed creative and "interesting" interpretations. But at some point, an interesting interpretation becomes frivolous and therefore fraudulent.

In one case finding a frivolous interpretation to be fraud, a contractor placed additional fill above the fill lines specified in the contract drawings and billed the government for that extra fill, even though the contract provided that the contractor was to be paid only up to the fill lines. The contractor admitted that it billed for fill over the lines, but said that there was an interpretation of the contract to support it. The contract clearly contradicted the contractor's interpretation. In addition, its subcontractor told the contractor that its interpretation was wrong. Moreover, the interpretation was contrary to industry practice. As one court put it, a contractor can be liable for fraud "even in the absence of any deliberate concealment or misstatement of facts. Under such circumstances, when the contractor's purported interpretation of the contract borders on the frivolous, the contractor must either raise the interpretation issue with the government contracting officials or risk liability under the federal fraud statutes."

CHAPTER 19
Delay

Delay is a common problem with contracts of any sort, government or private. As strange as it may sound, in a government contract, the contractor assumes that the government will delay the project. But there is a limit to what a contractor has to assume. That limit is reasonable delay. A contractor assumes the risk only of reasonable delay. If the delay is unreasonable, a contractor is entitled to relief: more money, more time to complete the project, or both.

228. If a contractor finishes before the contract completion deadline but after the deadline it had set for itself, must the government pay delay damages?

It's possible. The government cannot delay a contractor for free, even if the project is completed by the deadline the government set for the project. This kind of government-caused delay is compensable to a contractor if the contractor intended to complete the project ahead of schedule, it had the capability of doing so, and but for the government delay, it would have completed the project early.

This seems to go against common sense. If the government delays a contractor from completing a project but the contractor still completes the project by the government's deadline, the government has not prevented the contractor from finishing on time from the government's perspective. But the problem is that while the work was completed on time for the government, it was not done on time for the contractor. So it makes sense that the contractor is entitled to delay damages. This is true even though the government was never notified of the planned early completion date.

A contractor must establish its intent to perform the contract on the feasible and attainable accelerated schedule. This intent must be supported by the contractor's actions and performance. For example, a contractor met the test for early completion damages. It had submitted a plan showing early completion, which the government had approved. It had made such progress on the project that when work was stopped, it was more than six weeks ahead of schedule. There was no evidence that the project was inadequately staffed. Nor were there any contractor-caused delays. The government was found liable for the delay. (*U. A. Anderson Construction Co.*, ASBCA No. 48087, April 27, 1999.)

229. Before signing a release for a time extension given by the government, what land mine should a contractor be alert to?

A time extension modification waives all previous excusable delays. Regardless of whether a release has been signed identifying the other causes of delay, a time extension modification waives all previous excusable delays. Once waived, the delay cannot be used to excuse a termination for default. The rationale for this is that once a modification dealing with time extensions for delays is signed, the slate is wiped clean. Previous delays—whether known or not, whether waived or not, whether subject to a release or not—are in fact waived. Importantly, however, claims for delay costs are not waived. Thus, the "silent" waiver applies to excusable delays, but not to compensable delays.

There is one exception, however: Claims for delay costs are not waived where the contract modification included neither a waiver nor release of claims nor was there evidence that the parties intended to include delay costs in the modification.

230. What is the Eichleay formula and what does it do?

Eichleay determines delay damages. The Eichleay formula is named after the decision that started it all: *Eichleay Corp.*, ASBCA 5183, 60-2 BCA ¶ 2688. The Eichleay formula is the math that calculates how much home office overhead a contractor lost due to government delay. When the government delays a project but makes the contractor "stand by" during the delay (that is, remain ready to resume the work), the contractor's home office overhead during that delay is paid for according to the Eichleay formula.

Eichleay damages can be a very contested issue. Both sides, government and contractor, seem interested in abusing the concept that clearly has its place under certain circumstances. The contractor often will throw into a delay claim a demand for Eichleay damages simply because there has been a delay in the contract, whether or not the government caused the delay and whether or not there has even been a delay. Not to be outdone, the government abuses the Eichleay concept by routinely refusing to acknowledge its validity. Contracting officers are usually reluctant to pay Eichleay damages.

Nevertheless, courts and boards routinely allow—and disallow as well—the use of the Eichleay formula in delay situations. Let's look at how the Eichleay overhead calculation is made, and what it is designed to pay the contractor for.

Any construction project should pay a company back enough money for all the company costs attributable to the project. Who can argue with that principle? So if the government hires a company to provide one person for a job, the government must pay the costs of that worker to the company, plus profit. That worker costs the company in two different ways. The worker costs the company directly by way of what the company pays the worker. This worker wage is the direct cost to the contractor and to the contract. But this worker wage is not the only cost to the company for this one worker. When this worker's time sheets are entered into the company accounting system by a data entry clerk, the time the data entry clerk spent entering the data should be paid for by the project.

It is physically possible that the data entry clerk's time could be precisely accounted for if the data entry clerk kept track of that part of the day devoted to entering the data for that one person on that one project. But that's unreasonable. It would take more time to record the data entry clerk's time on the project than it would be for the data entry clerk to enter the project worker's time in the company accounting system.

So companies make an assumption: The amount of time the data entry clerk spends on a project is equal to the percentage that particular contract is to all the company's business that year. So, if the project consisting of one worker is one-third of the company's revenue that year, that data entry clerk spends one-third of his or her time on the project.

To convert this assumption into dollars, the company creates what is called an "indirect cost pool." Like a swimming pool filled with water, the indirect cost pool gets all the indirect costs thrown into it. Indirect costs typically include what is called home office overhead. Home office overhead typically includes company costs like the electricity to keep the lights on, buying books for the library, and people completing time sheets and W-2s back at the office. And when a company is bidding a project, the company puts enough money into that project to pay for all the home office overhead expenses. So the company makes sure that, for as long as the project goes on, there's enough home office overhead in that project to pay the way.

The way home office overhead normally gets paid is that the company gets paid the direct cost of the worker and adds into it not only a percentage for profit but also a percentage for overhead. So, for every day a person works and gets paid for the direct cost to the company, the indirect costs of home office overhead attributed to that worker also come back to the company.

But what happens if a project goes longer than the company had anticipated? If a company allotted enough money for 100 days of home office overhead, thinking that the project would last 100 days, what happens if that project gets delayed by the government and stretches out over 120 days? First of all, the project budget doesn't have 120 days of overhead in it. How does the overhead get compensated?

The worker gets paid only for working. If the project is delayed, the worker doesn't work and doesn't get paid. Nor does the home office overhead get paid. Eichleay allows the company whose project is delayed to get paid the home office overhead that had not been paid due to the absence of a worker who gets paid by the hour.

Exactly how the Eichleay formula gets calculated is beyond the scope of this book. Generally, however, the delayed company does this:

- Step 1: The company determines how much the delayed contract is in dollars to the company's total work—say the delayed project was one-third of the company's business in dollars.

- Step 2: The company determines its total overhead during the project.

- Step 3: To make sure the delayed contract picks up its share of overhead (say, one-third), the company determines how much money that one-third of the overhead was.

- Step 4: That one-third portion of the overhead that the project should bear, in dollars, is then divided by the number of days the project lasted so that the company knows how much overhead that project cost the company every single day. Once it is determined how much overhead that project should bear each day, that dollar value is multiplied by the number of days the project was delayed by the government.

The result is unabsorbed home office overhead. It is considered unabsorbed because it was not picked up or paid. There were no direct billings to which the indirect overhead billings could be attached for that period of delay.

Having looked at what the Eichleay formula deals with, let's see how a contractor becomes entitled to Eichleay damages. As mentioned, the Eichleay formula compensates contractors for government-imposed delay. Here's what a contractor has to prove to get Eichleay damages.

The delayed contractor must prove that there was a period of delay caused by the government during which time the contractor could not have taken on any other jobs. In other words, the contractor was on standby waiting for the government to tell the contractor when to get back to work. The government, significantly, never sent the contractor home or imposed a stop work order. The government required workers to stay around, doing nothing, so that the government would have the workers on hand to implement immediately any modifications the government thought proper, allowing work to resume.

An interesting issue is whether recovery of home office overhead after government delay can be done only through a per diem basis consistent with the Eichleay formula, regardless of whether home office overhead was recovered on a percentage basis during contract performance. Courts have ruled that this is true.

But an interesting issue is raised here. One typical type of damage recovery allowed a delayed contractor is the unabsorbed home office overhead. During contract performance, of course, this type of overhead is typically billed on a percentage basis, for example, 10 percent of direct costs. However, when delay ensues, this type of overhead is calculated on a per day basis according to the complicated Eichleay formula.

Here's the problem: FAR 31.203 requires a single distribution base for allocating a given overhead pool, while precedent from the U.S. Court of Appeals for the Federal Circuit seems to sanction the use of a percentage basis during contract performance and Eichleay's per day calculation for delay. But none of the Court's decisions address this FAR provision.

231. Is the Eichleay formula applicable to modifications extending the contract?

No. Extended home office overhead for a project that gets extended, but not delayed, must be calculated by a fixed percentage method and not the Eichleay formula.

When a construction contract extends beyond the original completion date, it's not always because the government delayed the project. When the government makes the contract go on for longer than expected because work is added to it, extended home office overhead is a cost that contractors routinely add to their bill. In dealing with extended home office overhead, there is no delay. In that event, Eichleay is not applicable. Extended home office overhead for more work but no government delay ("pure contract extensions") should use a fixed-percentage markup of direct costs incurred.

A fixed-percentage markup is used because the rationale for Eichleay is no longer present. As one authority saw it, Eichleay was "an extraordinary remedy specifically limited to contracts affected by Government-caused suspensions, disruptions, and delays of work. In such situations the use of a fixed percentage formula to compensate for homeoffice overhead is rendered inadequate or 'absurd,' since the flow of revenue from direct costs—a percentage of which goes towards recovery of homeoffice overhead—is simply cut off or substantially reduced."

232. How detailed and precise must the calculation of liquidated damages be?

To some extent, it's the amount, not the process, that is the critical issue for liquidated damages. Reasonableness is the test. The reasonableness of liquidated damages depends on the reasonableness of the dollar value set for the liquidated damages, not the process by which the liquidated damages were established.

Assessing liquidated damages against a contractor is likely to bring a claim because doing so takes money out of the contractor's pocket. Two typical arguments against liquidated damages are usually raised: (1) the CO, in setting the level of liquidated damages, did not thoughtfully establish them as required by FAR 11.5, but rather went to an agency chart and picked liquidated damages on the basis of that chart; or (2) the liquidated damages amount was unreasonable. This latter argument is a better one, if not the only one, since court and board decisions have greatly minimized the importance of the process used to set liquidated damages. Using charts is acceptable.

But first, why are liquidated damages used? They're used when damages are uncertain or hard to measure. When a building is not ready on time, what is the loss to the government? Hard to say precisely. But that also says why it's hard for liquidated damages to be found unreasonable; it is difficult to conclude that a particular liquidated damages amount or rate is an unreasonable projection of what those damages might be.

The FAR sets out a detailed process to be used to set liquidated damages. What happens if the CO does not do this detailed calculation but instead simply goes to a chart? Agencies have prepared charts for use in liquidated damages situations. Typically, the chart lists dollar values of the project down the side of a sheet of paper (say, $100,000 to $250,000) and for each dollar amount shows a daily liquidated damages figure that should be put into a solicitation.

Courts and boards have taken the position that they will enforce liquidated damages clauses if the amount was reasonable for the particular agreement at the time it was made. As a result, it doesn't matter how the amount was calculated—use of a chart or not. All that matters is "Is the amount reasonable?" Or, as one court phrased it, "Is the liquidated damages amount extravagant, or disproportionate to the amount of property loss, as to show that compensation was not the object aimed at or as to imply fraud, mistake, circumvention or oppression?"

One decision found that there was nothing inherently unreasonable about a reduction of about one-fifth of one percent of the contract price per day ($3,157.00) on a phase-one construction contract to be completed in a short period of time.

233. Can the government pay delay damages if a subcontractor is delayed but the prime contractor is not?

When the government knows and approves of a subcontractor's duty to complete its work by a date certain, the prime and subcontractor are entitled to unabsorbed overhead for being put on standby by the government, even though the prime contractor completed the contract ahead of schedule.

234. Is all delay caused by a defective specification compensable?

Delay caused by a defective specification is usually, but not always, compensable. A defective specification doesn't always give a contractor a blank check on delay damages. While all delay from a defective specification is usually considered unreasonable, contractor-caused delay after a defective specification has been identified must be charged to the contractor.

After all, any contractor doing business with the government accepts the fact that in many cases the government can delay the contractor for free. Typically, the government can delay a contractor for free for "a reasonable amount of time," whatever that is. Usually, the government only pays for "unreasonable" periods of delay. One exception to this rule is delay due to defective specification. The general rule there is that the government pays for all delay. Since the government prepared the specification, if the contractor is delayed, the government should pay.

But delays caused by factors outside the government's control relieve the government of liability irrespective of its faulty specifications. If, for example, a contractor had submitted a request for a modification after the discovery of a defective specification, the only way that delay would be compensated would be if the delay was caused by the defective specification. If the delay after the defective specification was discovered was due to the government's reasonable consideration of a modification, the delay is not defective specification delay and is not compensable. Even though the delay *followed* a defective specification, the delay was not *due to* the defective specification—the delay may be due to the government's slow, but reasonable consideration of the modification.

CHAPTER 20
Changes

The changes clause is a clause that only an organization with the clout of the federal government could exact from contractors. You will not find a clause like the changes clause in the typical agreement between two private, nongovernment parties. When two people get together and agree to contract for some work, the parties agree that the work—for example, painting the outside of a house—will be done by one party and money—say $3,000—will be paid by the other party in exchange for the painting. That's the deal. Neither party can force the other party to change the deal. Of course, the parties can agree to change the original deal. But neither party can force the other to make a change to the contract.

The government is different. In a government contract, the government and the contractor agree that the government can force the contractor to agree to a change in the deal to which the parties previously had agreed.

235. What are the limits of the government's use of the changes clause?

There are limits, of course, on how far the government can go with changes under the clause. The clause itself puts two significant limits on the government freely using the changes clause to do whatever it wants to do. The first limitation is that any change can only be "within the general scope" of the original deal. The second limitation is that these scope changes can be made to only a limited number of areas of the contract. So some changes are off-limits to the government under the changes clause.

It's important to understand how the changes clause works. For the purposes of this book, we'll use the standard changes clause, FAR 52.243-4. The changes clause for other types of contracts, such as architect-engineer, services, supplies, and so forth, are all minor variations on this clause:

> (a) The Contracting Officer may at any time, by written order, and without notice to the sureties, if any, make changes within the general scope of this contract

GAO has several tests for determining whether a modification of a contract is beyond this scope.

One GAO test for beyond-scope modifications looks at "whether there is a material difference between the modified contract and the contract that was originally awarded. Evidence of a material difference between the modification and the original contract is found by examining any changes in the type of work, performance period, and costs between the contract as awarded and as modified."

For example, an indefinite-delivery/indefinite-quantity (ID/IQ) contract to engineer, furnish, and install systems and equipment had a modification that added a senior network project engineer and a network project engineer who had to be certified as Microsoft Certified Systems Engineers. GAO found that the modification, and thus the delivery order, were within the scope of the original contract. The original contract had software installation and integration work. Moreover, the added personnel had job descriptions that were similar to or identical with the job descriptions in the original contract.

But, housekeeping services are beyond the scope of a preventive maintenance contract. The solicitation and contract required "facility maintenance repair, such as HVAC mechanic, boiler operator, plumber/pipefitter, general maintenance mechanic, electrician, painter, carpenter, electronic technician, welder and kitchen equipment mechanic." Housekeeping was not within the scope of this solicitation and contract. In this case, GAO also looked at "various letters and memorandum from agency officials regarding the intent and purpose of the original contract [which] also support our conclusion." This included the memorandum of agreement between the agencies using the contract, which addressed "scheduled or predictive maintenance" and "repairs to real property."

Requirements contracts are different. Large increases in items under a requirements contract will generally not be beyond scope. So long as an agency has good faith business reasons for doing so, it may order any quantity of goods under a requirements contract without going beyond the scope of the contract. Thus, it is very difficult to go beyond the scope of a requirements contract.

The only limit is the good faith of the government. A good faith business reason justifies greatly underbuying or greatly overbuying items under a requirements contract. One board referred to a requirements contract as "a virtually open-ended agreement pursuant to which the federal buyer may place orders in any quantity, no matter how far removed from the contract estimate, so long as the agency's action reflects good faith business reasons. Such orders, by definition, must be regarded as within the scope of the contract as originally awarded." There can be no bad faith if the agency has a legitimate need to overbuy or underbuy items from a requirements contract.

236. How are ripple effect costs paid for?

One of the most convoluted sentences in the entire FAR is found in the changes clause:

> (b) If any such change causes an increase or decrease in the cost of, or the time required for, performance of any part of the work under this contract, whether or not changed by the order, the Contracting Officer shall make an equitable adjustment in the contract price, the delivery schedule, or both, and shall modify the contract.

What were the drafters of the clause trying to say? The drafters were trying to account for "impact costs." Here's the problem. When the government makes a change, it normally causes an increase or decrease in the cost of, or the time required for, the work that is getting changed. That's obvious.

What may not be so obvious is that the changed work can make the unchanged work more or less costly, or more or less time-consuming. In other words, changes affect not only changed work; changes can affect the cost of or time required for the performance of work that will not be changed.

For example, the government has a contract with a construction company to build a road onto the building site and then construct the building at the end of the road that was just built. As the road is being built, the direction of the road has to be changed because a Native American burial site is discovered in the planned path of the road. To get around the burial grounds, the road must be moved, doubling or tripling the cost of the road. Naturally, the government would modify the contract to increase the cost of and the time required for constructing the longer road.

However, there's no change whatever to the building to be constructed at the end of this road. Although there is no change in the building itself, the cost of constructing the building and the time to build it certainly change because travel costs over the road, which is now two or three times longer than anticipated, will inevitably drive up transportation costs of materials and increase the cost of and time required for construction of the building even though technically the building was unchanged by the order.

What this poorly worded FAR sentence is trying to say is that changes have ripple effects. A change not only affects the cost of the actual work being changed, but can also change the cost of unchanged work. And the changes clause allows the CO to pay a contractor for the impact that any change has on unchanged but more costly or more time-consuming work.

237. What are the time limits for a contractor submitting requests for equitable adjustments due to changes under the changes clause?

The language of the clause is much worse than the reality of it. The language is:

> (c) The Contractor must assert its right to an adjustment under this clause within 30 days from the date of receipt of the written order. However, if the Contracting Officer decides that the facts justify it, the Contracting Officer may receive and act upon a proposal submitted before final payment of the contract.

The clause seems to demand submission of equitable adjustment within 30 days. But that's not the way the courts and boards have interpreted it. The contractor must assert its "right" to an equitable adjustment within this period of time. So there certainly is no need under the clause to submit a formal proposal for equitable adjustment within the 30-day deadline.

What the clause seeks is notice to the government within 30 days. Regarding the apparent 30-day deadline, the courts and boards have interpreted the "deadline" to be not an absolute bar to filing a notice or a request for equitable adjustment. What the courts and boards look for is whether or not a contractor's failure to follow the 30-day deadline has in any way harmed the government. In legal terminology, the courts and boards look for "prejudice." And even when they find some type of harm to the government as a result of a contractor missing the 30-day deadline, the courts and boards typically do not forbid the contractor from filing the notice or request for equitable adjustment. What they do is increase the contractor's "burden of persuasion" in proving the claim.

As a practical matter, the only real deadline is that the notice or request for equitable adjustment must be received before final payment. As described in Closeouts (Chapter 15), the phrase "final payment" is a term of art. It has special meaning in government contracts. Simply because no more payments might be due under the contract is no reason to assume that final payment has been made and that there's no time left to submit a request for equitable adjustment under the changes clause.

238. Does the contractor have to carry out the change while fighting about it with the government?

Typically, contractors do have to carry out the change while the change is in dispute. Here's the language of the clause:

> (e) Failure to agree to any adjustment shall be a dispute under the Disputes clause. However, nothing in this clause shall excuse the Contractor from proceeding with the contract as changed.

The clause clearly makes any controversy over the amount of compensation for the change subject to the disputes clause. And it would seem from the second sentence that a contractor, under all circumstances, must keep working on the contract while the dispute over the adjustment lasts. But notice the language that's used. The clause says that "nothing in this clause" excuses a contractor from keeping on the job while the fight over the money goes on.

But there is another clause that may excuse the contractor from proceeding with the work. That's the disputes clause itself, which does not require a contractor to proceed with work if the dispute involves an issue that "relates to" the contract.

This "duty to proceed" is tricky. As long as the work called for by a change under the changes clause is not beyond the scope of the contract, a contractor must proceed with the work. Contractors do not have the legal luxury of stopping work to litigate. One big exception is for work beyond the scope of a contract.

For example, a company with a contract to "demilitarize" bombs was told to double the number. It turned out that the number was not doubled, but only increased by about 20 percent. But in any event, the increase in the number of bombs was not the critical issue. What was critical was whether the amount of 3000 bombs, as demanded by the CO, was beyond the scope of the contract. The Court of Appeals for the Federal Circuit concluded that it was not. The main reason was that the total number of bombs to be demilitarized over the course of the contract was not changed. "If the contracting officer had required a significant change in the total number of bombs that Alliant was required to process, the contracting officer's directive might have been construed as a drastic modification in the terms of the option...." Moreover, Alliant could not prove that production for a higher rate over a shorter time "would be more costly than lower production for a longer period." Alliant was not forced to make a beyond-scope change and therefore had the obligation to proceed with the work. (*Alliant Techsystems, Inc. et al. v. United States,* U.S. Court of Appeals for the Federal Circuit No. 98-5016, 98-5044, May 28, 1999.)

239. If a contractor is forced to agree to a modification under the changes clause, is the modification valid?

Duress forcing a contractor to sign a modification will nullify the modification. Here's the rationale. A contract must be a voluntary meeting of the minds. As a result, an agreement that is coerced is voidable by the party being coerced. Duress can void contractual obligations if there is proof that one party involuntarily accepted the terms of the other, circumstances permitted no other reasonable alternative, and the circumstances were the result of coercive acts of the other party.

This is, however, very difficult to prove. Often, "duress" to a contractor is simply the fact that the contractor has to accept a bargain that it does not like. It's not that it's forced on it by the government.

Moreover, a contractor must raise the duress issue soon. It cannot wait several years before raising it. A four-year delay in claiming duress is too long. Duress must be alleged within a reasonable period of time.

240. Can anyone other than the contracting officer bind the government?

Only someone with authority to legally bind the government can in fact bind the government. The rationale for this principle is that strict control over taxpayers' money is critical. And the best way to maintain this strict control is to allow only those authorized, such as COs, to bind the government (i.e., to be able to legally commit taxpayers' money).

Exceptions to this principle fill volumes. Like any legal principle, there are exceptions that develop to ensure fairness. Over the years, a number of exceptions have been developed to make sure that the principle is not so rigidly applied that injustice results.

241. What is imputed authority?

One exception is imputed authority. The heart of the imputed authority principle is that the CO's representative or technical representative is the CO's eyes and ears. That being the assumption, it's fair to hold the contracting officer responsible for what the CO's representative does because it is assumed that the CO's representative does the job assigned: reporting information to the CO and being the CO's spokesperson.

For example, a company continued to work for the government during an option year even though the option had never been executed by the government. In fact, neither side had signed the option. There was no dispute that the contractor actually did work for the government during the option year. The government refused to pay for the company's services because there was no signed contract. The Armed Services Board of Contract Appeals found that an implied-in-fact contract existed based on the CO's representative's involvement.

242. What is apparent authority?

There is an exception that the government does not have. Although the private market has an exception to the authority principle—apparent authority—the government does not. Apparent authority is authority that does not exist in fact, but only in appearance—it's authority that seems to exist with the knowledge and assistance of the principal. In simple terms, if a principal allows someone to appear to be the representative of that principal, the "agent" can in fact be treated as an agent even though it is not. For example, a McDonald's changes over to a Wendy's on April 1. McDonald's must strip the location of all its logos on March 31 because if the facility opens April 1 as a Wendy's, but it appears to be a McDonald's, McDonald's could be sued for a rotten hamburger sold by the facility, even though the restaurant is legally a Wendy's. Because McDonald's allowed the facility to represent itself as a McDonald's, McDonald's can be held legally liable.

Apparent authority does not exist in government contracts. For example, a government supervisor could allow someone with no authority to use the office of someone with authority. If a company comes into the office, sees an unlimited warrant on the wall, assumes that the warrant belongs to the person using the office, and signs a contract with that person with no authority, the company cannot enforce the contract. If the government employee without authority were to attempt to commit the government legally, the government could disavow the employee's unauthorized acts.

CHAPTER 21
Equitable Adjustments

The government owes the contractor more money at many points in the contract administration process. Changes or modifications to the contract present the most common situation where an equitable adjustment has to be made. But there are other points in the process as well: differing site conditions, variations in estimated quantities, and delay.

When the government owes the contractor money, the government should make an equitable adjustment of the contract. Notice the word *equitable*. The idea is that any adjustment to the contract that the government makes must be fair, equitable, and reasonable.

But as the voluminous litigation over equitable adjustments shows, reasonable people can be miles apart on what's equitable. Amid all these opinions about *equitable*, there are several basic principles that the government and the contractor have to follow.

243. What is the starting point for calculating an equitable adjustment ?

The most basic starting point in determining an equitable adjustment is cost. An equitable adjustment is based on cost. This presents two seemingly valid arguments that contractors would like to make. The first argument, from a contractor's perspective, is that changes in the basic contract should be based on the price at which the item was bid in the basic contract. For example, if a contractor won the contract by bidding a price of $300 per fire sprinkler head, it seems reasonable to the contractor to get paid $300 per sprinkler head if the government issues a modification for more sprinkler heads.

But that's not the law. The law says that equitable adjustments are based on cost—the cost to the contractor for the additional items. If the contractor actually pays $100 for the heads, that's what the contractor starts with for an equitable adjustment.

A second argument contractors like to make is that an equitable adjustment should be based on the value of the change, not the price. Obviously, there can be a big difference. For example, in the classic case that established the "cost, not value" principle, the contractor was told to change the brick to be used on a building. Instead of a basic brick, the government wanted a decorative brick. The contractor managed to get the premium brick at the price of the basic brick. So when the contractor asked for an equitable adjustment for the change in brick, the contractor wanted to be paid for the value of the brick, say $3 per brick, rather than the actual cost of the brick, say $1 per brick. Incidentally, the contractor got that price because it managed to get a good deal at the quarry.

The contractor had an interesting argument. The contractor argued that its company had increased the value of the government building by using the better brick. So it would be unjust enrichment of the government if the government paid the basic brick price for the premium brick. A second argument the contractor made was that the government should pay the value of the brick as the basis for the equitable adjustment so that contractors are encouraged to use smart business techniques in carrying out changes. Paying the contractor for the value of the item would do that, in the contractor's view.

Neither of these arguments was successful. The court ruled that the starting point of any equitable adjustment was the actual cost of the item to the contractor.

Cost, however, is simply the starting point. The fact that a contractor actually spends a specified amount for an item doesn't end the discussion. There's the concept of reasonable cost. A contractor could have bought snow shovels in the middle of a blizzard, when prices would be higher, when it should have bought them in September. The government will pay for a cost only if the cost is reasonable. And the burden is on the contractor, not the government, to prove that the cost is reasonable.

244. How much profit should a contractor make on an equitable adjustment?

A second component of an equitable adjustment is profit. A contractor is entitled to profit on an equitable adjustment. There are some exceptions to this. For example, an equitable adjustment to a contractor for a suspension of work cannot include profit because the suspension of work clause on its face says that profit should be excluded from any equitable adjustment under that clause.

How much profit should a contractor make on an equitable adjustment? The standard answer is that a contractor should make the same profit on the equitable adjustment as on the underlying contract.

There are, however, exceptions that allow the profit to be higher or lower depending on the circumstances. For example, a contract started out with relatively easy work. A contractor would unload container ships several times a week. Then after Desert Storm began, the work increased significantly. Sometimes there would be two or three ships a day to unload. As a result of this great increase in work, the contractor had to hire more people and had to set up more complex accounting systems. When the government made an equitable adjustment to the contract to pay for this extra work, it did not want to pay a higher profit. The contractor took the case to a board, which found that the contractor was entitled to a higher profit. The contractor got a higher percentage profit than on the underlying contract because the work had become more difficult.

On the other hand, where a modification to a contract is a relatively simple task with very little risk and very little effort on the contractor's part, the government has an argument for putting a lower profit on the equitable adjustment.

245. When work is taken from a contract and different work is added, how is that priced?

Pricing modifications that reduce the amount of work a contractor is to do can be tricky. The first step is to calculate what the original work would have cost. In these so-called "deductive changes," the principle to keep in mind is that the change should keep the contractor in the same position, in terms of profit, that the contractor would have been if the work originally contracted for had been carried out.

This can have some strange results. For example, the government started out wanting a buried electrical wire system but changed to a less expensive overhead wire system. The government said the original system would have cost the contractor $60,000 and the modified, overhead system would cost $20,000 so the government deducted $40,000 from the contract. The only problem for the contractor was that the contractor had made a bad bid for this part of the contract. The electrical subcontractor had left out some equipment. As a result, the contractor bid $34,000 for what the government said was a $60,000 job. So naturally, the contractor objected to the government deducting so much money. As the contractor put it, the government was taking $40,000 from its contract and making it pay $6,000 of its own money for doing the modification work.

The argument has superficial appeal because it seems unfair. The problem, however, is not the government's "would have cost" approach. The problem is that the contractor made a bad bid. If the contractor had carried out the original work, the contractor would have lost a lot of money. And since the contract started out with a bad bid, the loss in that bad bid has to be carried over to the modification.

From that viewpoint, it's hard to feel sorry for the contractor. As a practical matter, the contractor would have lost a lot of money doing the original work since the original work would cost $60,000 and the contractor bid only $34,000. So the contractor would have lost $26,000 doing the original work.

Fortunately for contractors that make good bids, a very profitable contract that is modified by deducting a very profitable item has to maintain the same profit percentage on the new work. For example, if a contractor can win a bid by pricing a $7 item at $12—a huge profit margin—this $5 profit margin would get carried over into any modification in the contract.

The would-have-cost principle, however, is often difficult to apply. What if the original work had allowed the contractor to keep the income from work to be done? Since that work won't be done, the income won't be made. Is the contractor's loss of income to be considered a damage of the modification for which a contractor should be compensated?

No. For example, a contract allowed the contractor to keep the money from the sale of rock excavated from the site where a building was being built. But problems developed with the use of approved disposal sites for the rock. So a modification to the contract was made. Rock would no longer be disposed of off-site. Instead, it would be used onsite as fill. As a result, the contractor could not longer sell the rock. When the time came to put a price on the equitable adjustment, the contractor wanted to get credit for the loss of income it experienced now that the rock would not be disposed off-site and sold, bringing in additional income.

The government was against giving the contractor money for this loss of income. It argued that the changes clause promised the contractor payment for the increased cost of performance, meaning, to the government, only the out-of-pocket costs associated with a modification. The government did not believe that a loss of income was a cost of performance. The government also argued that the loss of income was speculative, in that it would be hard to establish how much money the contractor would have made selling the rock on the private market.

The board agreed with the government that the modification could not address the amount of income allegedly lost from the nonsale of the rock. It agreed with the government's argument that the amount of loss would be too remote and speculative to be recovered. "In general, losses related to other, unrelated contracts and related to general loss of business may not be recovered as part of an equitable adjustment." The board concluded that the loss of income amount could not be considered part of the equitable adjustment. (*SAE American*, PSBCA No. 3866, March 31, 2000.)

246. Sometimes the same kind of government action can be compensated under various clauses, with different dollar consequences. How does this work?

The deductive changes discussed above are one example of that. In a deductive change order, the government takes work off a contract, But there's another way the government can take work off a contract: It can do a partial termination for convenience that terminates or reduces the work under the contract. So the same kind of government activity, reducing work under the contract, can be done under either of two clauses.

What is the difference if one clause is used rather than the other? The lawyers and accountants will care if the government uses a deductive change order and not a partial termination for convenience. The reason they care is that their fees for helping a contractor prepare a partial termination for convenience settlement proposal are costs that the government must pay to the contractor under a partial termination for convenience. But if a deductive change order is used, the costs of the accountants and lawyers probably would not be paid for by the government.

Various clauses can affect how the government pays for the delay. In a construction project, for example, delay can be paid for under any one of three clauses. The delay can be paid for under the suspension of work clause, the differing site conditions clause, or the changes clause.

Under the suspension of work clause, the government pays only for delay that stretches out to an unreasonable amount of time. In addition, the suspension of work clause does not pay a contractor profit.

Delay can also be paid for under the changes clause. For example, if a contractor wastes time working with a defective government specification, that delay can be paid for under the changes clause. The advantage of using the changes clause here is that under a defective specification delay claim, all delay attributed to the defective specification is compensable. No consideration is given to what amount of delay is reasonable and what amount of delay is unreasonable. All delay, reasonable or unreasonable, attributable to a defective specification is compensable.

Delay can also be paid for under the differing site conditions clause. When differing site conditions are encountered (for example, discovering harder rock than the government anticipated at a construction site), a contractor can get paid more for doing more work associated with the harder rock. But what typically happens when harder rock is discovered is that the project gets delayed for some period of time to allow the government to decide what to do about the rock. Once the government decides what to do, it will tell the contractor how to proceed. While the government is considering how to fix the problem, there's usually a period of delay. When the government implements the fix, it will use the changes clause.

Typically under the changes clause, the equitable adjustment includes profit. So in calculating an equitable adjustment for differing site conditions, it's possible for the government to inappropriately add profit to the delay. However, delay under the differing site conditions clause (that is, the delay that occurs before the differing site conditions are fixed) should be compensated using the suspension of work clause, which does not allow profit on top of the delay.

247. Can an equitable adjustment include the costs of a consultant like a lawyer or an accountant?

It depends on how the consultant is used. But the FAR clearly makes these costs allowable. In FAR 31.205-33, the term *professional and consultant services* is defined as:

> . . . those services rendered by persons who are members of a particular profession or possess a special skill and who are not officers or employees of the contractor. Examples include those services acquired by contractors or subcontractors in order to enhance their legal, economic, financial, or technical positions. Professional and consultant services are generally acquired to obtain

information, advice, opinions, alternatives, conclusions, recommendations, training, or direct assistance, such as studies, analyses, evaluations, liaison with Government officials, or other forms of representation.

A CO must consider the following factors in FAR 31.205-33:

1. The nature and scope of the service rendered in relation to the service required

2. The necessity of contracting for the service, considering the contractor's capability in the particular area

3. The past pattern of acquiring such services and their costs, particularly in the years prior to the award of government contracts

4. The impact of government contracts on the contractor's business

5. Whether the proportion of government work to the contractor's total business is such as to influence the contractor in favor of incurring the cost, particularly when the services rendered are not of a continuing nature and have little relationship to work under government contracts

6. Whether the service can be performed more economically by employment rather than by contracting

7. The qualifications of the individual or concern rendering the service and the customary fee charged, especially on nongovernment contracts

8. Adequacy of the contractual agreement for the service (e.g., description of the service, estimate of time required, rate of compensation, termination provisions).

The focus of the U.S. Court of Appeals for the Federal Circuit is much simpler: benefit to the contract. "Costs incurred in connection with contract performance or contract administration should ordinarily be recoverable because they normally 'benefit' the contract purpose" [citing *Singer Co. v. United States*, 568 F.2d 695, 721 (Ct. Cl. 1977)] and "reimbursement of [these costs is] in the best interest of the United States" [citing H. Rep. No. 169]. Benefit to the contract purpose, whether in its work performance or administration, is therefore a prerequisite for allowability.

One common government response to a contractor's desire to get consultant costs back directly, as a direct cost, is that consultant costs, like attorneys' fees, are included in a company's overhead and indirect cost pool. But classifying these costs as indirect would be unfair. As one board of contract appeals has stated: "We have previously held that legal fees and other costs incurred in preparing and submitting contract claims to the CO are allocable as direct costs of the contract to which they relate, and that "to regard the expenses as indirect costs would . . . unfairly and inequitably burden other contracts."

Sometimes whether consultant costs will be allowed is right in the contract. For example, a government lease provision promising payment of costs for seismic work may include, as a direct cost, the costs of an attorney who worked with local government authorities to ensure compliance with local seismic requirements. A modification allowed a contractor to be reimbursed "for the cost of the seismic work" associated with the alteration and expansion of a post office. During the course of the seismic work, attorneys were needed to work out problems the city had with the retrofit. When the work was completed, the landlord tried to get the attorneys' fees reimbursed. These costs were found to be reasonable costs incurred in the course of performance, and the contractor was entitled to recover them.

CHAPTER 22
Claims

The government and a contractor sometimes get into arguments. Usually these arguments get solved informally. But sometimes they don't. In those rare cases where the parties cannot solve their problems peacefully, it becomes necessary to litigate them. A claim is a formal fight between the government and a contractor. Either one—the government or the contractor—can file a claim.

248. What does a claim consist of?

Claims typically have three parts. A claim is not just the money involved. A claim also involves interest and costs.

Interest

A claim starts to earn interest as soon as it is received by the contracting officer. The rate changes every six months and is never as high as what the banks charge their customers to use their money. But while the interest rate is not high, it beats what banks are paying for CDs. The important point is that interest can add up. If a large claim takes several years to resolve, the interest can be in the thousands.

Costs

It costs money to make a claim. Sometimes a contractor needs an accountant to help determine how much money was lost on the claim. Other times, like when contractors lose money because the government has delayed them, the contractors may need the help of an expert in construction scheduling or delay analysis. Or the government claims a contractor's work was defective so the contractor needs an expert to say the work was industry standard and correct. Or the claim is complex and the contractor needs a lawyer. The money spent for these experts is called "claim costs." And a contractor can get these costs back.

Both of these components of a claim can add up. One small claim resulted in a judgment for approximately $45,000 for the claim, about $8,000 for interest, and almost $40,000 for costs—the accountants, the lawyer, and deposition expenses including air fare to the scene of the project.

249. What is the difference between a request for equitable adjustment and a claim?

The big difference between a request for equitable adjustment (REA) and a claim is interest. A claim earns interest; an REA does not. It's important, however, to thoroughly understand their differences, and the claims process in general.

The Phone Call to the Government

The first step in the claims process is usually the phone call to the CO or technical person putting the government on notice that something is wrong. This is not a claim. No interest is running.

The Letter to the Government

The government's typical response to the phone call or other oral notice of a problem is to get the contractor to put it in writing. Then the contractor sends a letter to the government describing the problem. Of course, this letter could be more than simple notice to the government that there is a problem. It could be a request for an equitable adjustment or it could be a claim. Usually, though, it's too early in the process. The contractor doesn't know exactly how big a problem it will be, or how to fix it, or all its consequences, or how much it will cost to fix it. Without this information, a request for equitable adjustment or claim is premature. A contractor is usually not ready at this early stage to get too formal, by filing either a request for equitable adjustment or a claim.

Investigation and Preliminary Negotiations

The contractor and the government then try to gather information on the issue and negotiate over whether the contractor is due more money and, if so, how much more.

The Request for Equitable Adjustment

At some point in the process, the contractor knows what the problem is and how much it will cost the contractor. The contractor will then send a formal written REA to the government.

On the other hand, it's possible that the contractor's negotiations with the government have convinced the contractor that the government doesn't want to settle the issues or doesn't have the money to settle. If so, the contractor may decide to file a claim at this point.

The Claim

If the REA doesn't get the contractor more money, the contractor usually will file a formal claim demanding a CO's final decision.

More Information Gathering and Negotiation

Often, the CO does not want to issue a CO's final decision until he or she gathers more information and tries to negotiate some more with the contractor. Settlement discussions could take place at this point.

The CO's Final Decision

When a CO receives a claim, the CO must issue a formal CO's final decision that resolves the claim.

The Appeal to a Board of Contract Appeals or Court of Federal Claims

If the contractor is not happy with the CO's final decision, the contractor can appeal the decision. The contractor can appeal to a board within 90 days or within one year to the Court of Federal Claims. The contractor cannot do both. The contractor must make an "election," or decide between the two options.

However, none of these steps in the claims process is set in concrete. For example, it is possible for the first notice the contractor gives the government requesting more money to be formally labeled a claim, and thus be more than just a simple notice that there is a problem. Or the contractor could skip the REA and go straight to a claim.

The claims process also involves the government, since there are numerous occasions on which the government wants to file a claim against the contractor. Examples are the assessment of liquidated damages and excess reprocurement costs.

One common mistake the government makes in asserting claims against the contractor is that the government does not go through the CO's final decision process itself. Often, it simply adds on to a contractor claim a government counterclaim that has never had a CO's final decision. The absence of a CO's final decision is critical because this decision sets the boundaries for any further appeal. Generally, issues that are not addressed in that document cannot be heard by a board or a court on appeal. And while a board or court will let the parties to an appeal argue their case with some deviations from the CO's final decision, they cannot hear appeals of claims not included in that decision.

For example, a CO issued a final decision over money due the government for a 1978 contract. The contractor fought it in court. The government then filed a counterclaim for government recoveries based not only on the 1978 contract, but also on a 1984 contract. The court threw out the counterclaim since there had been no CO's final decision on the 1984 contract. All the court could deal with was what the CO had dealt with. The CO had not addressed the 1984 contract. While the court could consider a request for more damages from the same claim considered by the CO, the court could not consider the claim if it had never been considered by the CO in the first place.

250. When should the contractor start out with a request for equitable adjustment? And when should the contractor go straight to a claim?

A contractor might start with a request for equitable adjustment when the following is true:

- The contractor is in a long-term relationship with the government and doesn't want to rock the boat

- The contractor does yet not have final cost figures so the contractor does not know how much money it will be asking the government for

- The issues are complex or involve technical matters, and the contractor needs an expert.

A contractor might start out with a claim when the following applies:

- The contractor knows there is no likelihood that the government is going to voluntarily part with any of its money without a fight because there is no money available for an REA

- Animosity on both sides is so high that no amount of negotiations will pry money out of the government.

251. How does a contractor make a claim?

How the contractor makes a claim depends on what the claim deals with: whether the contractor wants more money, wants an interpretation of contract language that is confusing, or wants something legally called "other relief."

Claims for Money

Depending on the dollar amount, a claim for money has three or four simple elements:

1. *A sum certain.* To make a claim, the contractor must demand a specific dollar amount from the government. There can be no claim if the contractor tells the CO vague things like "I demand fair compensation for this" or makes other unquantified demands that lack a specified dollar amount.

2. *Specific demand for a CO's final decision.* The contractor must demand a final decision from the CO. There's nothing difficult about this. The contractor simply

states, "I demand a final decision of the contracting officer on this issue."

3. *Stated basis and amount of the claim.* The contractor must tell the CO the rationale for filing the claim. For example, it could be having to do extra work without additional pay, encountering a differing site condition without getting any additional money, being delayed by the government, or having the government make the contractor responsible for warranty work when the damage is not the contractor's fault.

4. *Certification.* If the money the contractor wants is more than $100,000, the contractor must certify the claim. The exact language the contractor must use is stated in the particular disputes clause in the contract. The contractor must simply parrot back in the letter to the CO the words of the clause. If the contractor doesn't use the exact words, the CO may think that the contractor is trying to avoid the certification because the contractor cannot truthfully say all that the certification requires.

For years, the government and contractors argued over the correct words of the certification. The fight was not over words per se. It was over the entitlement to interest that accompanied a properly certified claim. If the government could prove that the claim was not properly certified, it could invalidate the claim and save itself a lot of money in interest.

But it got to the point where more time and effort were being spent on the certification than on the underlying claim. In 1992 Congress decided to simplify the certification process. The FAR now has a "defective certification" provision at 33.201. The FAR defines a defective certification as "a certificate which alters or otherwise deviates from the language in 33.207(c) or which is not executed by a person duly authorized to bind the contractor with respect to the claim. Failure to certify shall not be deemed to be a defective certification."

If a claim has a defective certification, FAR 33.207(f) says: "A defective certification shall not deprive a court or an agency board of contract appeals (BCA) of jurisdiction over that claim. Prior to the entry of a final judgment by a court or a decision by an agency BCA, however, the court or agency BCA shall require a defective certification to be corrected."

But there is a significant limit on the use of the defective certification provision. It applies only to "technically" defective certifications, not to those certifications that are intentionally defective. The Congressional history of the correction law gave some examples of what could be corrected: a "certification with each document submitted as part of the claim when all claim documentation is not submitted simultaneously, missing certifications when two or more claims not requiring certification are deemed by the court or board to be a larger claim requiring certification, and certification by the wrong or incorrect representative of the contractor."

Defective certifications that are knowing and intentional ones—ones that miss the mark by miles—cannot benefit from the defective certification provisions. In one case, the board analyzed the legalese that accompanied the first REA and found that the language used was nowhere near the precise language that Congress demanded. It concluded that the first certification was not correctable and therefore was not a claim that could be appealed.

What attachments usually go with a claim? If the contractor has documentation that helps the case, the contractor should send it along to the CO. Typically, this would include invoices or canceled checks showing that the contractor actually spent the money that it's seeking reimbursement for.

Legally, however, the contractor doesn't have to send any documentation along with the claim. The CO also cannot refuse to issue the contractor a final decision on the claim on the basis that the contractor didn't provide enough supporting information. If the CO thinks there is not enough supporting information, the CO can deny the claim. The CO cannot refuse to issue a final decision on the basis of lack of information.

What is the advantage to providing as much documentation as possible? It is perhaps better to look at it the other way around. First, there is no advantage to withholding information. The contractor should give the submission the best shot possible from the very beginning. Second, there could be a big disadvantage in withholding information. It all centers on attorneys' fees and costs. Giving the CO as much information as possible takes away one of the government's arguments that prevent the contractor from getting attorneys' fees if it wins.

Here's why. There is a general rule that the government pays attorneys' fees if the government forces a contractor to litigate to get any claim money. But if the government refuses to give the contractor any money because the contractor has not proved its case, the government may not have to pay attorneys' fees. If the contractor has a good case but the contractor has not given the CO the supporting information to prove it, the board or court could find that the CO's denial of the claim was justified. In that case, the contractor would not be entitled to any attorneys' fees or costs, even though it won the claim.

Claims for Interpretation of Contract Terms

Every contract is full of language problems that must be solved. Whenever the contractor says that the contract means one thing and the government says that it means another, the contractor has a claim over contract interpretation.

And while these issues will involve money down the road, they don't involve money right now. So a claim for money is not yet appropriate. (The contractor certainly could provide the disputed goods, etc., and file a claim for the additional cost.) The immediate issue, however, is "what does it mean?" That makes the claim one involving the interpretation of contract terms. The contractor can file a claim that forces the government to give the contractor a formal answer to any contract interpretation issue. And it's much easier than a money claim. There is no need to provide back-up or invoices or to certify the claim.

How does the contractor file a legally sufficient claim over a contract interpretation issue? The contractor sends the government a letter describing the controversy: what the contractor thinks it means and what the government has told the contractor it thinks it means (if it has done so). The contractor ends by demanding a formal decision of the CO on the issue.

There is no need for a certification, and there is no need for back-up materials such as invoices. A one-page letter will do it.

Claims for "Other Relief"

What is this catch-all "other relief"? Typically, it is a claim involving a termination for default. When a contractor asks the government to reconsider its termination because there was an excusable delay, such as the government slowing the project down, that's a claim for "other relief." Also, asking the government to reduce or eliminate the assessment of liquidated damages could be "other relief."

How does the contractor file a claim for other relief? The contractor simply sends the government a letter describing what happened and why the contractor wants relief. As in a claim for contract interpretation, the contractor does not need any certifications. But the contractor should include support for its claim. For example, if the contractor thinks the government delayed it, the contractor should send the government copies of documents that support this belief.

252. What documents does the contractor have the right to see on filing a claim?

When a contractor files a claim, it has a right to see what documents the government has that support or hurt its case. These documents come to light through the discovery process.

The standard for the release of these documents is that "relevant but not privileged" documents are releasable. One type of privilege, the informant's privilege, has been mentioned. Others are the attorney-client privilege and the work product privilege. A more detailed discussion of privilege is beyond the scope of this book. But relevancy is not.

The eight essential elements of attorney-client privilege are: (1) where legal advice of any kind is sought (2) from a professional legal advisor in his capacity as such, (3) the communications relating to that purpose, (4) made in confidence (5) by the client, (6) are at his instance permanently protected (7) from disclosure by himself or by the legal adviser, (8) except the protection be waived.

The attorney work product privilege protects from disclosure documents prepared in anticipation of litigation. They are discoverable only if they are really needed. This means that documents prepared by a consultant to the government are not protected. The consultants are not clients of the government attorney. Also not privileged are a government lawyer's drafts of the CO's final decision if the attorneys were acting as the CO's "ghost writers." Nor are the drafts of the CO's decisions prepared by government attorneys covered by the attorney work product privilege, because the purpose of those documents is to fulfill the Contract Disputes Act and the FAR requirements of preparation of the CO's decision in this matter. They are not prepared because of litigation.

Interestingly, it pays a CO to write legibly—illegible documents can be released.

253. Is there a statute of limitations on filing a claim?

There are two, sometimes three, statutes of limitations on filing claims.

One is six years, which applies to all claims. The contractor must file the claim within six years of the claim accruing, although it's still unclear at this stage exactly what "accrual" means. The six-year statute of limitations is new within the past several years; no cases have been decided that provide any meaning to the word "accrued."

The contractor must also observe other deadlines depending on the specific clause under which the contractor seeks relief. These deadlines are found in the specific clauses. The changes clause, for example, has two additional deadlines. This clause says that any claim must be filed within 30 days and before final payment. As a practical matter, the 30-day deadline is not strictly observed. The "before final payment" deadline, however, is strictly observed.

So the contractor should carefully read the clause under which it is seeking help. It probably contains deadlines in addition to the six-year statute of limitations applicable to all claims.

254. Does it matter what clause the contractor uses?

It does matter—sometimes dramatically—what clause the contractor uses to seek a claim; it can really affect the amount of money the contractor will get. Every claim involves at least two clauses: the disputes clause and another clause. The disputes clause describes the process for getting the help authorized by the other clause. In government contracting, some types of harm can be covered by more than one clause.

Reducing the work under a contract—often referred to as de-scoping or deductive change—can be done either as a deductive change order under the changes clause or as a partial termination for convenience under the termination for convenience clause. Typically, minor (10 percent) reductions can be done under the changes clause. Larger changes must be made under the termination for convenience clause. The difference is that the contractor can get settlement costs, such as the costs of having an accountant tally up the damages or legal fees, under the termination clause, but not under the changes clause.

Delay is even more complex. The contractor can get delay damages under the suspension of work clause, the changes clause, and the differing site conditions clause. One big difference is that under the suspension of work clause, there is no profit. Thus, a contractor would try to avoid making its claim under that clause. Under the differing site conditions clause, any delay waiting for the government to decide how to fix the condition gets compensated under the suspension of work clause (no profit). But if the delay is due to a defective specification, the delay gets paid for under the changes clause, which does include profit.

255. Does the contractor have to keep working on the project while it has a claim pending?

Generally, the contractor does have to keep working on the project while it has a pending claim. Specifically, it depends on what disputes clause is in the contract—the basic disputes clause or the alternate disputes clause.

If the contractor has the basic disputes clause, it's difficult to walk away from the project until the government resolves the claim. If the contractor does, the government can terminate the contract for default, according to the disputes clause at section (i), which says: "the contractor shall proceed diligently with performance of the contract. . . ." However, there is one exception—when the dispute "relates to" the contract—to having to keep working under the basic disputes clause. This exception allows the contractor to walk away from the project while the contractor fights it out with the government.

Where does the contract say that? In clause (i), it says: "the contractor shall proceed diligently with performance of the contract, pending final resolution of any . . . claim . . . arising under the contract. . . ." Most claims "arise under" the contract. Some, however, "relate to" the contract. Since the basic disputes clause requires the contractor to proceed only for claims arising under the contract and not claims relating to the contract, the contractor can stop work if the contractor has a claim that relates to the contract. For example, disputes about wrongful government withholding of payment, or when the government interferes with the work or does not tell the contractor what to do when it has promised that it would, are disputes that relate to the contract.

A contractor must be very careful, however. If the contractor believes that a dispute relates to a contract but in actuality it only arises under the contract, the contractor is in default and could be penalized for not continuing with the work.

The second disputes clause, called alternate I (FAR 52.233-1), offers the contractor no choice—the contractor must keep working while the dispute is worked out with the government. The contractor cannot walk away from the project while the government resolves the claim. The contractor must proceed pending resolution of any claim ". . . arising under or relating to" the contract. Thus, the contractor has no grounds for stopping the work.

However, if the contracting officer makes a "cardinal change" to the work, a contractor may abandon its work. In one case, the government tried to add more work to a postal route. The contractor refused to do the work and won an appeal of the government's termination of the contract. The judge said that "an exception to the duty to proceed exists in situations in which the government has attempted to effect a change which fundamentally alters the party's contractual undertakings." How significant must a change to a contract be to make it a cardinal change? Admitting that there is no easy answer, the court in this case cited factors such as "(i) whether there is a significant change in the magnitude of work to be performed; (ii) whether the change is designed to procure a totally different item or drastically alter the quality, character, nature or type of work contemplated by the original contract; and (iii) whether the cost of the work ordered greatly exceeds the original contract cost." *Keeter Trading Co. Inc. v. The United States,* U.S. Court of Federal Claims No. 05–243C, July 19, 2007.

256. Does the government have any time limits for responding to the claim?

This too depends on the particular disputes clause in the contract. It also depends on the amount of the claim. So first the contractor must read the clause at section (e) to see what time limits are imposed on the government. Currently, claims $100,000 and under must be resolved within 60 days, but only if the contractor specifically asks in writing for a decision within 60 days.

Claims over $100,000 must be resolved within 60 days or the CO, within 60 days, must give the contractor a date by which the contractor will get an answer. The CO cannot waffle on this. A promise from the CO that he or she will respond by "October 29, 1999, barring unforeseen circumstances" is not good enough. The promise to respond by October 29 was a waffle because it was qualified by the "unforeseen circumstances" language. The CO did not give a specific date by which he or she would issue a CO's final decision.

257. Can a contracting officer stall indefinitely and simply fail to issue a contracting officer's final decision?

A CO can stall indefinitely, but it doesn't hold up the process. A CO must follow the time limits described above. If the contractor doesn't get an answer by the deadline, the contractor has received what is called a "deemed denial" from the CO. The CO's silence is considered to be a denial. The contractor then can write the BCA that handles the claim and ask it to order the CO to issue a CO's final decision. Bottom line: the government cannot stall.

258. What about arbitration?

Arbitration is a possibility. The disputes clause at clause (g) allows the contractor and the government to agree to alternative dispute resolution (ADR). The contractor should explore this possibility because it can be very effective in quickly resolving the dispute.

What is ADR? Basically, it's an attempt to keep the dispute from the courtroom and have it arbitrated in the conference room. Various boards have various forms of ADR. Ask the board handling the case what alternatives it provides for ADR.

259. What if the contracting officer gives only partial relief? What does the contractor have to lose if it appeals?

The contractor has the potential to lose quite a bit if it appeals.

The contractor has a tough decision. Does the contractor take what the CO has offered and run, or does the contractor gamble and go to the board or court for more? It is a gamble because going for more jeopardizes what the CO gave the contractor. For example, if the CO gives the contractor $20,000, but the contractor thinks it should receive $40,000, the contractor could appeal the CO's decision and try to get the extra $20,000 from the board or the court. But the contractor could fail to get the extra $20,000 and worse, the board could order the contractor to return to the government the original $20,000. Simply because the CO gives the contractor some money does not guarantee that the contractor will get at least that much if the contractor goes to a board or court.

260. What are the deadlines for appeals?

If the contractor wants to appeal, it must appeal to the board within 90 days of receiving the decision or to the court within one year. A contractor should not wait until the last minute. These deadlines are strictly followed; there are no exceptions.

261. What are the advantages of going to the board or the court?

The advantage of appealing to the board is that the board is cheaper and less formal. Contractors can handle the appeal by themselves.

Appealing to the board can also help a contractor save money. First, a board can decide a claim based solely on paperwork in the file that the contractor submits. The contractor does not need to have an in-person hearing in Washington, D.C., or anywhere else. Some small dollar claims can be handled very effectively this way—no travel, no time spent in hearings, no post-hearing briefs or summaries. Just the existing paperwork.

Second, and best of all, a board has small claims and accelerated procedures. The small claims process is for claims less than $25,000, for which an answer will be given within 120 days. There is no appeal to a higher court, the Court of Appeals for the Federal Circuit (CAFC). The accelerated procedures are for cases under $100,000 and can be appealed to the CAFC. In both the small claims and accelerated processes, discovery through written interrogatories and depositions is available, but the boards like to keep things simple and streamlined. So the possibility of unlimited discovery is not great if these two processes are used.

Hearings can be long or short depending on the case's complexity. One-day hearings are possible, but so are month-long ones. Hearings can take place in Washington, D.C., or elsewhere, depending on the circumstances. For example, if many of the witnesses are out of town, the board will travel.

The Court of Federal Claims generally requires the contractor to have a lawyer, thus making it a much more expensive option. It's a good option, however, when the 90-day deadline for appeals to the board has passed. This court becomes the only option at that point.

Appealing to the Court of Federal Claims could be expensive. The court is much more formal than a board. Hearings are usually held in Washington, D.C., although like the board, the court will travel.

262. When does the interest clock start to run?

Interest starts to run from the day the CO receives the claim.

The interest is simple, not compound; the interest rate changes every six months.

263. Can the contractor get paid for filing a claim?

It costs money to file a claim. The contractor might need an accountant to help develop cost figures. The contractor also might need an attorney to help with the process. It takes up the contractor's time and the contractor's staff's time. The contractor can recover these costs depending on when—at what point in the claims process—the contractor spends the money.

For claims cost purposes, there are only three points in the process:

1. The request for equitable adjustment

2. Preparing the claim that goes to the CO

3. Appealing a CO's final decision to the Court of Federal Claims or a board.

When the costs are incurred is critical:

1. *Allowable* REA costs: These are the costs of the extra help the contractor needs to complete the request for equitable adjustment. In one case, the government wanted a contractor to do additional construction work. The extra work required environmental clearances from the local government. The contractor didn't know anything about how to get them, so it hired an attorney to help. The contractor was reimbursed for the attorney's fees because they were considered to be costs associated with the request for equitable adjustment.

2. *Unallowable* claim preparation costs: The government will not pay the contractor to sue it. When the contractor prepares the claim itself that will go to the CO, the costs are on the contractor's tab.

3. *Allowable* claim litigation costs: If the contractor has to go to a board or a court to get the money, the contractor may well get the costs back. If the government

forces the contractor to litigate to get any money for the claim, and the contractor wins, the government will usually have to pay attorneys' fees and costs. This is because of the Equal Access to Justice Act (EAJA).

264. What are Equal Access to Justice Act (EAJA) costs? What costs can the contractor get back from the government under EAJA?

Congress did not want government lawyers on a salary to file abusive lawsuits against taxpayers and force taxpayers to hire attorneys to fight the government. In passing EAJA, Congress ruled that if the government litigates, it had better have a good argument. If the government has not thought out its legal position, it may well end up paying attorneys' fees and costs.

For the contractor to recover the attorneys' fees and costs paid, the contractor must successfully jump through three hoops:

1. *Eligible parties:* It must be an "eligible party." Individuals with a net worth of $2,000,000 or less are considered eligible parties, as are companies with fewer than 500 employees and a net worth of less than $7,000,000.

2. *Prevailing parties:* The contractor has to win, or "prevail," some part of the claim to qualify for attorneys' fees and costs. If the contractor loses completely, it doesn't matter how bad the government's argument was—the contractor must pay its own expenses. On the other hand, the contractor does not have to win completely. Winning just a small part of the claim makes the contractor eligible for attorneys' fees and costs.

3. *Government has bad facts or bad law.* In legalese, the government pays unless its facts and law are "substantially justified." The government can lose and still not have to pay attorneys' fees and costs, as long as it had a good argument.

The contractor can get back: accountants' costs, attorneys' fees, transcript costs, and hotel costs, but not the cost of the time fighting the claim. (It gets back attorneys' fees at the rate of $125/hour.)

265. Can the government come after the contractor and make the contractor pay its costs if the contractor loses?

It's rare that a losing contractor pays the government's costs. The rare cases where a contractor would be forced to pay the government's costs involve frivolous cases.

One way the U.S. judicial system discourages frivolous lawsuits is by making losers in litigation pay, for the litigation completely, for simply the court costs, or some other amount. The problem is that discouraging one litigant might discourage other litigants who have a good argument but can't gamble their money on winning. Courts in the United States usually are very sympathetic to litigants, finding frivolous lawsuits only on rare occasions.

First, let's define a "frivolous" case. Simply because an appeals court does not issue a decision on an appeal does not make that appeal frivolous.

For example, a company was sued by an individual who served as his own lawyer. He lost in the federal district court and appealed to the CAFC. He lost there, too. The court did not even issue an opinion in the case. The company then went back to court to get damages for filing what the company thought was a frivolous case. (No doubt, the individual himself probably thought that the company's retaliation damages suit itself was frivolous.) The court did not find the suit frivolous and took the opportunity to discuss frivolous cases.

The court was not prepared to call the case frivolous simply because it had not issued an opinion in the case. "This case, like some others we hear, was an easy one to decide. The trial court's explanation for its decision was clear and sound and no useful purpose would have been served by our writing an opinion." Deciding a case without a written opinion shortens the time the parties have to wait to get a case resolved. Issuing no opinion "indicates our view that the appeal lacked merit, but not necessarily that it was frivolous."

But, if cases that had little merit were to be considered frivolous, "we would be assessing substantial damages. That is not our practice, at least currently. No doubt, if that were our practice, many poor appeals would not be brought, the courts would be less congested, and meritorious cases would receive more prompt hearings and decisions. However, parties who lost their cases in a lower tribunal would be seriously deterred from pursuing an appeal, which, to the intermediate appellate court level, is usually a matter of right." Appeals allow more judges to decide whether the first court made a mistake. Such appeals are particularly helpful when the issue is a straight issue of law, like the interpretation of a contract.

The court acknowledged that the U.S. system is "currently biased toward maintaining open courts rather than deterring appeals. It favors the allowance of appeals, even in cases having little chance for success, without subjecting appellants to an undue risk of damages for a frivolous appeal." Thus, simply because the case had little merit was not enough to make it frivolous.

The court identified two types of appeals it considered frivolous. The first type is an appeal that is "frivolous as filed" because it raised issues "beyond the reasonable contemplation of fair-minded people," and "no basis for reversal in law or fact can be or is even arguably shown."

A second frivolous appeal is one that is "frivolous as argued" because the litigant "has not dealt fairly with the court, has significantly misrepresented the law or facts, or has abused the judicial process by repeatedly litigating the same issue in the same court."

Neither of these types of appeals was present here. Here, the plaintiff raised the same issues on appeal and doing so "is hardly a ground for a conclusion of frivolousness. The whole point of an appeal is to claim that the court below erred in its conclusion as to arguments raised."

But if an appellant simply raised issues without saying why the lower court was wrong, that could be a frivolous case.

The court summed up well the traditional American view of courts on frivolous cases: "We regret the fact that non-meritorious appeals are brought as much as do winning appellees. However, the doors of the courthouse must remain open for losing appeals as well as winning appeals." (*Lawrence N. Sparks, V. Eastman Kodak Company,* U.S. Court of Appeals for the Federal Circuit, No 00-1049, October 31, 2000.)

There have been cases, however, where the government has been paid for its costs by a losing company.

But it's the reverse of the usual situation where a winning contractor gets its attorneys' fees and court costs back from the government under EAJA. This law benefits only the contractor—it does not apply to the government.

Government procurement personnel often wonder why turnabout is not fair play. Why can't the government get its costs paid for by a losing contractor? Although it is not widely known, the government often gets back some of its court costs when it wins a case. This is allowed not by EAJA but by court rules. Typically, items like transcripts and copying charges (but not attorneys' fees) are assessed against a losing contractor in the Court of Federal Claims and the Court of Appeals for the Federal Circuit.

One way to get a losing contractor to pay the government's costs is if the contractor doesn't get more from the court than it got from the CO's final decision. For example, a contractor sued the government in the Court of Federal Claims for claims relating to delays, differing site conditions, and defective specifications. When the litigation was over, all that it won was what the CO had allowed in the CO's final decision plus the amount of contract hold-back that the government had conceded the contractor was due. Technically, the contractor "won" because these two amounts, about 2 percent of what it had sought, were part of the final judgment.

At the end of the case, the government asked the court for costs. One of the rules of the court allowed the court to give the "prevailing party" its costs. The critical issue was whether the government was a prevailing party. Technically, the government had to pay the contractor when the case was over, so the contractor argued that the government was not a prevailing party.

The court did not agree. Part of the contractor's recovery was conceded by the CO. The other part was sought by the contractor under the belief that the amount had not been previously paid to it when in fact it had been, certainly by the time the case was coming to its conclusion. The court found the government to be a prevailing party and awarded it its costs.

266. Can an invoice be a claim?

An invoice can be considered a claim under certain circumstances.

The Contract Disputes Act (CDA) clearly separates routine requests for payment such as invoices from nonroutine requests for payment such as claims. In the definition of *claim* in the disputes clause and in FAR 33.201, invoices and other routine requests for payment are distinguished from claims: "A voucher, invoice, or other routine request for payment that is not in dispute when submitted is not a claim. The submission may be converted to a claim, by written notice to the CO as provided in 33.206(a), if it is disputed either as to liability or amount or is not acted upon in a reasonable time." Thus, an invoice under certain circumstances may be a claim. There are two critical requirements: the certification and a "dispute."

Invoice Was Not a Claim—No Certification and No Dispute

A contractor sent the government a final invoice after the cost-plus-fixed-fee contract was over. Since the invoice was for more money than was left in the contract, the CO sent it back. She said that the government could not pay because the invoice included an overrun for which the government was not responsible. When the contractor appealed the CO's decision to the board, the board found that there was no claim. First, the invoice was not in dispute when submitted so it could not be a claim. Second, it was not certified as required by the CDA.

Invoice Was a Claim—Certification and Dispute

During a contract, the government and the contractor disputed several points, including whether a modification was the result of a defective specification and whether certain items should be included in the percentage completion of the progress payments. After the contract was terminated for default, the contractor submitted an invoice that billed the government for, among other things, progress payments consistent with the contractor's arguments on percentage completion and contrary to the government's arguments on that issue. The contractor's letter gave the CDA certification.

The board found this invoice to be a claim. It had been submitted after the termination for default and concerned the contractor's rights to payments for a specific percentage completion. The board said that the invoice "could not be considered a routine request for payment and even if it were, was disputed."

267. What does it take to make a termination for convenience settlement proposal a claim?

It takes a dispute. Unless the parties to a termination for convenience settlement have reached an impasse in their negotiations over the settlement proposal, no interest will be due on the amount eventually paid by the government.

Figuring out when a termination for convenience settlement proposal is a "claim" is tricky. When a contract is terminated for convenience, the parties begin to negotiate a settlement. Letters go back and forth. When does a claim exist and interest start running on the settlement proposal?

A contractor submitted a settlement proposal to the government that was audited by DCAA. The government agreed to give the contractor 90 percent of the amount recommended by the audit. Settlement negotiations over the remaining amount dragged on for months and through three termination COs. At one point, the contractor asked the government to negotiate a settlement or issue a CO's decision. At no point, however, did the contractor specifically demand a CO's final decision from the government. Eventually the parties settled the termination. The contractor wanted interest, but did not receive it from either the government or a court.

As the court viewed it, a settlement proposal is theoretically submitted to the government for the purpose of negotiation, not to get a CO's decision. As a result, when a termination settlement proposal is submitted to the government, it is not claim. Once negotiations reach an impasse, the settlement proposal can become a claim.

An impasse is reached, according to the court, when there is "an explicit request for a CO's decision or by some other conduct implying a desire for the issuance of a CO's decision." More specifically, before a termination for convenience settlement proposal could be a claim, there had to be "objective evidence" that the parties had reached an impasse. The rationale behind requiring objective evidence is that to require anything less would leave far too much ambiguity in the definition of an impasse and allow a finding of an impasse even though both parties were going through further negotiations.

Previous decisions showed what facts indicated an impasse:

- "Fruitless" negotiations

- Subsequent written requests by the contractor that the CO "settle" its claims

- Unilateral decision by the CO, i.e., an adjudicated claim

- Refusal by the CO to consider the contractor's termination settlement proposal, in which case there was an impasse as soon as the CO received the submission

- Contractor's explicit request for a final decision, in conjunction with the CO's refusal to meet to negotiate.

The situation here was missing objective evidence that the negotiations had reached an impasse and a clear indication by the contractor that it sought a final decision. The settlement between the parties showed that the contractor had not abandoned negotiations—a requirement of the court.

CHAPTER 23
Terminations

Every contract allows a party to terminate the contract if the other party is not doing what it promised. Obviously, this is true of government contracts. Every government contract has a termination for default provision that lets the government end the contract if the contractor is not doing what it is being paid to do. It is very important that these terminations be done correctly. If the government terminates a contract for default when it has no right to do so or does the termination incorrectly (like not giving notice in some situations), the termination becomes a termination for convenience, which allows the defaulting contractor to recover damages. As the courts and boards often say, a default is a "drastic remedy" that has to be invoked properly.

268. What are the most common mistakes the government makes in doing a termination for default?

Clearly, the most common mistake is that the government does not think through carefully the way it is doing the termination for default. There can be terrible mistakes in judgment in a termination for default.

The standard default clause (FAR 52.249-8) says that:

> (a) (1) The Government may, subject to paragraphs (c) and (d) below, by written notice of default to the Contractor, terminate this contract in whole or in part if the Contractor fails to—

(i) Deliver the supplies or to perform the services within the time specified in this contract or any extension;

(ii) Make progress, so as to endanger performance of this contract (but see subparagraph (a)(2) below); or

(iii) Perform any of the other provisions of this contract (but see subparagraph (a)(2) below).

* * *

(g) If, after termination, it is determined that the Contractor was not in default, or that the default was excusable, the rights and obligations of the parties shall be the same as if the termination had been issued for the convenience of the Government.

Notice that the clause says that if there is a default, the government *may* terminate the contract for default. The government does not *have* to do a termination for default. The heart of the decision to terminate a contract for default is a CO's exercise of discretion—the CO thinking through whether it would be in the government's interest to terminate the contract for default and ending up with a decision that makes sense.

The classic examples of the failure to exercise discretion properly are cases where the government terminates the contract for default when all the contractor needed was a few more days to get the work done. In one case involving the Government Printing Office, the CO terminated the contract for default when it turned out that the proposed delivery would have occurred only several days after the deadline if it had been extended as it should have been.

Another example of how the government does not wisely exercise its discretion is when the government pays too much for a replacement contract. When the government does a termination for default, it should not come out of the process a loser. For example, when it terminates a $2 million per year contract only to end up paying $6 million per year, the decision to terminate is not a sound exercise of discretion. In one case, the VA stayed in a clinic that it said was not built properly for nine months. The judge commented "... if the VA had permitted, Moreland could have performed all the necessary repairs quickly and without interrupting the VA's operations. The building was entirely safe for occupancy. Faced with this relatively simple and painless option to move forward under the existing lease, the contracting officer opted instead to terminate the lease for default and move to other facilities nine months later. In doing so, the cost of the VA was approximately $4 million per year greater than if the VA had remained in the medical clinic facility. This was an irrational decision by any measure, and one that could not have resulted from the exercise of reasoned discretion." *Moreland Corp. v. The United States,* U.S. Court of Claims No. 03-2154C, April 18, 2007.

Here are some other examples of the CO abusing discretion by terminating a contract.

Bad Faith

The bad faith of a CO's representative (COR) as well as COR conduct in the COR's financial interest will invalidate the termination for default.

Bad faith shows from the way the contractor is treated by the government. Telling a contractor to treat the COR like Jesus Christ and the CO like God is not only a dumb career move; saying these things also makes it difficult for the government to show how its termination for default was done in good faith.

In this case, a COR on a maintenance contract told the contractor's employees that, in the words of the COR, they should think of him as Jesus Christ and the CO as God. Other people heard the COR say that he would run the contractor off the contract. Others heard him say to the contractor's president that he would break the contractor. Still others heard the COR say that he needed some overtime to pay for his house. When the contractor had to work overtime to correct the supposedly unacceptable work, the COR also had to work and got paid overtime. So the COR had a financial interest in the contractor working overtime. Eventually, the contract was terminated for default. The contractor appealed and won.

First, the court discussed the famous traditional standard for proving bad faith: "well-nigh irrefragable proof of bad faith." The court said that, if you think about it, this is way too high a standard because "irrefragable" means impossible to refute. To the court, this phrase simply meant a higher standard of proof than the famous standard of criminal law "beyond a reasonable doubt." Too high a standard of proof "would appear to insulate government action from *any* review by courts—no matter how egregious." The court therefore used a lower standard and looked for "evidence of some specific intent to injure" the contractor.

It found plenty. The COR's "Jesus Christ" comparison "showed the COR to be a contracting official without a proper understanding of his role." His personal animosity was clear from his "break'em" statements. The remaining issue was, must the entire government contract administration staff be tarred by the conduct of one person? The government argued that there were other government employees who acted professionally. The court did not agree: "The CO's failure to inquire into and remedy the COR's bad faith coupled with the lack of evidence that the CO exercised independent judgment in applying the [inspection] standards of the contract results in the court's finding of bad faith on the part of the government in administering the contract." The court converted the termination for default into a termination for convenience. (*The Libertatia Associates,* U.S. Court of Federal Claims No. 93-459C, May 23, 2000.)

Insufficient Proof of a Contractor's Failure to Make Progress

To support a decision to terminate a contract for default for failing to make progress, the government must demonstrate that there was no reasonable likelihood that the contractor could complete the project within the time remaining.

The government faces two significant problems when it terminates a contract for failure to make progress: It carries the heavy burden of proving the default, and it must also prove that the contractor could not have finished the project within the time remaining.

A U.S. Postal Service contractor was delayed in the construction of a post office because the CO and the COR did not respond to the contractor's plans for changes the Postal Service wanted. Nor did the Postal Service employees return the contractor's phone calls. If they had, the project could have been completed on time. Eventually, the CO issued a termination for default. If, by the day the CO defaulted the contractor, she had given the necessary approvals asked for by the contractor, the contractor could have finished the project on time with the help of an accelerated work schedule.

The government was wrong to terminate the contract. For the government to win, it had to prove that there was no reasonable likelihood that the contractor could complete the project within the time remaining. It could not prove this. If the contractor had gotten government approvals and had accelerated its schedule, the contractor could have completed the project on time. Moreover, the government failed to cooperate with the contractor on resolving the design problems, making the delay an excusable one.

269. Are cure notices needed before doing all terminations for default?

A cure notice is needed only when the contractor would not be sure when the deadline is. In a supply contract for widgets to be delivered by April 1, the contract can be terminated on April 2 without a cure notice because the company, who is a party to the contract, is presumed to know the deadline.

Cure notices are used when the government does not believe that the contractor can finish the job on time. They are also used to warn the contractor that it may be terminated for default for violation of another part of the contract.

270. The government can charge the defaulted contractor for the excess costs of reprocuring the materials that should have been bought under the defaulted contract. How does a contracting officer do the reprocurement correctly?

When carrying out a reprocurement following a default, the CO does not have to get the lowest price, but only a reasonable price, which is then passed on to the defaulted contractor.

One of the biggest penalties a defaulted contractor bears is paying the excess reprocurement costs. When a defaulted contractor causes the government to pay more to get the goods from another company, the government has the right to pass on any extra costs incurred to the defaulted contractor. The government, however, cannot go out and buy a premium product and claim that the contractor must bear the price. The government has the obligation to mitigate the damages the defaulted contractor must bear. Importantly, when the government does not mitigate damages, it may lose its right to recover all the excess reprocurement costs.

A defaulted contractor argued that the government did not mitigate the defaulted contractor's damages in reprocuring loose-leaf products: The CO did not take into account a decline in paper prices prior to awarding the reprocurement contract to the next low bidder at its original price. A board of contract appeals ruled the reprocurement has been done correctly.

The Bureau of Labor Statistics (BLS) data relied on by the CO showed that the price of paper used in the contract had increased only slightly each month from the time the bids were received to the time the reprocurement contract was let. The CO had verified the BLS data. Moreover, the paper used in the contract had a price reduction of less than 1 percent and paper was only one-third of the contract's cost. A new competition would result in a price reduction of only $700. While prices might have gone down in the following months, prices known to the CO at the time he made his decision went down only slightly.

271. On what grounds can the government terminate for convenience a newly awarded contract?

The cure for everything—competition—will justify the government doing a termination for convenience during a solicitation. To properly terminate a contract for convenience shortly after award, the government need not prove a cardinal change. It must simply prove that the termination furthers full and open competition.

In one case, the government underestimated by 450 percent the amount of work that was required under a requirements contract. The CO believed that this error affected the pool of potential bidders and terminated the contract for convenience. The court agreed. To justify a termination for convenience during competition, the government did not have to prove a cardinal change (i.e., a beyond-scope change) to justify the termination for convenience. All the CO had to demonstrate was that the statutory requirements for full and open competition had been affected.

CHAPTER 24
Fraud

Because the government spends so much money on procurement, the possibilities for fraud in procurement are great. The government has given itself a number of weapons to fight fraud; as a result, a contractor can pay dearly if it tries to defraud the government.

272. What are the government's remedies for contractor fraud?

Treble damages for one. Forfeiture of the claim for another. And in some cases, forfeiture of the entire contract proceeds. Sometimes, all of the above.

In one case of fraud, the contractor had an interesting interpretation of the word "incurred" as in the phrase *incurred costs*. It submitted as incurred costs material costs that had never been invoiced and in some cases costs for material that had never been received. The contractor even conceded that its material costs were not amounts actually paid to companies or reflected on invoices. For example, the contractor considered as an incurred cost "unbilled escalation" which, in the words of one court, occurred when a company did not bill or invoice the contractor for an increase in material costs, despite the fact that the contractor's purchase orders contained escalation clauses that typically triggered a price increase on a certain date. The contractor felt that the escalation price increase was an "actual cost" because it believed it would eventually owe it to its companies.

The court came down hard on the contractor. Federal remedies for fraud, the court noted, are "cumulative and not in the alternative." The court found the contractor liable under several statutes. First, under the Special Plea in Fraud provision of the U.S. Code, fraudulent claims are forfeited. Second, under the False Claims Act, the contractor can be liable for civil penalties if it violates its duty to examine "its records to determine what amounts the government already has paid or whether payments are actually owed to subcontractors or vendors." Third, the Contract Disputes Act allows the government to recover the false or unsupported portion of a claim that can be tied to misrepresentation or fraud.

This fraud case was more like "aggravated stupidity." When the contractor submitted the claim close to the end of the contract, it had almost all the invoices for the materials used in the contract. Yet it submitted the total amount of the purchase orders with its companies whether or not they had been paid or had even sent the contractor an invoice. The court held that the contractor's actions forfeited the almost $4 million claim, imposed a $10,000 civil penalty, made the contractor pay the government the unsupported portion of the claim ($223,500), and made the contractor pay the government's costs of review. (*UMC Electronics Co.*, U.S. Court of Federal Claims No. 93-709C, June 23, 1999.)

Terminating a contract for default is another remedy that the government has for fraud in government contracts. Curiously, the clause itself does not specifically allow a default simply on the basis of fraud. However, failure to perform a contract clause is one specified reason to terminate a contract for default. And a contractor's overbilling can be construed to be a failure to follow the contract clause demanding accurate invoices and can therefore be used as a basis for terminating for default.

In one case, the contractor's conduct was outrageous. The president of the company prepared invoices without even looking at the company files. The invoices were simply copied from previous invoices. Because the agency had corrected mistakes in invoices in the past, the company president relied on the agency correcting the invoices she prepared. She considered her invoices to be scratch or draft invoices. A board upheld the agency's termination for default of the contract.

273. With all these remedies, what is the contracting officer's role when fraud is discovered in the claims process?

In two words, stay out. Leave it to the U.S. Department of Justice. COs should not address a fraud-tainted claim. In fact, a CO is prohibited by law from handling any claims involving fraud.

The disputes clause of a contract (typically FAR 52.233-1) seems to give the CO broad authority to handle all kinds of claims: claims arising under or relating to a contract. In fact, the CO's authority has been called "all disputes authority." But amid all this authority is one type of claim that is excluded from a CO's authority: a claim that has fraud associated with it. This type of claim not only cannot be handled by the CO—it is beyond the jurisdiction of the courts and boards.

One case had an interesting twist: The CO had no authority to handle the claim even though an official fraud-fighter in the government, the Air Force's Office of Special Investigation (OSI), had concluded that it would not pursue the fraud allegations against the contractor, mainly for procedural reasons.

A contractor submitted invoices that the government thought were forgeries. Later, the government did a termination for convenience. The CO denied the contractor any money for a settlement of the termination for convenience due to the "apparently fraudulent invoices," in the words of the CO. The contractor appealed to the court, where it lost as well. The court concluded that the CO was not authorized to issue a CO final decision because the Contract Disputes Act removes fraud from the CO's consideration. Regardless of what OSI thought, the CO still believed there was fraud in the submission of some payment vouchers. So the CO's final decision was unauthorized and invalid.

274. What is this landmine for contractors called an "implied certification"?

It's hard to believe that the submission of something as simple and ordinary as an accurate monthly invoice can be considered a False Claim Act violation. But it can if the invoice requires the contractor to certify that it is complying with federal law when in fact it is not.

This landmine is called an *implied certification.* Implied obligations can present a real problem because they are implied. They are not written down anywhere because they are so obvious. So the absence of something in writing makes implied obligations—like the implied certification—very subtle.

Courts have recently been finding implied obligations in invoices. They are finding an implied certification of contract compliance attached to requests for payment made by a contractor to the government.

In violation of federal laws, a government contractor was disposing of chemicals associated with a government contract. The president of the company knew that the company was not complying. Nonetheless, the company submitted routine invoices. There was no *express* certification on the invoices that the company was complying with Environmental Protection Agency regulations or any other regulations. A court found that the invoices had an implied certification that the contractor was complying with federal laws. And it was not.

The court based its decision on the legislative history of the False Claims Act. The Senate Judiciary Committee said that the FCA applied to "a claim for goods not provided or provided in violation of contract terms, specification, statute, or regulation."

Other courts have also found violations of implied certifications. The Court of Federal Claims found a violation when an 8(a) firm submitted invoices to the government after signing a prohibited comanagement agreement with a subcontractor that made the 8(a) firm no longer an 8(a) firm. In another case, a court found a violation of an implied certification when a Medicare provider submitted invoices for payments knowing that the provider was not complying with all Medicare requirements. In a third case, another appeals court found a violation of the FCA when a contractor knowingly omitted from progress reports material information concerning noncompliance with the program it had contracted to implement.

The "knowing" violation requirement is critical. Inadvertent violations are no problem legally. The standard for "knowing" is that the contractor knew, or recklessly disregarded the risk, that its implied certification of compliance was false.

But there are limits to the implied certification. In one case, a bounty hunter looking for a reward argued that invoices violated the FCA because they were signed by a former government employee who, in the eyes of the bounty-hunter, was violating the federal anti-revolving door statutes imposed on former government employees. A court ruled that this interpretation was a stretch: "a false certification of compliance with a statute or regulation cannot serve as the basis for a qui tam action under the FCA unless payment is conditioned on that certification. By itself, breaking the law is not enough. It's the false certification of compliance that creates liability when certification is a prerequisite to obtaining a government benefit.

Courts will infer certification from silence, but only where certification was a prerequisite to the government action sought.

275. Can government contractors violate the False Statements Act?

Certainly, they can. And there is one classic landmine resulting from a loophole recently closed.

Contractors are also subject to the FCA. Government contractors must be careful of what answers they give to questions from the government. The truth, and the whole truth, is required. Because of the way the law is interpreted, it is better to remain silent in response to a question by the government agent in a government inquiry rather than answer "no." A "no" can be considered a lie.

This can be a common problem. Government contractors talk to a lot of different federal officials during the course of their contract. Contractor candor has always been the best policy. But absolute candor is required.

The problem is the "exculpatory no." When a person answers "no" to a federal inquiry, can a person answer no solely to protect its rights under the Fifth Amendment? Some courts had given people the right to say "no" because "yes" would be self-incriminating.

That's no longer true. The False Statements Act makes it a crime to give "any" false statement to government agents. And when you think about it, the Fifth Amendment does not give a person the right to lie. It gives people simply the right to remain silent. There is no constitutional privilege to lie to government agents.

Acronyms

ACO	administrative contracting officer
ADR	alternative dispute resolution
ASBCA	Armed Services Board of Contract Appeals
B&P	bid and proposal
BAFO	best and final offer
BCA	Board of Contract Appeals
BLS	Bureau of Labor Statistics
BOM	bill of materials
BPA	blanket purchase agreement
CAFC	Court of Appeals for the Federal Circuit
CAS	Cost Accounting Standards
CASB	Cost Accounting Standards Board
CBA-IPI	CMM®-Based Appraisal-Internal Process Improvement
CCASS	Construction Contractor Appraisal Support System
CDA	Contract Disputes Act
CDRL	contract data requirements list
CIA	Central Intelligence Agency
CICA	Competition in Contracting Act
CIO	chief information officer
CLIN	contract line item number
CMM®	Software Capability Maturity Model®

CO	contracting officer
COR	contracting officer's representative
COTR	contracting officer's technical representative
COTS	commercial off-the-shelf
CPCS	Competitive Performance and Continuous Surveillance
CPSR	contractor purchasing system review
CR	clarification report
CR/DR	clarification report/deficiency report
DCAA	Defense Contract Audit Agency
DID	data item description
DoD	Department of Defense
DOL	Department of Labor
DR	deficiency report
EAJA	Equal Access to Justice Act
EVMS	earned value management system
FACNET	Federal Acquisition Computer Network
FAR	Federal Acquisition Regulation
FARA	Federal Acquisition Reform Act
FASA	Federal Acquisition Streamlining Act
FCA	False Claims Act
FCCOM	facilities capital cost of money
FOB	free on board
FOIA	Freedom of Information Act
FPR	final proposal revision
FSS	Federal Supply Schedule
G&A	general and administrative
GAO	General Accounting Office
GEIA	Government Electronics Industry Association

GFP	government-furnished property
GPO	Government Printing Office
GPRA	Government Performance and Results Act
GSA	General Services Administration
GSAR	General Services Administration Regulations
GWAC	government-wide access contract
GWP	government-wide programs
HUBZone	Historically Underutilized Business Zone
ID/IQ	indefinite delivery/indefinite quantity
IFB	invitation for bid
IFN	item for negotiation
ISO	International Organization for Standardization
IT	information technology
JWOD	Javits-Wagner-O'Day Act
KPA	key process area
LTD	live test demonstration
MAS	multiple award schedule
NASA	National Aeronautics and Space Administration
NCMA	National Contract Management Association
ODC	other direct costs
OFPP	Office of Federal Procurement Policy
ORCA	Online Representation and Certification Application
OSBU	Office of Small Business Utilization
OSI	(Air Force) Office of Special Investigation
PEA/OFPP	Procurement Executive Association & Office of Federal Procurement Policy
PM	program manager

PPI	past performance information
PPIMS	past performance information management system
PRO-Net	Procurement Marketing and Access Network
REA	request for equitable adjustment
RFP	request for proposals
RFQ	request for quotes
SB	small business
SBA	Small Business Administration
SB/SDB	small business/small disadvantaged business
SCE	software capability evaluation
SDB	small disadvantaged business
SEI	Software Engineering Institute
SIC	standard industry codes
SOW	statement of work
SSA	source selection authority
SSEB	Source Selection Evaluation Board
UNSPSC	(Dun & Bradstreet's) Universal Standard Products & Services Classification
WBS	work breakdown structure

Index